PRAISE FOR *IN YOUR CREATIVE EL[...]*

"Claire brings a fresh voice and a brilliantly [...] [...]verse perspectives to the question of creativity in business."
Dr Sara Jones, Centre for Creativity in Professional Practice, Cass Business School, City, University of London

"I'm always looking for a quick fix but it's not something you can normally attain when you're trying to expand your mind and improve your skillset. This is a fascinating read and a breath of fresh air because you can read the whole thing or dip in chapter by chapter for a quick fix. The author takes an in-depth look at creativity in a way that's enriching as well as educational and with a wonderful lightness of touch that keeps it accessible and user-friendly. Bridges deftly distils an impressive body of research and insights into each chapter with helpful case studies and provocative questions thrown in along the way to keep readers on their toes. It's also funny, which is such a rare quality in a business book. This book has filled me with inspiration, practical tips and confidence – and now the hard part, putting all that into practice!"
Eleanor Conroy, Communications Director at Global Radio

"A comprehensive toolkit for fine-tuning your creative engine. Wherever you may consider yourself to be on the creativity spectrum, from inexperienced novice to seasoned pro, you will find something in here to spark a thought, prompt a reflection or motivate a change."
James Rutter, Brand Director, COOK

"This is a great book for really democratizing creativity. From Punchdrunk to Google to the NHS and Pixar – these are really different companies with differing staff and cultures, and the book proves that anybody, any organization, can up the game in terms of creativity. Running a business and succeeding is not just about having great ideas yourself but about really understanding how to scale creative thinking – and that's hard. The book offers a great toolkit for managing creativity and building creative thinking systematically into an organization and its culture. In terms of business value this book proves that creativity can truly add value to the bottom line and improve employee satisfaction."
Greg James, Chief Strategy & Development Officer, Havas Media

"I honestly can't fault this book. The whole area of creativity is misunderstood by the majority. But what enlightened CEOs and MDs realize is that creativity is no longer some exotic, optional extra. It's a strategic issue. I've read many books on creativity and In Your Creative Element is the most refreshingly original yet. It provides accessible, down-to-earth and practical tools to unlock individual and company creative potential. It's for anyone who believes in the power of creativity to drive the bottom line."
Stuart Yeardsley, Creative Director, 3 Monkeys Zeno

"Creativity in business – the Holy Grail of success and so often noticeable mainly by its absence. This will quickly become the go-to book on the subject, vital as it is to the future of my industry, and of so many others."
Francis Ingham, Director General, PRCA

"Creative thinking seems to have been regarded as one of the inexplicable dark arts by many senior managers. This book demystifies creativity, showing – practically – how your brand can walk the walk while so many others merely pay the topic lip-service. Don't believe what some 'creatives' might tell you – your own creative instincts can not only be honed but mastered over time using the nuggets of insight within. Read it, love it, do it!'
Arif Haq, Head of Creative Capabilities, Contagious Insider

"I believe that we all have the ability to be creative – it is a muscle that can be exercised and as such all people have creative ability if they try. This book is almost a toolkit – or perhaps personal trainer – for accessing that creativity. The use of the periodic table as an analogue of creative elements is original and brings science to the often felt 'wooliness' of the creative process."
Jason Perfitt, former Commercial Director, Pfizer UK

"I was delighted to share my story in this brilliant new book. I was always a creative dreamer as a child, thinking it was second best to other characteristics that would get you a job, so to speak. Over the years I've learnt that creativity is essential, not just about the talk of ideas but equally how to make them happen. This is what this book does, it creates possibility and a belief everyone is creative. My experience is that creative leaders know how to build trust, connect with people, inspire them and are great at enabling change. Using the elements is a smart and accessible way to lead conversations about creativity whether you work in a non-profit or commercial organization. As well as my story, the book is packed with dozens of practical examples about how individuals and businesses can raise their game in relation to this important topic. I'm particularly pleased to add to the dialogue about purpose and hope that by sharing my personal story others will be inspired to dig deep and explore their own values in relation to creativity, and other important areas, to really find meaning and satisfaction in their work and life."
Jackie Lynton, Social Change Activist and Founder, IHO People

In Your Creative Element

Element

The formula for creative success in business

Claire Bridges

KoganPage

Publisher's note

Every possible effort has been made to ensure that the information contained in this book is accurate at the time of going to press, and the publishers and author cannot accept responsibility for any errors or omissions, however caused. No responsibility for loss or damage occasioned to any person acting, or refraining from action, as a result of the material in this publication can be accepted by the editor, the publishers or the author.

First published in Great Britain and the United States in 2017 by Kogan Page Limited

2nd Floor, 45 Gee Street	c/o Martin P Hill Consulting	4737/23 Ansari Road
London	122 W 27th Street	Daryaganj
EC1V 3RS	New York, NY 10001	New Delhi 110002
United Kingdom	USA	India

ISBN   978 0 7494 7732 5
E-ISBN   978 0 7494 7733 2

British Library Cataloguing-in-Publication Data

A CIP record for this book is available from the British Library.

Library of Congress Control Number

2016958923

Typeset by Graphicraft Limited, Hong Kong
Print production managed by Jellyfish
Printed and bound in Great Britain by CPI Group (UK) Ltd, Croydon CR0 4YY

For James and Luca

CONTENTS

Art meets science
in the Periodic Table
of Creative Elements.

The table above attempts to answer the question
What does it take to be creative in business?

It is inspired by the original periodic table that was
designed in the 1800s to create order and illustrate
trends of then known elements to predict properties
of unknown elements.

Key

Values	Definitions	People	Creative mind	Culture	Purpose	Process

Periodic Table of Creative Elements

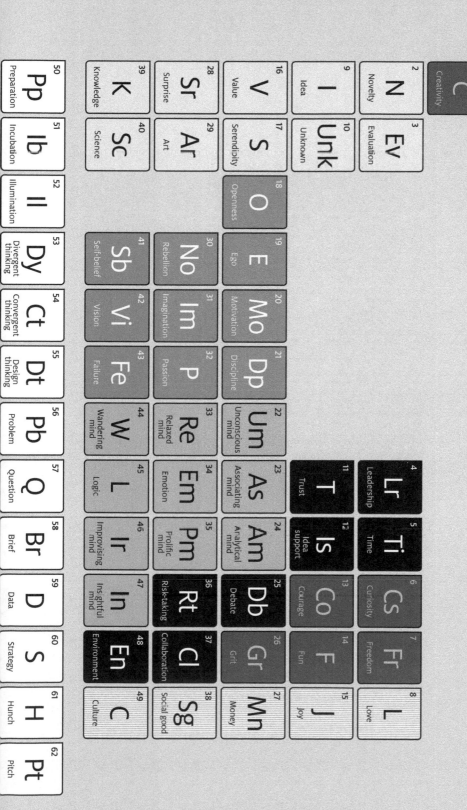

ABOUT THE AUTHOR

Claire Bridges is Chief Spark and Founder of leading creative training consultancy Now Go Create, whose philosophy is that everyone can be creative.

The book features proprietary work undertaken by the author for her MSc in Innovation, Creativity and Leadership from the Cass Business School at City, University London. Claire is one of only 55 people in the world to hold this qualification. This study is complemented by 20 years front-line experience in the creative industries.

Claire has worked at MD and Creative Director level for some of the world's biggest brands in her previous 20-year PR career, including Starbucks, Kellogg's, Unilever, P&G and Danone. Claire's passion and focus is the practical application of creativity for business, training companies and individuals how to be more creative. Now Go Create run workshops around the world that last from three hours to week long creative leadership intensives and ongoing programmes.

Now Go Create work with clients including Sky Media, Pret A Manger, Save The Children, ASOS and many of the world's leading PR, digital and media agencies. Claire has worked on thousands of creative projects and trained over 10,000 of people around the world.

Claire is in demand as a speaker, consultant and judge for creativity awards. She works annually as part of the training faculty at the prestigious Cannes Lions Festival of Creativity working with creative professionals from all around the globe, alongside the best creative talent in the world. Claire served on the PR Jury at Cannes in 2014, a rare accolade for those working in the creative industries, reviewing thousands of creative campaigns, a privilege and highly illuminating experience.

Find out more about our leadership and training courses at www.nowgocreate.co.uk and follow @nowgocreate

CONTRIBUTORS

Elizabeth Lovius is a leadership coach with over 20 years' experience, and has worked with thousands of professionals all over the world. Elizabeth coaches leaders to discover the source of their creativity, leadership and wisdom enabling them to lead collaborative cultures that deliver results.

In her early career at IBM, with a background in training, creative problem solving and process improvement, Elizabeth went on a journey to discover what makes people perform at their peak. In IBM, as a transformational change facilitator, she developed and led a team of 200 change agents to implement cultural change. She has experience in a variety of business sectors including: retail, manufacturing, IT, banking, government, healthcare, creative media, social enterprise and sport.

Clients have included the leaders of: The Body Shop, The Big Issue, itsu, ITV, Kahoot!, Charlie Bighams, CookFood, Pret A Manger, the English RFU and WPP group. Elizabeth is author of *Facilitating Genius* – a workbook – and is currently writing her second book on leadership.

Kate Magee is a writer, editor and business journalist who has spent the past decade covering advertising, communications, PR, marketing, social trends and creativity. She has written for several titles including *BBC News Magazine*, *Brand Republic*, *Campaign* (Asia, UK, US), *Marketing* and *Management Today*. As well as working on freelance projects (such as this book), she is currently the Associate Editor at *Campaign*, the advertising industry's most influential media brand, where she is in charge of the analysis and opinion on the site, weekly magazine and iPad app. She was previously Associate Editor at *PR Week*, where she was in responsible for all the long-form content and special projects for the brand. She has discussed her views on BBC Radio 4's *Today* programme, *Sky News* and in *The Guardian*.

Dr Ben Martynoga is a neuroscientist and science writer. He's been at the forefront of academic research into brain development for a decade and a half. He's now a visiting researcher at the new Francis Crick Institute in London. He recently swapped his white coat for a pen, leaving his full-time lab role to focus on writing. Driven by curiosity, Ben relishes explaining complex scientific ideas for as wide an audience as possible. His writing has appeared in print and online publications including the *Guardian* and the *Financial Times*. He regularly interviews high-profile scientists, from Sir Paul Nurse to Jane Goodall, for the *Financial Times*. He has a regular slot writing science and innovation features for *The Long + Short* magazine. Ben is also in demand as a speaker. He's presented at Cheltenham Science Festival and talked about the neuroscience of creativity at the Wellcome Collection and The School of Life.

Mike Peake is a journalist and web content consultant with more than 25 years' experience in newspapers and national magazines. He began as a beat reporter on the local weekly near his hometown in the north-west before London and the thrill of glossy magazines lured him away for more than a decade of celebrity interviews and international travel. For five years he ran the features desk on the then-popular *FHM magazine*, and was at the now-defunct title throughout what many people perceive as 'the glory years'. In 2006 Mike left London to pursue a life away from the city; he has now been freelancing for a number of titles – from the *Daily Telegraph* and *Sunday Times* to *Harrods Magazine* and *Country Life* – for 10 years. Mike is currently working on 'yet another' movie idea, this time a blockbuster aimed at children.

ACKNOWLEDGEMENTS

This book has very many people to thank for the research, insights and interviews that inform it. *Knowledge* K and *collaboration* C are the two key elements that characterize this experience; in particular working with Ben Martynoga, Elizabeth Lovius, Kate Magee and Mike Peake. Thank you for the brilliant writing, guidance, insights and hard graft.

My sincere thanks go out to the talented creatives and innovators who so generously shared their stories and their work. Particular thanks to Jackie Lynton for choosing to share her inspiring story with me, and to Unity's Gerry Hopkinson and Nik Done for letting me nose around and get under the skin of their agency's brilliant creative culture.

Here is the full list of interviewees featured in the book. My gratitude to them all:

Michael Acton Smith, Mind Candy

Felix Barratt, Punchdrunk

Claire and Rupert Callender, The Green Funeral Company

Wendy Clark, DDB

Bruce Daisley, Twitter

Harry Dromey, Channel 4

Kelly Finnegan, Man V Beast (who also did the brilliant visuals in the toolkit)

Chris Gallery, Mother

Cindy Gallop, IfWeRanTheWorld and MakeLoveNotPorn

Arif Haq, Contagious Communications

Duane Holland, DH Ready

Gerry Hopkinson and Nik Done, Unity

Jason Hughes Sky Media

Sara Jones, Cass Business School, City, University of London

Jackie Lynton, IHOP –In Hope of People

Vicki Maguire, Grey London

Sandy Middleton, Racepoint Global

Anahita Milligan

Ramzi Moutran, Memac Ogilvy & Mather Dubai

Damien Newman, Central

Keith Reinhard, DDB

Petra Sammer, Ketchum

Damon Statt, Mischief PR

Matt Trinetti, The Escape School

John Wardley

John Whiston, ITV

Stuart Yeardsley, 3 Monkeys/Zero

From the academic world, heartfelt thanks to the faculty on the Masters in Innovation, Creativity and Leadership (the MICL) at Cass Business School, City, University of London. Without them this book would never have come to be. In particular Dr Sara Jones for her extensive guidance and advice through the early drafts, and her invocation of grit during later ones. Mary Ann Kernan for her assistance and encouragement in relation to getting the work published. Professor Clive Holtham's derivé sowed the seeds for the Creative Safari. Andy Wilkins introduced me to CPS, which provided a formal framework for 20 years experience on the ground.

Thanks to my friends and colleagues; Anahita for her always-on-the-money advice and practical input, and to Lucy Francis for being my right hand woman and holding the fort. To my mum, Jayne Bridges, for the proof reading and editing.

Thanks to clients past and present for their anecdotes, stories and support, including Ian Watson and Sam Redman at Prêt A Manger. The early supporters, and later readers – thanks Rimi Atwal, Jason Purfitt and Stuart Yeardsley for your feedback and input, which made everything better. Steve Latham at Cannes Lions Festival of Creativity for his support, and access to the archives for my research. And of course Jenny and Charlotte at Kogan Page for your support and unwavering enthusiasm for the project.

Most importantly thanks and love to my partner James for his support through the highs and lows of the creative process and being a brilliant and wise sounding board.

Thank you everyone! I hope you enjoy the book you helped to create.

Introduction

Why I wrote this book and how to use it

What does it take to be creative in business? This is the question this book sets out to address. Creativity can be intimidating and subjective, and the information on the subject overwhelming.

When I first became responsible for driving creativity in a 100-strong PR agency owned by WPP, one of the world's biggest marketing companies (where ideas were its lifeblood) it dawned on me that despite being labelled 'creative' myself, I didn't know any formal techniques or processes. Throughout my 15-year career up to that point, I had used my intuition and just got on with it. I honed my skills on the job learning through trial and error and from some talented folk along the way.

When I became a Creative Director, I went looking for the answers to the many questions I had:

- Is it possible to develop personal creative confidence, skills and behaviours?
- What processes and tools exist to make creativity more deliberate and sustained?
- How could I help my teams to be more creative?
- What does a thriving creative culture look like?
- What does it take to lead creativity?
- What could I learn from neuroscience that would help me and others to be more creative?

I immersed myself in the subject, reading everything I could find and set about learning and practising the creativity tools that I didn't even know existed when I started. *In Your Creative Element* is the handbook I wish I'd been given when I first became responsible for driving creativity and innovation in that business and beyond. Think of it as your curated guide to creativity – with the what, the why and the how combined.

The creative director role was the genesis of my obsession with the subject, which drove me to pursue an MSc in Innovation, Creativity and

Leadership at Cass Business School at City, University of London. Studying the academic research into creativity helped me to assimilate my practitioner experience and added science to my 'gut-feel' approach.

Through my studies and day-to-day training practice, I discovered that there is no 'one-size fits all' approach to creativity. We all have personal and cognitive preferences, life experiences, differing educations and upbringings, cultural contexts and working environments that all have a bearing on our approach. This book aims to share what academics and professional practitioners have to say on these subjects and to share my own good, bad and ugly personal experiences.

Mind the gap – the business case for creativity

Currently more people work in the creative industries than at any time before in UK history. There are 2.62 million creative roles, accounting for 1 in 12 UK jobs and the creative industries contribute £8 million an hour to the UK economy (Department for Culture Media and Sport – DCMS – 2014), a total worth of £ 71.4 billion per year. Even if your job title or sector doesn't fall into the DCMS description, creativity has been identified as the most essential skill for navigating an increasingly complex business world according to a global study of CEOs (IBM, 2010).

The World Economic Forum (WEF, 2016) has identified critical thinking/problem solving, creativity, communication and collaboration as four crucial competencies required as key skills to bridge what they term 'the 21st century skills gap'. Character qualities including curiosity, grit and leadership all also important in addressing the talent shortage.

Adobe's 'Creative Dividend' report found that 'companies that embrace creativity outperform peers and competitors on key business performance indicators, including revenue growth, market share, and talent acquisition' (Adobe, 2014). While 82 per cent of people agreed that businesses benefit from creativity, only 11 per cent asked said that their current practices are aligned with creative working. A further 61 per cent of senior managers felt that they do not compare well with firms recognized for their creativity and 10 per cent believed that their firm's practices were actually counter-creative.

You will be familiar with innovative brands like Uber, Apple, Google and Virgin. Creativity is not accidental in those ground-breaking organizations: there are deliberate processes, mindsets and environmental factors at play that anyone can learn from. But creative success is not dependent on having the resources of a million-dollar business or being listed on the FTSE 100.

I've deliberately focused on a wide range of sectors to show creativity in action for small businesses and well-known brands alike. We all know about creative 'geniuses' like Steve Jobs too but how can we mere mortals be more creative in our day-to-day work?

Three broad areas are covered in the book in order to help you develop and expand your knowledge of the subject:

- your individual creativity;
- creativity in teams;
- a culture for organizational creativity.

Chapter by chapter, you will reinforce your awareness of where you already excel and develop a strategy to further play to your strengths. We'll also explore where you might have a blind side. Additional focus will capitalize on your investment in order for you to reach your creative potential. After all, getting out of your comfort zone is the essence of creativity!

There are naysayers who say that creativity cannot be taught and who believe that it is the purview of the few. Or, that you have to wait for the muse to appear in her own sweet time. This book is not for those people. I believe that creativity is both art and science, and that whoever you are, whatever job you do, whatever industry you work in, there are ways of stacking the creative chips in your favour and establishing the ideal conditions to create something truly original.

The periodic table of creative elements

With ever-decreasing attention spans and the rise of visual media – from Instagram to emoticons – the periodic table of creative elements provides a visual shortcut to the contents of the book.

The table is a nod to the collision of art and science and is loosely based on Dmitri Mendeleev's original 19th-century periodic table designed to create structure and illustrate trends of then-known elements designed to predict properties of then-unknown elements. I liked the idea of adding order and logic to the concept of creativity – considered a 'dark art' by some and a science by others – as well as highlighting the known and unknown.

The full table is at the front of the book.

New radicals and creative thinking in the NHS

To bring the academic research and the elements to life I've interviewed many remarkable people. One case study features in several chapters: an inspiring story of the power of creativity to catalyse change in an unlikely institution. Thinking differently can be challenging in the commercial sector where profits and competitive advantage are the prize, so imagine trying to mobilize a radical grassroots movement for change within an institution like England's National Health Service – the fifth biggest employer in the world. Yet a group of change makers, including Jackie Lynton, did just that.

As former Head of Transformation in the NHS, Jackie was one of the key people behind NHS Change Day – a grassroots movement that invited staff to publicly pledge to improve patient care. It resulted in 189,000 pledges and is now an annual event. NHS Change Day is a social movement (which typically questions an established state) that began as a Twitter conversation and which has since spread to 10 provinces globally.

Leading innovation charity NESTA named NHS Change Day one of 50 'new radicals' and recognizes Jackie as a 'rebel thinker' who champions diversity of thought. The only healthcare entrants in the world, NHS Change Day were winners of the 'Leaders everywhere challenge' prize awarded by the *Harvard Business Review* and McKinsey M-Prize for management innovation.

Jackie is now a social change activist and a passionate advocate for the power of storytelling. She believes that living your purpose can drive extraordinary achievement. Jackie has generously shared her own story which is an inspiring, real-world and world-leading illustration of many of the creative elements: courage, grit and openness.

The structure of the book and how to read it

The book is designed to be dipped in and out of depending on your mood, need and attention span on any given day. The aim is to stimulate your thinking and to provide the building blocks for an action plan to up the creative ante for you or your company. Working through the book you'll discover your own unique creative formula using a combination of the elements.

Each of the nine chapters is made up of its different elements and is interspersed with creative coaching questions (reflecting on where you are now in relation to each element) and creative experiments (practical things to do right now) sprinkled throughout each chapter. These questions have been developed in collaboration with uber-coach and leadership expert Elizabeth Lovius who works with 'rockstar' CEO's and elite sportspeople to keep them on their 'A game'.

Of all human activities, creativity comes closest to providing the fulfillment we all hope to get in our lives. Call it full-blast living.
Mihaly Csikszentmihalyi, 1996

I suggest that you begin with Chapters 1 (Definitions) and 2 (The values of creative people). Your perspective on these two topics will inform your world view on creativity and will affect how you read the rest of the book.

Chapter 3 explores the characteristics of creative individuals. What makes us define one person as creative over another? What behaviours can we adopt to be more creative in our working lives?

In Chapter 4 we'll investigate the inner workings of the creative mind with neuroscientist Ben Martynoga. Chapter 5 asks what creative companies do differently to those that stagnate, or even worse, die? We'll explore the eight elements that contribute to a thriving creative culture. Why does creativity matter? What do we use it for? Having a shared purpose is key to creative companies.

Chapter 6 – covering Purpose – explores how love and money collide in the mission-driven business and how to create meaning for yourself and your people.

The idea that we can deliberately shape and influence our personal creativity is a relatively modern one. In Chapter 7 – The creative process – I'll share different frameworks to approach creative challenges and add structure. Chapter 8 delves into the practical business of 'making', or being creative, with a range of tools and techniques to help conquer the blank page, and ways to evaluate your ideas.

The final chapter brings it all together and looks at how you can create a personal action plan – or one for your organization – and put it to work back at the ranch, along with your personal creativity formula.

Let's blast off.

Definitions 01

This chapter looks at these 10 creative elements:

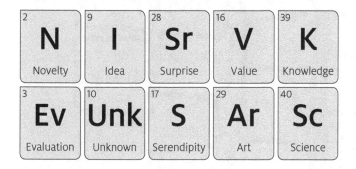

What is creativity?

Creativity is almost infinite. It involves every sense – sight, smell, hearing, feeling, taste and even perhaps the extrasensory. Much of it is unseen, nonverbal, and unconscious.
Pioneering creativity researcher E Paul Torrance, 1998

This chapter shares research from some of the key thinkers in creativity, along with definitions to help inform your work and creative conversations. I'll share how companies like Google and Heineken use shared definitions to shape their work, and my go-to definition. We'll also look at factors beyond the rational, including serendipity.

Creativity is a famously tricky thing to define:

Figure 1.1 Typical one-word definitions of creativity from workshop delegates

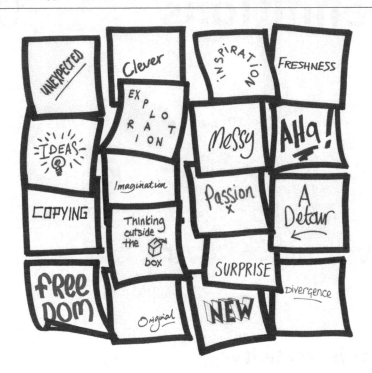

I've evaluated many definitions, asked business leaders and hundreds of professionals in our workshops for their thoughts on creativity. Here's a selection:

Michael Acton Smith, internet entrepreneur and founder of UK entertainment company, Mind Candy says:

> I think creative people are very curious and I think I am, too... I think that mindset of always being open and excited and looking at different things rather than being stuck in a rut (as many people are) exposes you to new ideas and you start to be able to connect the dots between different industries. That's when the more creative things start to emerge.

Matt Trinetti, co-founder of The Escape School believes that 'creativity is simply letting the little things stirring inside you come out and play in the real world. Ideas, sentences, art, businesses, movements. Anything really. It's giving space for things to emerge from you and through you, and then unleashing those things into the world.'

Bruce Daisley, UK Managing Director at Twitter told me that 'creativity isn't a skill, it's a practice'. Ed Catmull (2008), President at Pixar and Disney Animation Studios might agree. He observes:

People tend to think of creativity as a mysterious solo act, and they typically reduce products to a single idea: This is a movie about toys, or dinosaurs, or love... However, in filmmaking and many other kinds of complex product development, creativity involves a large number of people from different disciplines working effectively together to solve a great many problems.
A movie contains literally tens of thousands of ideas.

'No organization is creative,' says NASA's Jim Hodges (2011): 'People are creative, but the organization can foster or inhibit the creative by how work is conducted and how individual initiative is encouraged.'

Jackie Lynton (2016) is the former head of transformation at the National Health Service (NHS), whose story features throughout the book. She told me: 'Creativity for me is connecting with people, making things happen, and having hope for what is possible. When someone says the word "can't" I get excited because there could be a way, a possibility of something waiting to be born and [we shouldn't] impose limits on ourselves.'

Do you have your own definition?

While there are many and varied responses, answers tend to lend themselves to key aspects of creativity. Michael Acton Smith and Matt Trinetti focus on the *person*. The go-to response of 'thinking outside of the box' refers to *process* and Ed Catmull describes the output or *product* as well as process. NASA refers to aspects of environment or *place*.

Figure 1.2 The 4Ps of creativity

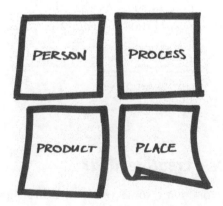

These categories are known as 'the 4Ps' (Rhodes, 1961). I'll look at them later in the book.

Creativity and innovation – one and the same?

These two terms are frequently used interchangeably, but there are key differences. When the conceptual idea tips into being a concrete product that's where creativity and innovation meet. The UK Department of Business, Innovation and Skills (2010) says innovation is 'the successful exploitation of new ideas'.

I have predominantly used the term 'creativity' throughout the book, but of course nascent ideas lead to innovations. The economist Theodore Levitt (2002) writes: 'Ideas are useless unless used. The proof of their value is their implementation. Until then they are in limbo.'

Below are my go-to definition and three examples of how a shared definition can benefit a business.

For application to business problems, I admire creativity guru and UK government adviser Sir Ken Robinson's definition of creativity as 'the process of having original ideas that have value' (2013).

 **Novelty**

I like the definition above because one can dismantle the concepts into manageable chunks – *process* suggests that there is a systematic way to approach a problem, *original* brings in the idea of *novelty* as a way to measure the *idea*.

 Idea

So what makes a creative idea?

Millward Brown work with some of the world's biggest companies to research and develop brand marketing campaigns. They define a big idea as 'a game-changer'. It shifts paradigms and turns category convention on its head. It must 'resonate, be disruptive, have talk value, transcend cultural and geographic boundaries and stretch the brand without straining credibility or believability.' (Hernandez, 2012)

Vicki Maguire, Executive Creative Director at advertising agency Grey London (responsible for award-winning advertising campaigns for Volvo and the British Heart Foundation) describes what makes a great creative idea for her:

> It's a mix of experience and gut feeling. If it answers the brief perfectly. If you can see it having a role in culture. If you can see people talking about it, writing about it in the press. If that idea's time is right, it's a good idea. Ideas have an energy that's infectious. If the team are excited and there's a buzz around it, then it's a good idea. (Maguire, 2016)

Sr Surprise

When evaluating ideas, I like to add a further dimension. Researchers in the field of Artificial Intelligence, Maher and Fisher (2012) bring together the criteria 'novelty, value and surprise' as ways to assess creative designs.

The aspect of surprise, for me, reflects the emotional aspect to creativity – invoking a feeling, a visceral response to an idea or a product.

V Value

Value suggests that the idea (or product or service) must be useful to the creator. Sales of course come under this element, as does return on investment (ROI), share of voice, brand reputation scores and shifts in behaviour.

CASE STUDY   Simples! How creative thinking and a talking Russian meerkat helped double the value of comparethemarket.com

Prior to 2009, price comparison websites were a low-interest, highly commoditized category with little differentiation. In a category where market share is determined by spend, www.comparethemarket.com were behind all their competitors, compounded by a long and unmemorable name (Campaign, 2009).

Responding to these challenges, and inspired by the highly successful Cadbury's gorilla ads, Aleksandr Orlov – a Russian meerkat aristocrat – was created, to play on the similarity between the words 'meerkat' and 'market'.

According to advertising agency VCCP, who created the campaign, one small footnote in the brief provided the unlikely insight for the final creative idea.

> We asked the creatives if they might be able to find a way of introducing a cheaper term or phrase into the advertising that could exist alongside 'market'… The cost per click on meerkats was in the region of 5p (market was £5)… So we rebriefed the idea to the creatives asking them to create layers of character, warmth and affection. Aleksandr Orlov was born.
> (campaign, 2009)

The integrated campaign has evolved over the past seven years to include prime-time TV sponsorship, merchandise and PR with a social media presence at its centre. Using Sir Ken Robinson's (2013) creativity definition above 'the process of having original ideas that have value' – the briefing story gives us a sense of the process involved behind the strategy and the creative idea.

The search strategy was smart and original. Using 'meerkat' as a way around the cost per click for the more expensive word 'market' ultimately led to the mascot's creation. For me, this epitomizes creative thinking at its best – if you can't outspend the competition, outthink them.

In the UK insurance category the Churchill's dog had previously been used effectively, and using characters itself is not new. Think of Tony the Tiger (Kellogg's) or the Cadbury's Gorilla, which inspired this campaign. Orlov's character builds on what has gone before. For this category, the work was groundbreaking and upped the creative ante for the whole category, spawning other character-led campaigns from competitors.

There is no doubting the value that the comparethemeerkat campaign has delivered – a year's worth of objectives were met nine weeks after its initial launch with the cost per visit reduced by 73 per cent and quote volumes increased by over 83 per cent (*Campaign*, 2009). The campaign doubled the value of the brand (*Daily Mail*, 2014).

Was the campaign surprising? A talking Russian meerkat and the use of storytelling and humour in this space was unexpected. The campaign also shows *risk-taking* Rt in challenging the norms of the category. The character has made an impact in popular *culture* c with the meerkat's catchphrase 'simples' being included in the *Oxford English Dictionary* (2016).

With 68,000 Twitter followers and demand outstripping supply for merchandise, customers have high levels of engagement with Orlov. The ad agency commented: 'We couldn't differentiate rationally. People were sick of the rational stuff and weren't really listening.' Their strategy in one word was *love*. We'll explore the elements of *emotion* Em and *logic* L further in Chapter 4.

So would you define the campaign as creative, and in what ways?

There will always be subjectivity and questions about how novel, or surprising or valuable something is (one could begin perhaps to apply a scale or rating) but having a clear and agreed definition can make discussing creative ideas easier, as we'll see with Heineken's Creative Ladder below.

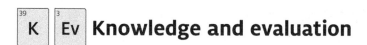 **Knowledge and evaluation**

Any output of the creative process is subject to scrutiny and consideration as to its merits. In order to decide how creative something is you'll need to apply your *knowledge*, which is also required for the element of *evaluation*. In Chapter 4 I'll bring together insights from neuroscience and psychology to understand how we make decisions, along with evaluation tools in Chapter 8.

Dr Ruth Noller (2001), one of the leading contributors to the field of creativity research, created this equation:

$$C = fa(KIE)$$

This suggests that creativity is the interaction of knowledge, imagination and evaluation. f is a mathematical term that means everything inside the brackets is affected by what's outside – the 'a' represents a positive attitude.

'Knowledge is essential for judging the products,' says Ferran Adrià, three-star Michelin chef and founder of the much-lauded (now defunct) restaurant El Bulli. Adrià is widely regarded as one of the most innovative chefs on the planet. He describes the years spent experimenting, tasting and gaining experience as 'the mental palate' which all contribute to a 'chef's mental database' (Adrià and Soler, 2012). His famous 'deconstruction' process uses traditional ingredients that are creatively transformed, preserving the original flavours so that they are identifiable to the diner in some ways, while being completely surprising in others.

▶

Take Adria's version of the classic Spanish omelette (Carlin, 2011):

First, he reduces the old-fashioned tortilla to its three component parts: eggs, potatoes and onions. Then he cooks each separately. The finished product, the deconstructed outcome, is one-part potato foam... one-part onion purée, one-part egg-white sabayon. One isolated component is served on top of the other in layers, and topped with crumbs of deep-fried potatoes. The dish, minuscule, comes inside a sherry glass.

This description of Adria's process perfectly sums up combinational creativity (Boden, 2004) – the rearrangement of existing ideas (here, ingredients) to create something new.

Why defining creativity matters for your business

There are still businesses that see creativity as little more than a cosmetic: a final touch of lipstick to make a product look more appealing. They are profoundly wrong... Applied creativity can be as central, as integral and as functional as any operating system; and should be expected to be so.
Phil Lader, WPP Chairman, 2014

A shared understanding and definition of creativity can help to set the direction and creative ambition for a business, and act as a filter for which ideas to pursue.

Heineken's creative ladder

The creative ladder is a process designed to produce creative work: 'So brilliant, it will be remembered when we're all dead,' says Søren Hagh, Heineken Global Marketing Executive Director (Magee, 2015).

One of the challenges around creativity is identifying a common language that people can understand and share. Hagh explains: 'People have different interpretations of what it is... there can be misunderstanding and people shy away from discussions around it.' (Magee, 2015)

The award-winning marketing team at Dutch brewing company Heineken has found a way to do this using their 10-step 'creative ladder' as a framework to evaluate ideas. The company uses the ladder to define what great work is, and to evaluate its own creative output as well as that of other brands.

Figure 1.3 Heineken's creative ladder

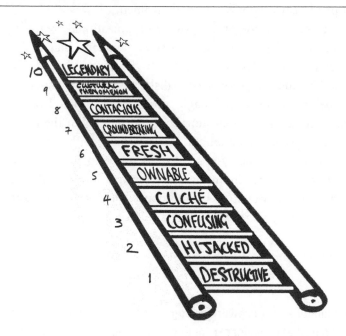

The company believes that clichéd work will not have a positive impact for example, and strives for work high on its scale. Arif Haq is an ex-PepsiCo marketer who now leads the creative capabilities practice at Contagious Insider, the consultancy hired by Heineken to develop the ladder. He says: 'Initially Heineken came to us and simply said "We need better creativity." The first question that came to mind was obviously "What do you mean by better?" Without a universally understood definition, you can expect lots of frustrating hours spent wasted between clients and their peers, with their bosses and most definitely with their agencies. When clients, who generally aren't creative professionals, don't have a consistent language to evaluate creative work, they tend to fall back to their safe space which is quite often overly subjective disqualifiers that aren't very helpful in building better work. Stuff like "I don't like cats" or "My wife won't like it" (they sound ridiculous, but I've heard them in real life).

'This is when we came up with the idea of the ladder. It was based on the idea of Leo Burnett's Global Product Committee scale, only more practically focused for clients rather creatives. Full credit to Heineken – they absolutely saw the value of it from the start and have continued to embrace it. The real power of the ladder is not in the 1–10 number (that's really just so we can benchmark over time) but rather in the descriptions of each rung. I've seen clients use that language verbatim in creative discussions and it transforms their ability to have meaningful conversations about an area in which they have not previously been professionally trained.'

'There are many factors in improving organizational creativity, but one of the critical ones is having a consistent language that allows you to define what it is and what it is not. Creativity is frankly a discipline with a disproportionately high level of bullshit merchants who try and hide the topic behind a curtain of magic and mystery. What I've seen is that by having a lingua franca that aims to build literacy in the topic, creative capability can absolutely be taught. We're dealing with a complex part of human cognition, but when you see a marketer who at the start of the day is convinced they are not in any way creative get introduced to a tool like the ladder, and you watch their confidence blossom right there in front of you, it's incredibly worthwhile' (Haq, 2016).

Tip

Use the ladder as a framework to judge and improve your existing ideas. Think about what components your company might find useful and create your own.

Heineken also has an internal creative council, comprising its agencies' creative directors and internal marketers to encourage collaboration and debate.

Google's moon shots

Google CEO and co-founder Larry Page doesn't believe in making small improvements – he's looking for breakthrough ideas that will change the status quo. Google calls this process 10x – making any product 10 times better than its competitors. Google X was established in 2010 to try to imagine the seemingly impossible – the self-driving car and Google Glass were born out of this process.

Page explains (Levy, 2013):

It's natural for people to want to work on things that they know aren't going to fail. But incremental improvement is guaranteed to be obsolete over time. Especially in technology, where you know there's going to be non-incremental change. So a big part of my job is to get people focused on things that are not just incremental. Google calls these big bets 'moon shots'.

> **Tip**
>
> Be clear what kind of creativity you are looking for – if it's breakthrough or incremental – and add some real ambition to the problem statement.

Paddy Power's mischief department

Bookmaker Paddy Power's creative ambitions are clearly articulated. In order to drive bets, its' 'Mischief Department' has hijacked sporting events to create headlines across the world's media. The department's name drives a clear creative direction, one that points to risk-taking and pushing boundaries. Stunts have involved Stephen Hawking, the Vatican, illegal immigrants and the Amazon rainforest. Despite being a listed company Paddy Power's says it has a 'tongue-in-cheek attitude' to marketing.

Harry Dromey was Paddy Power's chief Mischief Maker from 2013 to 2015. He told me: 'The riskiest thing is to be boring. You need an element of risk to make great creative work. You also need to foster a culture, the right atmosphere and the attitude. Things get lost to consumers if messaging is bland.'

So far, so rational. But what about our next element – the unknown?

10 Unk The unknown

Despite all the research and debate, there is still much that is unknown in relation to creativity. By reason alone, it is still beyond comprehension. It may be surprising to read that the president of one of the most successful creative companies on the planet, Pixar's Ed Catmull (2014) believes in the importance of this element. In *Creativity, Inc* he writes: 'The mechanisms that keep us safe from unknown threats have been hardwired into us since before our ancestors were fighting off sabre-tooth tigers with sticks. But when it comes to creativity, the unknown is not our enemy. If we make room for it instead of shunning it, the unknown can bring inspiration and originality.'

S Serendipity

The element of serendipity – the faculty of making happy and unexpected discoveries by accident – also plays its part in creativity. Fleming's discovery of penicillin is a well-documented example of finding what you're not looking for. His accidental observation of bacteria in a Petri dish led to his Nobel Prize in 1945.

Swiss engineer George de Mestral invented Velcro following a walk with his dogs when he noticed that tiny burdock burrs had attached themselves to their fur via their tiny hooks.

Many writers include chance, luck, fate and magic in their descriptions of creativity.

In *Big Magic* (2015) Elizabeth Gilbert writes: 'The Greeks and Romans both believed in the external daemon of creativity... who lived within the walls of your home and who sometimes helped you in your labours.' The Romans called this your genius – your guardian deity, the conduit of your inspiration. Which is to say, the Romans didn't believe that an exceptionally gifted person *was* a genius; they believed that an exceptionally gifted person *had* a genius.

Shakespeare refers to them in his sonnets, and later the Romantic poets like Blake and Coleridge invoked the muse for creative inspiration. Rudyard Kipling noted that he had a supernatural 'daemon' that commanded him to write the *Jungle Books* and *Kim*.

Even today innumerable songwriters, designers and artists cite their 'muse' as inspiration. The realm of the arts is where society is perhaps more inclined to acknowledge the concept of the unknown and unexplainable in relation to creativity.

Ar Sc Art and science

This periodic table would not be complete without a nod to art and science – creativity is often described as a blend of these two elements and there are many books dedicated to both areas.

Picasso is often named when I ask people to list the creatives who inspire them, along with a business maverick like Sir Richard Branson. Scientists crop up less often.

By necessity, scientists are champions of rationality and logical ninjas. Logic is a crucial pillar of the creative process, but this fact tends to get overlooked in favour of the idea of an 'aha!' moment that erupts out of the blue.

The focus of this book is 'applied creativity' for business, but there are many elements that apply whatever the creative endeavour; the need for grit, failure, passion and imagination to name but a few.

CREATIVE EXPERIMENT

THE ARMCHAIR JUDGE

Challenge yourself, your definitions of creativity and your objectivity. From the suggestions in this chapter, pick some criteria to evaluate ideas against – perhaps 'novelty, value and surprise' (Maher and Fisher, 2012) or the Heineken creative ladder. Now use these criteria as a lens to judge anything creatively, in your field or beyond. It will challenge your thinking and push you to really explore *why and how* something is creative.

Take the list and apply it to a product, service or idea out in the world. You could set up your own 'creative counsel' with a group of your colleagues and compare notes.

Find relevant examples from your sector – perhaps The Grocer New Product Awards, Thinkbox TV Planning Awards, the Cannes Lions Festivals of Creativity, Innovation or Healthcare or The Webby or Shorty Awards. Whatever your industry benchmark is, pick 5–10 pieces of work to assess. Using your criteria, take 10 minutes with a coffee and evaluate the work.

Pay attention to your initial (emotional) responses, apply some of the thinking and criteria in this chapter, and then reassess. You could try using the evaluation matrix tool (see Chapter 8) and allocate each item a score.

- What do you notice about your responses?
- How easy do you find it to be objective?
- What might you do differently next time you have to judge creative ideas?

REVIEW THE CHAPTER

- What's your personal definition of creativity?
- Do any of the quotes included above particularly resonate with you?
- Do you think that you look through any of the lenses more than the others – a person-centric, process, product or place approach over any of the others?
- Would your team benefit from a shared understanding? What about your organization?
- How do you think the definitions affect how you might evaluate creativity?
- What might you do differently at work having read this chapter?

Table 1.1 Definitions

Element	Key question	Which area most interests you in terms of developing your personal or team action plan and finding out more? Rate your interest level out of 10.
Novelty (N)	How new or original is the idea, product or any other output?	
Idea (I)	What defines a creative idea for you or your company?	
Surprise (Sr)	Is there an element of the unusual or the unexpected in the idea or product?	
Value (V)	What is the value of the idea both to the creator and the intended audience?	
Knowledge (K)	Could you improve your knowledge in your own or a related field to improve creative ideas?	
Evaluation (Ev)	What criteria do you apply to your own or others' creative work?	

Table 1.1 *continued*

Element	Key question	Which area most interests you in terms of developing your personal or team action plan and finding out more? Rate your interest level out of 10.
Unknown (Unk)	What do you think about the role of chance, magic and luck in relation to your own creativity?	
Serendipity (S)	Do you have any personal experience of serendipity?	
Art (Ar)	Do you relate to aesthetics, beauty and the need for self-expression associated with being artistic?	
Science (Sc)	Do you relate to the order, logic and process associated with science?	

IN A NUTSHELL

A shared understanding and definition of creativity can help to set the direction and creative ambition for a business and act as a filter for which strategies to pursue. Later on, the definitions can act as criteria by which to judge your own and others' ideas. As a starting point it's useful to have your own definition and if you're running a team or a company to have a collective definition that can act as the North Star for your initiatives.

DIG DEEPER

Ken Robinson's 2006 TED Talk 'Do schools kill creativity?' challenges notions of what creativity is, how it relates to intelligence and what it means for education.

The values of creative people

This chapter looks at these six creative elements:

1	6	7	13	14	26
Cr	**Cs**	**Fr**	**Co**	**F**	**Gr**
Creativity	Curiosity	Freedom	Courage	Fun	Grit

Each of us has many, many maps in our head, which can be divided into two main categories: maps of the way things are, or realities, and maps of the way things should be, or values. We interpret everything we experience through these mental maps.
Stephen Covey, 2013

This chapter focuses on mindset and explores the six values that research shows are helpful for being creative. We'll see how values drive creativity at Netflix, why The Royal Navy measures cheerfulness, how curiosity sparked the idea for the most shared advertisement of 2013 for the United Nations, and why being gritty aids creativity.

Values are the guiding forces in your life – your internal life compass

Values embody your beliefs and attitudes. Essentially they act as a lodestar or map to direct decision-making at times when the answer eludes you. Whether they are consciously or unconsciously held, values are usually quite stable, but can change in relation to (big) life events or when you deliberately revaluate and question whether they are no longer helpful.

Values are the foundations that underpin your world view, influencing the way you make decisions and judge those of other people. Values are key to motivation. If our values help determine our thoughts, feelings and actions, then it's useful to explore whether the values we hold help or hinder our personal creativity. Otherwise no amount of savvy problem-solving techniques, processes, inspiration (or perspiration) will help.

One of my important values is having fun (an acknowledged boost for creativity) so 'the fun factor' is a filter through which I make decisions on both a personal and professional basis. However playfulness can lead to inertia or tetchiness if I consider an activity dull or boring. In theory, I also crave adventure, but when balanced against one of my other important values – security – this wins hands down, which explains why I have never quite got around to booking that sky-dive.

Understanding my need for security has forced me to re-evaluate how I approach the generation of new ideas and risk-taking so I deliberately push myself out of my 'comfort zone' in order to move forward. As acquiring wealth can make us feel more secure, our attitude to money is also a value in itself, but it can conflict with the freedom 'value'. For me this means I can be rebellious or stubborn if I have to juggle income with choice (do I want to work with this person or client?). None of this is right or wrong, it just *is*. For me this is useful to remember when I feel uncomfortable in creative or other situations. Do you recognize any of your values here, and what impact do you think they have on you creatively?

There are hundreds of possible values

Shalom H Schwartz is a leading authority on the subject. He proposed 10 universal values (which act as a gateway for many other values) that are recognized across all major cultures (Zanna, 1992). The universal values and some commonly associated with these are:

Table 2.1 Values

Universal value (Schwartz, 2012)	Example values (adapted from Schwartz, 2012)
Self-direction	Freedom, curiosity, creativity, openness to change, control, mastery.
Stimulation	Excitement, variety, novelty, challenge.
Hedonism	Pleasure, enjoying life, fun, self-indulgence.
Achievement	Ambition, intelligence, self-respect, competency, grit.
Power	Authority, wealth, social recognition, social power, preserving public image.

Table 2.1 *continued*

Universal value (Schwartz, 2012)	Example values (adapted from Schwartz, 2012)
Security	Concerned with social order, national security, a sense of belonging.
Conformity	Politeness, obedience, self-discipline, maintain status quo.
Tradition	Moderate, devout, detached, humble.
Benevolence	Friendship, responsibility, forgiveness, honesty, loyalty.
Universalism	Equality, wisdom, beauty, social-justice, peace, nature, harmony.

When values are activated, they become infused with feeling. People for whom independence is an important value become aroused if their independence is threatened, despair when they are helpless to protect it, and are happy when they can enjoy it.
Shalom H Schwartz, 2012

Take a look at Schwartz's list above. Are there any values that you clearly identify with? Any that you reject straight away?

Imagine the values of three different people:

- A venture capitalist might hold the values associated with power: wealth, competition, authority.
- The founder of a social enterprise could have values associated with universalism like equality, social justice, benevolence and responsibility.
- An artist's universal values may be a combination of stimulation, hedonism and self-direction expressing freedom, creativity and beauty.

Our values drive our behaviour – the venture capitalist's motivation is to make money for themselves (or others) so the behaviour is spending money on themselves and demonstrating wealth and power. The social enterprise founder makes money but puts the profits to wider good so their behaviour is sharing and collaboration. The artist may create for the rewards of self-expression, beauty and mastery of their craft with little consideration for financial matters.

Now take a moment to imagine what values the British royal family might hold. What do you imagine the values of the Kardashian family might be? If you worked for one these 'firms' which values do you think would best support the generation and development of ideas?

As former head of transformation in the NHS Jackie Lynton was one of the key people behind NHS Change Day – a grassroots movement that resulted in 189,000 staff pledges.

My values: integrity is important, basic respect for each other despite hierarchy, in hope of people and the human spirit, what can we do for others, contributing to a higher purpose that is bigger than ourselves and helping people to grow. For me fun is also a strong value, as is courage. Start with finding your own story of who you are and know your values. When you live your values it builds resilience by reminding you why you do what you do.

Can you identify which universal values Jackie's list reflects?

Researchers Dollinger *et al* (2007) found that values including tradition, conformity, security and power are not helpful to creativity (as you may have surmised from thinking about the two different 'royal' families.)

The first three elements in this chapter – *creativity*, *curiosity* and *freedom* are all related to self-direction which is positively associated with creativity. Dan Pink's work on motivation, which we'll consider later, also supports the importance of these self-directed values, including mastery.

Cr **Creativity**

Why are you reading this book? As Jay-Z said, 'You coulda been anywhere in the world, but you're here with me, I appreciate that.' Obviously creativity is a key value for you.

In order to create the right environment in which to be more creative, it's helpful to establish a set of goals:

- As far as creativity is concerned, what specifically do you hope to achieve or be able to do, that you can't do now?

- What is motivating you?
- What are you prepared to do to achieve your goal?
- Will you need any help?
- Are you ready?
- Let's go!

Throughout the book you'll find coaching questions, designed to help you determine where you are now in relation to each of the elements. This is the first and it's a bit longer than the others as your views in relation to this chapter will inform how you digest the book.

CREATIVE COACH

What do you stand for? Working out your personal values

If you already know about your values and want to dive straight into the other elements, skip this exercise and head straight to page 30. If you've got 15 minutes to dig a bit deeper then grab a coffee and come on in.

We have values in four different core areas of our lives: family, career, health and relationships. Creating a values statement in order to set the direction is a standard exercise for many leaders and businesses, and one you may well be familiar with.

If you don't already have a clear idea of your personal values, the exercise below is the good place to begin. For teams, this can be a powerful way to start thinking about a shared understanding of creativity and the starting point to build your personal, team or company creative manifesto. It's quite possible that your words and language may not be the same as Schwartz's and that's OK. Fun is not used as a word by Schwartz but it's clear that it relates to enjoying life. The priority is being clear on what's important to you (which, of course, you may already be).

Jim Kouzes and Barry Posner (2008) have worked with thousands of leaders around the world. This is their exercise to start eliciting and exploring your values.

They invite you to 'write a tribute' to yourself. Imagine you are about to attend an important event – perhaps your 70th birthday party or to win a lifetime achievement award in your industry – where your friends, colleagues and family will speak in your honour.

▶

What will people say about you and what you stand for that will make you feel proud and happy? To help, ask yourself some (or all) of these questions:

- 'What do you stand for?'
- 'What do you believe in?'
- 'What are you discontented about?'
- 'What brings you suffering?'
- 'What makes you jump for joy?'
- 'What are you passionate about?'
- 'What keeps you awake at night?'
- 'What's grabbed hold and won't let go?'
- 'What do you want for your life?'
- 'Just what is it that you really care about?' (Kouzes and Posner, 2008)

Ask yourself 'why?' at the end of each question.

Is a clear set of values and things that are important to you emerging? You might be wondering how to work out whether something is a 'value'. A really simple way of doing it is to think about a value as a big theme or concept, not a physical thing you can touch.

Now review your list. Rank the values you have in order of their importance to you. I like to do this on Post-its so they can be moved around easily. Live with the list for a little while. Looking at the list, do you feel happy and proud of yourself? Does it really get to the heart of what's important to you?

Take a look at your top three values. Consider whether they help or hinder you creatively. It doesn't matter if you don't have any values that are listed here. At the end of the chapter we'll ask to review the values shown to be helpful for creativity and assess their relevance to you.

Figure 2.1 Prioritize your personal values

Kouzes and Posner suggest that as a next step you write your own 'credo' memo. This is your personal statement to direct your wishes if you were not around to do so and should be punchy, no longer than one side of paper. Think about this as your own personal mission statement. Here's my credo memo:

> Life's too short to stare at a blank piece of paper. Reject mediocrity. Take a risk. Play more. Get outside. Dream big. Believe in yourself. Persist. Be magnetic. Drink tea. Get lost. Dance. Shower the people you love with love (thanks James Taylor). Be brave. Say yes. Sing. Eat more cake. Seek forgiveness, not permission. Surprise yourself.

What would yours be?

You could also initiate a writing a 'credo dialogue' with your team – each person writing their own credo memo and comparing what's important, looking for shared values and purpose.

Our next element is *curiosity*.

Cs Curiosity

We're driven by this relentless curiosity – which is the inventor instinct, the entrepreneur instinct, and what I believe is also the creative agency instinct of 'We can make this better' or 'We can do this in a different way.' With people like that, I know we've all got a fighting chance of being able to work together.
Unity co-founder Gerry Hopkinson, 2015

Curiosity is an intrinsic part of being human. As babies and children we have a basic drive to explore our surroundings. Instinctively, curiosity and creativity seem bound together – but how does one impact the other?

What's your CQ?

Personality expert Tomas Chamorro-Premuzic argues that in a world of information overload, curiosity quotient or CQ is as important to business as both intellectual and emotional quotients (IQ and EQ). He says that in an era of complexity 'people with higher CQ are more inquisitive and open to new experiences. They find novelty exciting and are quickly bored with routine. They tend to generate many original ideas and are counter-conformist' (Chamorro-Premuzic, 2014). He believes that CQ is also something that can be nurtured in an individual, which is useful in the pursuit of creativity: 'IQ is difficult to coach. EQ and CQ can be developed.'

There's a CQ test you can take written by Earl Nightingale the 'Dean of personal development'. Find his *Creative Thinking* audiobook and test on i-Tunes.

CASE STUDY

Unless it's breaking new ground we're not interested. Why bother doing something that's been done before?
Felix Barrett, Artistic Director and Founder, Punchdrunk, 2016

Since 2000, immersive theatre company Punchdrunk has created 20 must-see promenade productions. In 2013 Punchdrunk had a hit London show with *The*

Drowned Man: A Hollywood Fable. A Punchdrunk trademark: the audience members became anonymous behind Venetian beaked carnival masks while they silently followed the actors who moved around the different floors and spaces. Participants roved and followed the action they were drawn to, splitting up from their friends and following their curiosity. It was a sometimes disorientating, profound experience, as unlike any West End theatre production as you can imagine and an approach that has spawned many imitators and a legion of fans.

Felix Barrett is Punchdrunk's founder and Artistic Director. I asked him to explain what the world of business can learn about curiosity from his boundary-pushing theatre company. He told me:

> *It's often more powerful not to say anything at all and to create mystery. When we launched* Sleep No More *in New York we had zero marketing spend and it sold out. In a way we do the opposite of traditional marketing, and that's what attracts brands to us. We avoid the conventional and inspire word of mouth. We give the audience an experience and it lives on, becoming a personal story – 'you'll never guess what happened to me'. It's initially instinctual and emotional, not a cerebral response, and that leaves a serious imprint.*

Figure 2.2 Fernanda Prata and Jesse Kovarsky in Punchdrunk's *The Drowned Man: A Hollywood fable* (2013–14)

Punchdrunk empowers its audiences; brands should empower their consumers. Don't spoon-feed the audience, create a big whacking mystery! Complexity and curiosity are big drivers personally and professionally – if you don't show the whole picture, the unexpected and the unknown suddenly have important roles to play. You need to give yourself time to experiment, to develop ideas and play around with different concepts. Not everything has to be fully polished to engage and animate audiences. (Barratt, 2016)

Curiosity drives creativity

In 2013 unwomen.org ran a powerful campaign (see Figure 2.3, below) to highlight widespread sexism and discrimination against women around the world. The 'autocomplete truth' used real online auto-completed internet searches to expose negative, stereotyped and often shocking results in relation to women's rights.

The searches included: women cannot drive, women shouldn't vote and women shouldn't have rights.

Curiosity caused the team to dig deeper and re-evaluate something that was happening thousands of times a day. Using the hashtag #womenshould the shareable campaign allowed people all over the world to create their own version of the image on social media. With a budget of just US $3,000 the campaign was *Adweek*'s most shared advertisement of 2013, and won Social Good campaign 2013 (Ad Council), generated over 1.3 billion global impressions and won a coveted Cannes Lion Award for creativity and effectiveness in 2015.

Ramzi Moutran is Executive Creative Director at Memac Ogilvy and Mather Dubai, the advertising agency that created the idea. He told me: 'With a lot of topics, we think of them as "old" last-century issues, when actually the same problems are still amongst us if we look closer. The campaign proves that gender equality isn't there yet, and it's only the tip of the iceberg.'

Figure 2.3 The auto-complete truth campaign for unwomen.org

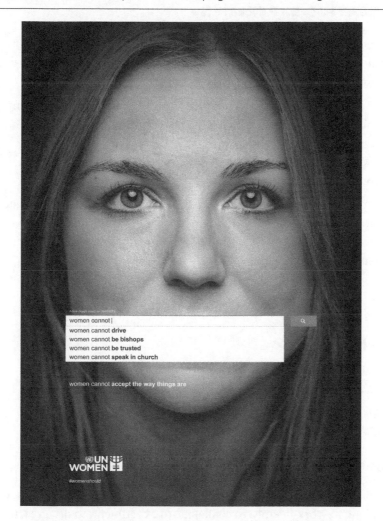

CREATIVE COACH

- How can you bring your passion for what intrigues and interests you outside work into the office day-to-day to spark creativity?

- Reflect on times when you have been highly curious and others when you have been utterly bored.

- What stimulates curiosity in you? How could you bring curiosity to what seems boring?

CREATIVE EXPERIMENT

- If you're trying to devise ideas for a product, service or concept, ask: what could we create that intrigues people to lean in and find out more?

- As an intro to your next creativity session, gather some random objects together and as a group, develop your curiosity muscle and ask about each one: Who made it, why did they make it? Who first made one? How did it come into existence? How many other uses could there be?

- For your next creative challenge make a list of people you consider to be curious. Choose them one by one and consider how they would approach the challenge. Don't censor, just step into their shoes. Now apply their thinking back to your challenge.

Fr | Freedom

The ultimate freedom for creative groups is the freedom to experiment with new ideas. Some skeptics insist that innovation is expensive. In the long run, innovation is cheap. Mediocrity is expensive – and autonomy can be the antidote.
Tom Kelley, IDEO, 2011

Freedom can take many forms – to make mistakes, to take decisions, to fail, to explore, to work flexibly, to challenge, to experiment, to disagree, to share information, to break the rules, to be unrestricted, to have free time and to decide where to work. For some people working around structures, rules and processes is stifling. The phrase 'ask for forgiveness, not for permission' is a common mantra for those working in innovation. Freedom is a core component of motivation which we'll explore more in the next chapter.

Google is famed for giving employees scope – 20 per cent time, flexible working, personal development time, choices over where to work, frequent breaks, bowling and mindfulness all on 'work-time'. They say they want to create the happiest, most productive workplace in the world. Research backs up what many companies like Google instinctively know – freedom results in more and better ideas and a happier workforce. Creativity researchers Patterson *et al* (2009): 'Innovative people are intrinsically motivated and autonomous; they are likely to thrive in organizations which allow them the freedom to choose how to work and when to work.'

How much freedom do you have in your work and how important is it to you?

Freedom is definitely a core value for me. When I was an MD, working with a 30-strong group, I made a radical (much-derided by many of my colleagues) decision. My job depended on my ability to give good counsel and to generate a never-ending stream of ideas for clients. I felt stifled by having to be in the office 24/7 and decided to work a four-day week to give myself the headspace, freedom and energy I felt I needed to do perform well. Clients were very supportive, but many people in the industry told me that it couldn't be done. Some were just incredulous that I didn't want to be in the office. When I became Creative Director I continued working four days a week and I know it made me better at my job. James Webb Young was a leading thinker in the advertising industry and in his classic 1965 publication, *A Technique for Producing Ideas* he refers to the curious 'tentacles of the mind'. I couldn't just switch off on those days out of the office and it gave me much-needed time and space to noodle on the client's problems.

But I know that some of my colleagues thought it signalled a lack of ambition and commitment. My desire for freedom trumped many other values (including the security of the monthly pay packet) and led to me starting my own business.

It seems I'm not alone.

According to Escape The City (2015) there are three key reasons why people leave big companies: 50 per cent want to start their own business, 64 per cent want more opportunities for more creativity, innovation and entrepreneurialism and 61 per cent want a greater sense of freedom, autonomy and independence in their working lives.

CASE STUDY　The corporate escapee

Matt Trinetti is a former IBM consultant who quit in 2014 to run The Escape School, part of escapethecity.org, a London-based initiative that helps frustrated city workers get out of the rat race and pursue more fulfilling (and often more creative) careers. Starting around a kitchen table, the founders wanted to do something different and their goal is to help one million people find work they love. I asked him:

Figure 2.4 Matt Trinetti, Founding Director of Escape the City's Escape School

How easy was the transition from the corporate world into an entrepreneurial, creative one?

'It hasn't been easy. Psychologically, working in the corporate world fantastically trains you to do things neatly, by the book, and not ruffle any feathers. Everything must have a purpose and that purpose is usually linked back to profitability and productivity. On the flip side, creative work isn't always polite, clean or profitable. So learning to be OK with creating just for creation's sake is a tough thing to accept. Professionally it's also difficult because the paths appear less linear and more uncertain.'

What's the biggest creative challenge you've had to overcome?

'There are a few. One is giving myself the permission to let my ideas play. Another is developing confidence in my ideas and my creativity. A third is persistently working at it – showing up and doing the work required to get better. I'm still in the process of "overcoming" all of these.'

When you see people at Escape School, is it refreshing to see these worker drones brimming over with creative ideas, or is it actually quite tricky to tease out their ideas?

'Every person is different. For some the ideas flow freely; for others it takes more work. Most people do have ideas though – the problem is that as soon as an idea comes, they're quick to judge and discount it. Too many ideas fail because they're instantly destroyed by the voices in people's heads telling them what they can and cannot do'.

CREATIVE COACH

What creates a sense of limitation for you?

- Is there a voice in your head holding you back?
- What is it saying?
- What if the opposite were true?

When was the last time you felt really free? What was that like and what enabled you to be free? Consider the following:

- How could you bring that freedom into your creative life?
- What processes limit your creativity at work? How could these be removed?
- If you are a leader, where are there opportunities for you to offer your employees more freedom? What benefits might come from that?

CASE STUDY   Freedom and responsibility – how values drive creativity for Netflix

The idea for Netflix was born in 1997 out of a simple problem when founder Reed Hastings incurred a US $40 overdue fine on the movie *Apollo 13* after he forgot to take it back to the video rental store on time.

Netflix was created and with it many of the conventions in the video rental market were scrapped – a flat-fee service for unlimited rentals, no late, shipping or handling fees and no return dates. The company didn't rest on its laurels and kept apace with technology moving into video streaming and the creation of original programming like *House of Cards*, challenging and outperforming the established TV networks. Today the company is worth US $25.5 billion. Flexibility and creativity are at the heart of the business. So how does Netflix do it?

Hastings has written a simple black and white PowerPoint deck on the Netflix culture, which has attracted 5 million views. 'Sheryl Sandberg has called it one of the most important documents ever to come out of Silicon Valley' (HBR, 2014). Find it on slideshare.net (entitled Netflix Culture: Freedom and Responsibility). It outlines how CEO Hastings and Patty McCord, then Chief Talent Officer, ripped up the rule book – not just on how the movie rental business operated – but on conventional HR policies too. They viewed traditional industrial models that were based 'on reducing variation (manufacturing errors)' as outdated, seeing this as opposite to what's needed in creative firms which is 'increasing variation (innovation)' (HBR, 2014).

The Netflix model is 'to increase employee freedom as we grow rather than limit it, to continue to attract and nourish innovative people, so we have a better chance of success.'

Responsible people thrive on freedom and are worthy of freedom.
Reed Hastings, 2011

Netflix has seven aspects of culture that reveal how creative leadership allows them to manage the balance between 'freedom and responsibility'. Examples include:

- Netflix has no 'fixed' working hours policy and many employees work evenings and weekends without being 'tracked.' This inspired the company to stop keeping track of vacation days. With the bare minimum of 'rules', people can take up to 30 days without approval. In order to stimulate creativity and physical wellbeing, leaders are encouraged to model the way and take long breaks.

- Rather than have compliance departments, rules and checks, the expense policy is just five words: 'Act in Netflix's best interests.'

- Netflix talk context, not control. They ask: 'Managers, when one of your talented people does something dumb, don't blame them. Instead ask yourself what context you failed to set' (Reed Hastings, 2009).

The company's stated aim is to be 'big and fast and flexible'. It's a model that relies on learning, growing and embracing change rather than standing still. Netflix focuses on encouraging high performance from its employees. If people make mistakes the mantra is to fix problems quickly. This is a common theme amongst other innovative businesses like Pixar and IDEO, as we'll see later.

 # Courage

Life shrinks and expands in proportion to one's courage.
Anaïs Nin, writer, 1939

Boldness, audacity, daring, guts, balls, fortitude, conviction, bravery, chutzpah. Whatever you call it, courage is inextricably linked with the act of creativity. If creativity is bringing something new into being then it means a move away from certainty. Creativity, big and small, requires a leap of faith, guts, a dose of courage. It just depends how big the shot. Courage is a key value for innovation and particularly important for leaders (Patterson *et al,* 2009).

Elizabeth Gilbert's *Big Magic* is a rallying cry to living creatively and she writes brilliantly about conquering fear. She writes that it is inevitable but boring, and creativity is much easier if you accept that 'basically, your fear is like a mall cop who thinks he's a Navy SEAL. He hasn't slept in days, he's all hopped up on Red Bull, and he's liable to shoot at his own shadow in an absurd effort to keep everyone "safe"' (Gilbert, 2015). Of course if you're being chased by a tiger, fear is useful, but we don't need those levels of anxiety flying around in our day-to-day creative lives.

Artist and creative coach Lisa Sonora Beam acknowledges how fear impacts creativity: 'Among the main deterrents to bringing new ideas into form are the emotional and psychological blocks of the creator. These blocks aren't a sign of weakness, they signal opportunities for our growth. Without the proper orientation to creative blocks, creating can feel like going off the deep end. That's why so few people dare to pursue their ideas very far' (Sonora Beam, 2008).

But why does 'going off at the deep end' scare us? What is it we're afraid of? While it's not always comfortable to do it is useful to dig a bit deeper.

In the past, a fear of being judged by others has had an effect on my ability to articulate my ideas. Will they be good enough? Am I an original creative thinker or will I just appear stupid?

Once an idea was signed off then the fear of judgment was quickly replaced by the fear of *failure*. Will the idea work? Will the media cover it? Will we be fired for spending the client's money and not showing enough return on investment?

Whatever it is that personally scares you Gilbert (2015) says, 'if you can't learn to travel comfortably alongside your fear, then you'll never be able to go anywhere interesting or do anything interesting'.

Trust me or sack me

Unity co-founder Gerry Hopkinson, on having the courage to sell ideas:

As much as we really do believe in having principles, having theories, having evidence and having data there's an over-reliance on those in our age. Great ideas generally get pushed over the edge by people who just say, you know what? I feel this is right and you're going to have to just trust me or sack me.

So the question becomes, how can we make you comfortable with that? Can we make you comfortable by doing a test? Can we make you comfortable by constant monitoring, can we make you comfortable by telling you that someone else has done it before? In the end it's not giving up on an idea and so bravery is individual but it's also collective. People are braver when they know everyone has got each other's back.

You can't be brave alone. You can be brave individually to a certain extent if you're not crapping yourself that you are going to get a bollocking or lose your job. If the institution you work for (or the client) engenders trust then at least you can have dissent, debate, argue and you can be more courageous.

CREATIVE COACH

- When have you had to show courage?
  - What happened?
  - How did that affect you?
  - What do you believe enabled you to be courageous?
- When you think about times when you've felt at your most creative, generated an idea in a group, sold a creative idea to someone else, or pushed for an unpopular option – how did it require courage?
- What do you think was the source of courage?
- Write down a list of all the things that scare you, in any part of your life, big or small. Think about some of the ways you've tackled fears before and if there are any strategies you could use now with any of your challenges.

CASE STUDY   Be courageous: stand for something

A bank is perhaps not the most obvious sponsor of the Sydney Gay and Lesbian Mardi Gras. ANZ, one of Australia's biggest, has been involved with the festival since 2007 and uses its owned media spaces – the cash machines all over the city – to spread a message of inclusion and diversity. Meet the 'GAYTM'.

In 2014 the campaign generated branded media coverage in over 70 countries around the world, created great viral content and allowed the bank to make a positive contribution to a global issue in a relevant way.

Supporting gay rights is not an obvious association for a highly conservative corporate entity like a bank. It takes a potential risk in alienating customers who do not support the cause and it would be easy to sponsor more traditional events that don't rock the boat.

Figure 2.5 ANZ Bank 'Gay TM'

Figure 2.6 The bank's ATMs were decorated, tattooed and embellished in the spirit of the event

CREATIVE EXPERIMENT

- When you tackle your next creative challenge explore how you could pick a fight or stand for something – what unexpected association can you make or what cause can you support?

- If you had to say your brand or service stood for something – what would it be?

Fun

Playing is an important thing because you know you've got to kind of let yourself go to be creative and you've got to allow the ridiculous things to happen.
Grayson Perry, artist, 2013

For many, the idea of showing any emotion in the workplace is a no-no. But does the notion that 'work should always be serious' get in the way of creativity?

My own experience in workshops reveals a dichotomy between navigating serious business issues and engaging in playfulness in order to find solutions. Fun is associated with lack of commitment and play is considered childish and the direct opposite to work. This is addressed by Tim Brown, CEO and President of IDEO, the award-wining global design firm, ranked as one of the world's most creative businesses. In his 2008 TED Talk *'Serious Play'* he talks about Guilford's 1995 divergent and convergent creative process (see page 167) and suggests that it is in the first phase, where many options need to be generated and explored, that playfulness may have the biggest role, with a more serious approach adopted in convergence – judging and selecting ideas. Fun and play can create an environment where *risk-taking* [Rt] is allowed, for a short while.

His colleague, IDEO Founder David Kelley talks about 'thinking with your hands' and the idea of quick and dirty prototyping has gained much traction in recent years across many different fields. The theory is that this hands-on approach is a development of the construction play that as small children we explore on a daily basis, but which diminishes as we get older – think Play-Doh or camp-building. The idea of role-play is also embraced at IDEO for service or experience-based products, although it is often approached with reluctance by clients at first. Ultimately Brown says: 'We think playfulness helps us get to better creative solutions. Helps us do our jobs better, and helps us feel better when we do them' (Brown, 2008).

Playfulness and humour is 'the spontaneity and ease that is displayed' (Ekvall, 1996) in the workplace, according to one of the leading researchers in this field, and his research shows it's key for creativity in business, as we'll see in Chapter 4. Csikszentmihalyi (1997) agrees that the ability to be playful and enjoy the creative process is important to generating creative ideas. If you're a tortured artist working alone in a garret or a songwriter pouring your heart out, then negative emotions can be powerful creative triggers. But if you're reading this with a view to increasing your creative output at work and working alongside other people, then we suggest that you deliberately foster positive moods; enjoyment, happiness and fun are to be pursued.

CASE STUDY   Banter and humour in the Royal Navy

Cheerfulness is a choice.
Andrew St George, leadership expert, 2013

The Royal Navy – a command and control organization responsible for stability on the high seas – is not necessarily one you would associate with fun. At the request of the Second Sea Lord of the Royal Navy, leadership expert and fellow at Aberystwyth University, Andrew St George spent time with every level of the Navy staff to document their approach to leadership, and was surprised with some of his findings.

He writes: 'No one follows a pessimist, and cheerfulness is a choice... The cheerful leader in any environment broadcasts confidence and capability, and the Royal Navy instinctively understands this. It is the captain, invariably, who sets the mood of a vessel; a gloomy captain means a gloomy ship. And mood travels fast'. The Royal Navy actually records the impact of cheerfulness in operations, concluding that the behaviour benefits difficult circumstances. It goes further in that it *actively* encourages fun through different activities. These include:

- Encouraging 'banter' – the gentle, playful and friendly exchange of remarks amongst all ranks from Sea Lord to junior sailors.

- Playing 'dogwatch sports' – informal games that fill dead time at sea.

- According to St George (2013), these are 'often trivial and nonsensical – passing a stick, for example, across an ever-widening divide. But besides cheerfulness, they encourage speed of thought, an outward-looking mindset, and a willingness to talk. Cheerfulness in turn affects how people sit, stand, and gesticulate.'

- Promoting humour through joke telling.

CREATIVE COACH

- When do you have the most fun? How could you use that to set up your next creativity session?
- What's the most playful environment you've ever been in? How could you replicate an aspect of that within your workplace?
- When was the last time you were so absorbed in play you lost track of time?
  - What were you doing? How could you bring more of that into your life?

CREATIVE EXPERIMENT

- Identify a game that has no purpose other than play. (Think Snap, Operation, I Spy or Lego). Bring it to your next creativity session as an icebreaker/stimulus/energizer.
- If you're with young children, watch them at play for a little while or even better get involved – notice what they do. What insights did you have into play?
- Create a space in your working environment that is designed to be playful. Make it bright, comfortable and stimulating. Have lots of things to play with such as pre-printed paper for origami, Keri Smith postcards (each one is a playful little life experiment) or put random objects in a paper bag as stimulus – I like to put postcards, weird food items and song lyrics in mine. Museum shops are good for sourcing different cheap and random items for workshops too.

Gr Grit

Grit is passion and perseverance for very long-term goals. Grit is having stamina. Grit is sticking with your future, day in, day out, not just for the week, not just for the month, but for years, and working really hard to make that future a reality. Grit is living life like it's a marathon, not a sprint.
Angela Lee Duckworth, TED 2013

The element of grit is a well-understood concept in relation to achievement in sport – this element can also be a crucial factor in turning ideas into innovations that see the light of day. Generating great ideas is just a tiny fraction of any creative success story. Different studies show that it can take anywhere from 50, 100 or even 3,000 crude ideas to be generated for one to make it to the real world (Isaksen *et al*, 2011).

Grit plays a key role in delivering those ideas, and applies to many other parts of life too. Grit is the ability to see things through when the going gets tough. It's about dealing with setbacks, being able to focus and completing the task in hand. There's often a part in the creative process where it feels too hard, where you can't see the wood for the trees and where the answer proves elusive.

Persist!

The importance of grit is beautifully summed up in a hand-written note by Pixar animator Austin Madison who has worked on films including *Ratatouille*, *WALL-E* and *Up*. As part of *The Animator Letters Project* (2010) he writes about the disparate parts of his creative process in a missive called 'Persist'. The first stage is when he is 'white-hot, in the zone, firing on all cylinders creative mode... ideas pour out like wine from a royal chalice and happens about 3 per cent of the time.' His rally-cry to persist comes from the rest of the time when he is 'in the frustrated, struggling, office-full-of-crumpled-up-paper mode... slog diligently through this quagmire of discouragement and despair.'

Though Austin was brave to admit it so publicly, it was a sentiment that many of us tackling a challenge will recognize only too well. The good stuff he talks of comes from another of the elements related to grit – *discipline* Dp , discussed more in the next chapter.

Finding your personal grit reserves can be a painful part of the creative process. Not knowing the answer and facing obstacles can feel overwhelming. It helps to know that this uncomfortable feeling is completely normal. As American artist Lisa Sonora Beam (2008) says: 'Feeling the difference between where we are right now and where we want to be is called structural tension. Being able to tolerate structural tension is a major key to accomplishing what we want.' Grit can be key to making it happen.

Research by Sidney J Parnes (1961), co-founder for the International Center for Studies in Creativity, showed that more and better ideas were produced in the second half of a creative session. He called this the 'extended effort principle' and it's useful to bear in mind when you or a group start struggling with ideas and start to feel frustrated, stuck or want to stop. Persist!

Grit is tenacity. It's the long game. What do you think is the average age of a Nobel Prize winner? (The answer's at the end of this chapter).

Dyson – sucking it up and showing grit

Inventor James Dyson first made a name for himself in the mid-1970s when he came up with an idea for a lightweight wheelbarrow, which used a ball instead of the traditional wheel. He next turned his attention to vacuum cleaners, having become frustrated by the lacklustre efforts of his machine – but it would take five long years (and 5,127 prototypes) before he got his product to market and another five years before his bagless invention could be hailed as a success. Where most people would have walked away, Dyson stuck with it, fuelled by self-belief and a rather large helping of grit. 'I became obsessed,' he told *Inc* Magazine. 'Most people thought I was mad' (2012). History proves that he wasn't. His personal fortune today is estimated at more than £3 billion.

How gritty are you?

The creative process can be frustrating and challenging. When there are big problems to be solved – be they environmental, financial, commercial, societal, economic, military or political – we need our best problem-solvers to have grit. With experience as a management consultant, teacher and now psychologist and PhD, Angela Lee Duckworth (quoted at the start of this chapter) believes that grit is an accurate predictor of success in any field. In her research she asked a simple question in a broad range of situations from West Point Military Academy to National Spelling Bees – 'who is successful here, and why?'

She defines grit as 'the tendency to sustain interest in and effort toward very long-term goals' (Duckworth *et al*, 2007) and has created a 'grit scale', which you can find online. A maximum score means you're extremely gritty, while a low score means you're not gritty at all. If you think you need more grit in your creative life, explore the grit scale. (For the record, apparently, I'm pretty gritty.) Finally, grit is a vital attribute when it comes to dealing with rejection. Without it, negative feedback will usually lead to capitulation, but with your grit reserves fully stocked you can find the energy to keep going until someone says yes.

One can only imagine and marvel at JK Rowling's grit levels when her first Harry Potter manuscript was being repeatedly ignored. The famously rejected also include Tim Burton, Madonna, Bono, Andy Warhol and Sylvia Plath, who wrote: 'I love my rejection slips. They show me I try.' (Kapadia Pocha, 2012)

CREATIVE COACH

- Where could you do with more grit in your creative life?
- How does grit (or lack of it) show up anywhere else in your professional life?
- Who do you know and admire (even grudgingly) for their personal demonstration of grit? What beliefs do you think they might hold that help them persevere?
- Know that you're in exactly the right place to help with grit – when you understand your values it's much easier to stick with something.

CREATIVE COACH

- Pick a project you have left on the shelf but know you really want to move forward. What would move it forward? *Start today.*
- Next creative session you run, push a little harder and longer when the ideas dry up. Use some of the creativity tools in Chapter 8. See what happens.
- Create some posters or postcards that promote gritty thinking and post them up where you and others will see them, like Samuel Beckett's quote: 'Ever tried. Ever failed. No matter. Try again. Fail again. Fail better.'

*The average age of a Nobel prize winner is 59.

REVIEW THE CHAPTER

- Have any of the elements below enabled your success so far in terms of your creativity?
- Which creative element do you most relate to in this section?
- Score yourself in terms of how important it is to you.
- Then rank the value of elements for yourself in priority order. What are you drawn to? (You may want to add some of your own values here too.) What wouldn't you ever compromise on?
- What do you need more of in your creative life?
- What are you going to do to get it? List three things you can start today.

Table 2.2 Values

Element	Key questions	Where do your strengths lie in relation these elements?	Which area would you most like to develop or explore further?
Creativity (Cr)	Have you set goals in relation to your personal creativity or for your team or company?		
Curiosity (Cy)	Are you able to follow your curiosity enough? How can you stimulate your curiosity even more?		
Freedom (Fr)	How free do you feel to remove the unhelpful limits that you or others set?		
Courage (Cg)	To what extent do you stand up for what you believe in? What stops you?		

Table 2.2 *continued*

Element	Key questions	Where do your strengths lie in relation these elements?	Which area would you most like to develop or explore further?
Fun (F)	How much fun are you having in your creative process?		
Grit (G)	How determined and purposeful are you? To what extent do you stick with things and power through?		

IN A NUTSHELL

We hold our values both consciously and unconsciously. They guide us and affect our decisions and behaviour. Some values have been shown to aid creativity – those that lead us towards mastery and enjoyment in life like curiosity, freedom and fun, while others like tradition and conformity can make creativity harder. The values we hold drive our behaviour and characteristics which is the subject of our next chapter.

DIG DEEPER

On leadership – Kouzes, J and Posner, B (2008) *The Leadership Challenge: How to make extraordinary things happen in organizations* 3rd edn, Jossey-Bass, California

On courage – Gilbert, E (2015) *Big Magic: Creative living beyond fear*, Bloomsbury Publishing, London

On perseverance – Duckworth, A L (2013) Grit: The power of passion and *perseverance. TED Talks Education.* Filmed April 2013. Available at TED.com

The characteristics of creative people

This chapter looks at these 10 creative elements:

18	19	30	41	20
O	**E**	**No**	**Sb**	**Mo**
Openness	Ego	Rebellion	Self-belief	Motivation

31	42	21	32	43
Im	**Vi**	**Dp**	**P**	**Fe**
Imagination	Vision	Discipline	Passion	Failure

Are you considering becoming a creative person? Too late, you already are one. To even call somebody 'a creative person' is almost laughably redundant; creativity is the hallmark of our species. If you're alive, you're a creative person.
Elizabeth Gilbert, writer, 2015

What makes us describe a person as creative? Can we change our behaviour to become more creative? Before you start this chapter, make a quick list of people who embody creativity for you. Why have you picked them? Can you pinpoint any of their characteristics?

Zaha Hadid, Steven Spielberg, David Bowie, Tracy Emin and Shakespeare all spring to mind for me, as do words like counter-culture, radical, maverick, visionary, rebellious, genius, loner and hard to manage. So far, so clichéd.

It's challenging to write about 'creative people' because as Elizabeth Gilbert's quote suggests, of course, everyone is creative. Yet society also seems to agree that some people either have, or demonstrate, more creativity than others. Research indicates that creativity is a complex soup of traits, behaviours, cultural and social influences as well as life experiences. That's before we add in the neuroscience of creativity, which we'll explore in the next chapter.

Before we delve further, a word from Carol Dweck, one of the world's leading motivation experts (whose research we'll hear more of later in this chapter), on the hot potato concerning whether a person's creative (or indeed other) abilities are set in stone:

> It's not nature or nurture, genes or environment... Of course, each person has a unique genetic endowment. People may start with different temperaments and different aptitudes, but it is clear that experience, training, and personal effort take them the rest of the way.
> Carol Dweck (2016)

I think it's also helpful here to refer to Margaret Boden who has lived a 'life scientific' working for decades in diverse subjects encompassing medicine, psychology, computer science and creativity, amongst other things. As we saw in the definitions chapter she makes a distinction between types of creativity.

'P' psychological creativity relates to an 'individual mind' – the person involved in generating the idea, and *'H' historical creativity* relates to the whole of human history (Boden, 2004). While most of us will never demonstrate the latter, neuropsychologist Rex Jung says 'creativity is common and genius is a lot more rare than we would believe' (2015).

If we want to explore creativity in all its richness, then Boden's distinction points us towards different types of people. I'm going to unpick some of the myths, stereotypes and generalizations about individual creativity and explore traits common to some 'H' creative icons as well as more modest, real-world 'P' examples to illustrate what it means to be a creative person in the broadest sense.

You may well already be familiar with Mihaly Cskiszentmihalyi and his work on flow. In *Creativity: The Psychology of Discovery and Invention* (1996) Cskiszentmihalyi interviewed 91 'exceptional' creative individuals who had made a difference in their field including scientists, photographers, composers, artists and novelists in his classic study of the creative process. The one word which sums up a creative person for Cskiszentmihalyi? 'Complexity'.

He suggests that creative people can navigate and embrace the full spectrum of personal qualities (many of which are opposing), while many of us behave in just one way. He writes about 'ten dimensions of complexity' – seemingly opposite traits of 'the creative personality' which are:

- *Physical energy and rest* – When required the creative person can concentrate for long periods with absolute focus – but downtime is just as important. 'They consider the rhythm of activity followed by idleness or reflection very important for the success of their work' (Cskiszentmihalyi, 1996). This behaviour is put in place to achieve goals rather than a genetic predisposition.

- *Smart, but naive* – The ability to flex between wisdom and childishness. One has to be able to keep an open mind and not allow our existing knowledge to impact our ability to generate new ideas. Imagine trying to 'unknow' your child's favourite nursery rhyme or the walk to work.

- *Playfulness and discipline* – As we saw in Chapter 1, fun is an important value for a creative life. In Chapter 2 we explored grit. Individuals and companies need to find a balance between these two dimensions for creativity.

- *Imagination and reality* – The ability to go beyond what is understood and accepted as the current reality and then to be able to ground your ideas in the real world. Robert Dilts (1996) modelled Walt Disney's creative process and broke it into three stages – the dreamer, the realist and the critic – which is a simple and useful process to follow to navigate this pairing.

- *Extroversion and introversion* – Creativity can be both a private and social process; not necessarily one or the other. While the idea of the lone creative genius pervades, Cskiszentmihalyi's interviews repeatedly show the need for feedback, discussion and the exchange of ideas.

- *Ambition and selflessness* – The need for both competition and cooperation, and the ability to balance one's ego and desire for recognition with the greater cause or problem in hand.

- *Psychological androgyny* – The ability to demonstrate both masculine and feminine behaviours – to be aggressive and nurturing, sensitive and rigid. This person 'doubles his or her repertoire of responses and can interact with the world in terms of a much richer and varied spectrum of opportunities' (Cskiszentmihalyi, 1996). Perhaps not so obvious in business, David Bowie and Grace Jones both embraced the importance of their male and female sides and artist Grayson Perry often appears as his frock-wearing alter ego, Claire.

- *Traditional and rebellious* – To break the rules, Cskiszentmihalyi argues that a person must know the rules, so they must be/or have been a traditionalist to some degree.

- *Passion and objectivity* – Without passion it is impossible to sustain interest and motivation in the long term and while helpful, to be overly objective can stifle an idea. The creative person must flex between these two behaviours.

- *Suffering and enjoyment* – This pairing probably brings to mind the image of a struggling artist or poet, but 'a badly designed machine causes pain to an inventive engineer, just as the creative writer is hurt by reading bad prose' (Cskiszentmihalyi, 1996). These are the highs and lows of the creative process.

O Openness

Your assumptions are your windows on the world. Scrub them off every once in a while, or the light won't come in. If you challenge your own, you won't be so quick to accept the unchallenged assumptions of others.
Alan Alda, actor, 1980

So, our first element in this chapter is openness. Openness to experience is one of 'the big five' personality traits according to theories developed over the past half-decade. It's up first, as it's fundamental to being creative.

Openness means being receptive to new experiences, to people, ways of doing things, ideas and cultures and to possibilities that don't yet exist. The definitive words for openness include curious, inventive, variety, adventure, independent and a willingness to try new things. Negative definitions are cautious, routine, consistent, traditional and straightforward.

Consider your experiences and evaluate your own openness to ideas. Have you ever had an idea so perfect that the minute it popped into your head, you immediately recognized it as the 'big idea?' If you work alone this mini-Eureka moment may have been a breakthrough and given you the solution you needed. But for many, particularly in a group brainstorming scenario, this attachment can actually become a real stumbling block. If you hold on too tightly to ideas in the early stages then you can quickly become blind or resistant to other options. This can be down to ego.

19	
E	**Ego**

Broadly defined as someone's sense of self-importance and self-esteem, ego is often frowned upon in the modern workplace because the goal, and the team are perceived as more important than the individual.

Too much ego is one of the worst traits often associated with creative types: 'Ego says "I can do no wrong", whereas confidence says "I can get this right"' (Henry, 2016).

What do Charles Darwin and a billionaire hedge fund manager have in common?

Think of something about which you have a strong opinion – maybe it's politics, religion, the death penalty or the type of food you love or hate. Do you really want your opinion changed? Be honest: the answer is probably no. This is down to your confirmation bias. British psychologist Peter Wason's 1960 experiment (and many others since) revealed that we seek out and manipulate information that backs up the opinions we already hold, rather than using the information to form new opinions. In fact, often after we are presented with information supporting the opposing case it only confirms to us, that our original position is correct!

You can think of confirmation bias as your internal 'yes man' (or woman) and it's definitely worth calling him (or her) out. It's a well-recognized phenomenon in the world of finance where this kind of skewed thinking can cost millions.

Charles Darwin may have been aware of this own confirmation bias and the potentially damaging effects of looking for evidence to support his theories, long before Wason's experiments. Darwin paid particular attention to any facts that contradicted his findings rather than dismissing them.

Why being two-faced is good for creativity

Researcher Albert Rothenberg (1971) analysed the process of creative geniuses including Pasteur, Einstein, Van Gogh and Mozart as well as Nobel Prize winners. He coined the terms 'Janusian thinking' to describe the ability to hold completely opposing views at the same time.

Being open to change is key in the fast-paced world of tech where firms must move fast or face irrelevance, explains Bruce Daisley, UK MD of

Twitter. He told me: 'You want people who have humility, otherwise you get confirmation bias. As soon as you think you know what the answers are everything you're doing leads back to those answers. When you sit there and you think "we have no idea what we'll be doing in six months", it gives you an openness, a sense of sort of open vulnerability that you've got to try and interpret the world fresh everyday'.

Sounds simple. Being open to ideas is a concept that is easy to grasp and seems obvious. Yet it is often much easier said than done.

I was once brought into a very successful business to work on a competitive pitch worth a potential £2 million (pretty good stakes in that industry). I brought in a team of bright sparks to help me and we began working through the brief. On the first morning of our conflab there was a knock at the door and the CEO of the agency came in and told us at length about his big idea for the pitch, telling us to 'just bear it in mind'. So we spent days talking to consumers and media, doing research, trying out the product, talking to partners. We thrashed out the options and some days later presented three very different routes to the CEO. By now at least 20 other people had been involved in the thinking and direction of the ideas, crititically evaluating the options. Can you guess where I'm going with this? Yep, the CEO decided that his original idea was still best and ran with it. They lost. We'll never know whether any of the other options were any better or worse, but they were never really under consideration.

CASE STUDY   Yes, and – lessons from improv

Stand-up comedy has become fashionable with executives and business schools in recent years, and creativity can be stimulated by thinking like a stand-up comedian:

- You're problem-solving on the fly.
- You have to listen, collaborate and be open to new ideas.
- You have to be vulnerable and open to failure.

A well-known improv exercise is called 'Yes, and...' The idea is that working in pairs you cannot use the word 'no' but must instead 'accept the offer' (whatever the other person says) and run with it, starting the sentence with 'Yes, and...' and building on what the other person has said, no matter how ridiculous or banal. The antithesis to 'Yes, and...' is 'Yes, but...' because when you say this you're blocking the other person.

At the outset you might feel like you're in an episode of *The Office*, but try brainstorming something, anything, using this response. It doesn't mean in your next meeting or workshop that you have to abide by the 'yes, and...' rules for a whole hour. Just try it as a warm-up exercise for 10 minutes or have a five-minute moratorium on 'no'. This is a fun way to suspend your judgment, even for a short while, and to build on ideas you might otherwise reject. Also, maybe you'll notice how often *you* say no or *but* in a creative session, or quickly squash someone else's ideas.

Harry Dromey, Group Marketing Manager at UK broadcaster Channel 4 (and former Head of Mischief at bookmaker Paddy Power) has benefited from improv. He told me: 'I draw from loads of different reference points – being curious means that you do different things, you need food for thought. I took a course in stand-up comedy, and it has done wonders in all areas. You're totally laid bare, and you go through thinking "oh my god it's so hard" and you have so much more appreciation of the work that goes in. Ideas don't just happen, they need work and it makes you better at creative work'.

CREATIVE COACH

- Consider your own openness to new ideas. Are you more comfortable with the familiar or do you prefer the new and different?

- What stops you from embracing or doing something differently?

- How could you actively seek out a new experience or point of view tomorrow?

CREATIVE EXPERIMENT

- When you've generated a number of ideas or options you like, choose one and deliberately find an opposing point of view or argument to your position.

- Find someone else to deliberately disagree with you. See more about *debate* Db in Chapter 5.

- Listen more than you speak in brainstorms or meetings.

- Try the 'Yes, and...' approach in pairs and see what this does to your ideas.

No Rebellion

> I come from the underground. I am never comfortable in the middle of the stream, flowing in the same direction as everyone else... my instinct is always to resist the pull of the obvious. It's not easy.
> Grace Jones (2015)

Creativity benefits from the 'crazy ones', the upstarts, troublemakers, outliers, wildcards or rebels, those who challenge 'the way things are'. This element probably represents the most stereotypical idea of what 'makes' a creative person.

Rebellion is not just for artists and musicians, it is a useful trait for business. As part of their research for *The Innovator's DNA*, the authors found two common themes amongst the highly successful entrepreneurs they interviewed (which included Amazon's Jeff Bezos and Michael Dell) '(1) they actively desire to change the status quo; and (2) they regularly take risks to make that change happen' (Christensen *et al*, 2011).

CASE STUDY   Ripping up the rulebook – the Green Funeral Company

> *We want to challenge absolutely everything about the funeral industry.*
> **Claire Callender, The Green Funeral Company**

Rupert and Claire Callender, the husband and wife team behind a small company in Devon, are challenging the status quo in an unlikely field. Self-proclaimed 'radical' undertakers who run The Green Funeral Company they offer an ecological alternative to traditional funerals. In a brilliant example of challenging norms and rules in a highly conservative field, the Callenders are disrupting the way business is done in the commercialized and corporate funeral industry.

They say:

> *We proudly call ourselves undertakers so there is no ambiguity about what we do. When we first meet you, we are unlikely to be wearing suits. We do not have a fleet of hearses and limousines. We do not employ bearers. We do not have a standard funeral, we do not use euphemisms. We do not consider faux-Victoriana and a mournful expression to be an assurance of respect and dignity. We have buried Generals and Lords, but we approach*

Figure 3.1 The radical undertakers – Rupert and Claire Callender

each funeral as unique. What is at the core of our work is honesty, acceptance and participation, even if that is just helping us to carry the coffin. In doing so, all of us become less of an audience and more of a congregation. (The Green Funeral Company website, 2016)

Citing influences including the DIY philosophy of punk, the communal experience of raving and crop circles, Rupert Callender told me more about shaking things up.

Are you a rule-breaker?

'Yes, I would certainly consider myself a rule breaker. I went to a minor public school, which encouraged – actually demanded – conformity. The deal was explicit: play the game and you will be rewarded with a place in the establishment. I knew from the age of 14 I wanted no part in it.'

What kind of emotions really drive you?

'I think that people have this idea that creativity is always about thinking something up that is positive, whereas my experience is that outrage at an existing flaw is a stronger driver. My own experiences of bereavement and funerals had been deeply damaging, so we started as ceremonial undertakers knowing what not to do more than we knew what we should do. That followed. Take a bad idea and tweak it better.'

Did you set out to change the status quo when it comes to funerals?

'We did. Reading the third edition of *The Natural Death Handbook* showed us that a great deal of current funeral practice, particularly how the body was dealt with and presented, along with all of the trimmings: the procession of cars, the cookie cutter rituals, in fact almost everything about it was wrong.'

Claire adds: 'Punk showed everyone that you can just set something up and run it out of your bedroom and that ethos was definitely how we started. We knew everything had to change and we had a Volvo, a plank and some ice packs to do it with. We wanted to challenge absolutely everything about the funeral industry and we still do'.

What were the challenges?

'We survived through a combination of naivety and zeal. We didn't realize quite how sewn-up the industry was, the power of the heavyweight corporate behemoths, the way that the bereaved were subtly disempowered. Often this was done with good intentions – people who choose to work in the funeral world are often altruistic, thoughtful people. It is the venture capitalists who see the opportunity that vulnerable, disorientated people make.'

Did the behemoths fight back?

'Luckily, we have been largely ignored by the mainstream. A lot of small independents that we have come into contact with like us and our approach. The corporates follow us from the shadows, just keeping an eye on us, but as an actual company, we are so small as to be barely a threat to anyone. It is ideas of empowerment, spiritual freedom, practical involvement, and the unthreatening biology of a dead body that is so disturbing to the large mainstream companies, all of whom trade upon ideas of tradition, fear, emotional blackmail and the bereaved's own feelings of helplessness to churn out funerals that mean nothing, help no one and cost too much.'

CREATIVE COACH

- Have you ever kicked against something or rebelled?
  - What was it? How did it feel to rebel?
  - What was the outcome?
  - What did you learn?
- How do you feel about conforming? To what extent do you think that impacts upon your creativity?
- What do you think would happen if you conformed less and challenged more? Can you absolutely know that is true?

A neophile is someone who is easily bored, loathes tradition and routine and craves novelty. You couldn't have an organization full of them; it would be an unmanageable mess. But if you do want to push the boundaries then channel your inner punk. Breaking the rules is a quick and easy way to trigger creative ideas and potentially disrupt the market in which you are working in. We saw in Chapter 2 how Netflix disrupted the movie rental business by tearing up the existing playbook. In 1989 First Direct changed the face of UK banking – a telephone bank, with no branches, open 24 hours a day and a focus on customer service.

CREATIVE EXPERIMENT

- List everything that is a 'rule' or established convention for your industry, category or business and then explore the opposite or challenge how that rule could be broken.

- Or tackle a taboo: what are the issues or skeletons in the cupboard for your business, industry or customers? What would happen if you brought one of them out into the open?

DISRUPTION IN AN UNLIKELY PLACE

Procter & Gamble's #touch the pickle campaign for the Whisper sanitary protection brand assumed huge cultural importance in India where women are urged not to perform their normal daily activities while menstruating. A jar of pickles is a kitchen staple in most Indian homes and the campaign encouraged women in an act of defiance to 'touch the pickle' – an action that according to 'mythology' would cause them to rot. Sparking conversation about this previously taboo subject, Whisper's share of voice grew from 21 per cent to 91 per cent with 2.9 million women pledging to 'touch the pickle jar' (adage.com, 2015).

Bringing innovation, education and much-needed disruption to the feminine hygiene category, 2015 start-up THINX won a *Time* Magazine 'best invention' award for its period-proof underwear. Even in New York City in 2016, the word period is still considered taboo, as the founders discovered when they tried to book outdoor ads using the word – being refused advertising slots on the grounds of taste. Founder Miki Agrawal said: 'We have a lot of work ahead of us. There is a real gender-equality problem on our hands. Tackling that through creating a category disrupting product is a great start' (Contagious, 2015).

Challenging the status quo requires a good dose of our next element – self-belief.

Sb Self-belief

It turns out that creativity isn't some rare gift to be enjoyed by the lucky few – it's a natural part of human thinking and behaviour. In too many of us it gets blocked. But it can be unblocked. And unblocking that creative spark can have far-reaching implications for yourself, your organization and your community.
David and Tom Kelley, *Creative Confidence*, 2013

Before you start this section, rate your creative confidence out of 10 *right now*.

I believe that everyone is creative, so I'm not asking you to rate your creative capabilities (because I believe in you!) but your *confidence in* those abilities. So, if it's 10/10 then you can probably skip this element but if you need a shot of creative confidence, read on.

In a comprehensive report prepared for innovation foundation NESTA, Patterson *et al* (2009) found that self-belief and confidence are crucial elements for innovation. Over time we can develop what are called 'limiting beliefs' which can impact our ability to do almost anything.

Frequently in our workshops, participants bemoan that 'I'm just not very creative.' Investigating this potentially damaging comment, often we discover this negativity is because as a kid they told they weren't creative or that currently their contributions are criticized by a colleague.

IDEO founders Tom and David Kelley's brilliant book *Creative Confidence* builds on psychologist Albert Bandura's notion of self-efficacy, which is a person's belief in their own ability to succeed in any given task or area. David Kelley's TED 11-minute talk is the perfect accompaniment to a cup of coffee. His rallying cry is for the world to stop labelling people as creative 'haves' or 'have-nots'. If you struggle with confidence he raises questions around self-belief that are worth exploring.

CREATIVE COACH

- What is your belief about your own creativity?
- How has that shaped how you engage with creative projects?
- Think of someone in your life who believes in you. What would they say to you about your creativity? What might be a more empowering belief?

Self-belief is linked to many other elements including *courage* |Cg| and *risk-taking* |Rt|. If you haven't already done so, visit those elements to discover practical ways to up the ante on your creative confidence.

|Mo| Motivation

Creativity is not a talent, it's a way of operating.
John Cleese, 1991

Motivation is the third most important employee characteristic for innovative working according to Patterson *et al*'s NESTA Everyday Innovation report (2009).

When was the last time you did something just for the sheer hell of it? For me it was jumping into an icy cold lake, having sat in an outside hot tub while on holiday mid-winter. There was no reason for it apart from a little exhilaration and fun, an example of what psychologists call 'intrinsic motivation'. Other examples of things that can act as intrinsic motivation include a sense of satisfaction or accomplishment, happiness, meeting a challenge or becoming better at something or getting into flow.

Csikszentmihalyi (2008) made the term 'flow' famous, following his research into the roots of happiness and what he calls 'optimal experience'. It is 'the state in which people are so involved in an activity that people will do it even at great cost, for the sheer sake of doing it.'

The opposite – 'extrinsic motivation' – include external factors like praise, rewards, pay, promotion and perks – all things bestowed upon us by someone else.

What does motivation look or feel like for you? When I'm motivated I'm bouncing around like Tigger from *Winnie the Pooh*, firing off ideas, a bit over-excitable, feeling driven and on-fire. Unmotivated me is frankly not too pretty, lacklustre, grumpy, physically not very active and unsure of where I'm going. Knowing your values and living them at work and at play can be a way to stay motivated.

CASE STUDY   Do you agree or disagree with the following?

- 'You have a certain amount of intelligence, and you can't really do much to change it.
- 'You can change even your basic level of talent considerably.'

The way you answer these questions reveals your mindset – your beliefs about yourself and your potential, according to Carol Dweck, a Stanford University Professor and a world-leading expert on motivation who has identified what she calls 'fixed' and 'growth' mindsets which have implications for creativity, amongst many other things.

The fixed mindset

People with a fixed mindset believe that their traits are just givens. They have a certain amount of brains and talent and nothing can change that. If they have a lot, they're all set, but if they don't... So people in this mindset worry about their traits and how adequate they are. They have something to prove to themselves and others. (Mindsetonline.com, 2015)

People with a fixed mindset have a tendency to avoid challenges, give up easily and ignore useful negative feedback, feeling threatened by others.

The growth mindset

People with a growth mindset, on the other hand, see their qualities as things that can be developed through their dedication and effort. Sure they're happy if they're brainy or talented, but that's just the starting point. They understand that no one has ever accomplished great things – not Mozart, Darwin or Michael Jordan – without years of passionate practice and learning.

Dweck compares tennis player John McEnroe and basketball player Michael Jordan as examples of sportspeople with a fixed or growth mindset respectively. Dweck notes that the supremely talented McEnroe loathed practice, didn't acknowledge his mistakes and routinely blamed others for his losses (hence his umpire spats). Compare this to Jordan who said in a Nike commercial: 'I've missed more than 9,000 shots. I've lost almost 300 games. Twenty-six times, I've been trusted to take the game-winning shot, and missed.' His raw talent required massive commitment, practice and grit enabling him to become the dominant force in the game owing to, Dweck argues, his growth mindset.

In the growth mindset people learn from criticism, find lessons and inspiration in the success of others and they persist in the face of setbacks (see *grit* Gr, Chapter 2).

Figure 3.2 Two mindsets, Carol S Dweck, PhD

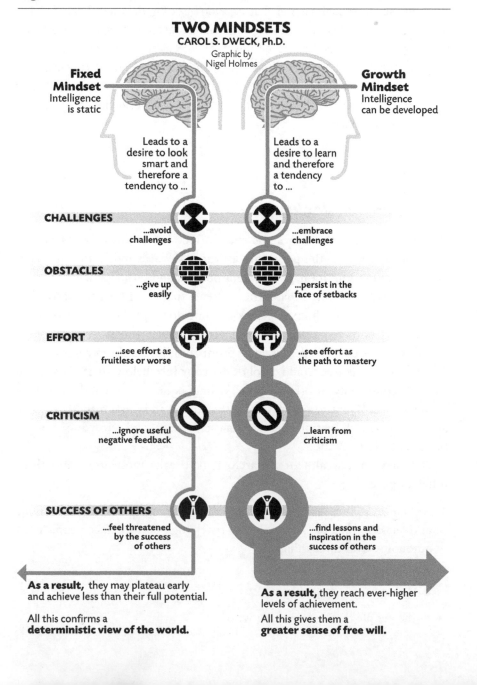

I've definitely worked for bosses with a fixed mindset and it was not conducive to long-term creativity. It meant that every time a sales pitch went badly, the potentially useful (albeit painful) negative feedback was dismissed rather than used as a way to learn and move forward.

There was always some other factor responsible for the loss – 'It was never a genuine pitch', 'they wanted a smaller/bigger company or 'it was a terrible brief'. It was never the hard truth that maybe the work wasn't really good enough, or that we didn't spend enough time or that we didn't ask the right questions. Coming second (or third or fourth) is painful but it should mean that something is taken from the experience and improved (mastery, in Pink's (2009) terms). The fixed mindset means that it's easier to place responsibility for any 'failure' outside of yourself, attributing blame, rather than taking responsibility and attempting to improve. If the finger is constantly being pointed at you, looking for someone else to blame is contagious.

People are not donkeys

We are all aware of the 'carrot and stick' principle and this maxim has long been the bedrock for the pervading attitudes towards motivation in many areas, including education, government policies and businesses.

In *Drive* (2009) Pink unpicks the elements that contribute to motivation and argues that since human beings are not donkeys then carrot or stick methods are outdated for the needs of 21st century business. As technology takes over the controlled mundane production-line tasks previously performed by people (see 'could a robot do your job' below) there is a move towards complexity in other job roles that require more subtlety. This is particularly relevant for creativity as the carrot and stick mentality could actually 'diminish performance, crush creativity and crowd out good behaviour' (Pink, 2009).

Drawing on a wealth of research, Pink breaks motivation into three different parts:

1 *Autonomy* – Our 'default setting' as human beings is 'to be autonomous and self-directed'. He argues that to reach high performance people need autonomy over three things:

- the task or job in hand;
- the time they do it; and
- the people they are working with.

We explore *freedom* Fr fully in the next chapter in relation to developing a creative company culture.

2 *Mastery* – Mastery is about 'becoming better at something that matters' to you and – as discussed above it begins with 'flow' – we have 'optimal experiences when the challenges we face are exquisitely matched to our abilities' (Pink, 2009). It requires a particular mindset and another of our elements from Chapter 1 – *grit* Gr.

3 *Purpose* – 'Humans, by their nature, seek purpose – a cause greater and more enduring than themselves. But traditional businesses have long considered purpose ornamental – a perfectly nice accessory as long as it didn't get in the way of important things' (Pink, 2009). But the world is changing.

What motivates us to create and what do we do it for? Purpose is the focus of Chapter 6 where I'll look at what all this means for creativity.

CREATIVE COACH

- What do you always find time for no matter what? What motivates you to do that? How is this linked into the values you identified in Chapter 1?

- Think of a time when you last created or did something for the sheer hell of it:
    - How did it feel?
    - What motivated you?

- Is there a pattern to what motivates you?

- How could you apply that to your creativity?

CREATIVE EXPERIMENT

- Take Pink's online assessment (www.danpink.com/drive.html) to find out more about what motivates you.

- If you are a leader, think about the overall motivation of your team. Consider the three different aspects of motivation that Pink discusses. Is there one that clearly stands out as an area of strength or a weakness?

▶

- How could you give people the chance to have more autonomy and self-direction?
- How do you encourage mastery?
- Is there a clear and inspiring purpose that creativity serves?

Im Vi Imagination and vision

There's a moment where the fantastic becomes possible, just barely possible, that's where the fun is.
Avatar director James Cameron, 2015

Imagination and vision are closely linked. Every new film, product, painting, invention, design, novel, app, piece of music or code starts with an idea, someone's vision that must be made real. Those people society proclaims 'creative visionaries' – Leonardo da Vinci, Steve Jobs, Alexander Graham Bell, Henry Ford, Bill Gates – all had the ability to see beyond now and look into the future. Originality requires a leap into the unknown, combining vision and imagination.

Scott Barry Kaufman is Scientific Director of the Imagination Institute, a research centre that focuses on finding out more about this element. He says that imagination has many different components: 'Idea generation, mental imagery, mental simulation, future thinking, pretend play, personal meaning-making, episodic memory, perspective taking, empathy, narrative generation and narrative understanding' (*Scientific American*, 2015*)*.

As the Cheshire Cat says in *Alice in Wonderland*: 'Imagination is the only weapon in the war against reality', echoing Cskiszentmihalyi's findings at the start of the chapter.

But letting your imagination run wild in a windowless meeting room on a Monday morning is not always so easy. Creativity tools can help spark the imagination (see Chapter 8) and there's a lot we can learn from neuroscience too. Ben Martynoga unpicks how our imaginative minds work in the next chapter, with some more practical ways to harness our brain chemistry to fire up ideas.

Could a robot do your job?

Currently computers cannot replicate the human imagination, but scientists are working on it. Research by Oxford University found that 'around 35 per cent of today's jobs are at high risk of being automated in the next two decades.' People in low-skilled and low-paid jobs (under £30,000) are most likely to be replaced by a machine (Cellon Jones, 2015). Today many jobs are automated; a proposition which only 10 years ago seemed inconceivable. Uber and Google are at the forefront of driverless cars (no more cabbie small-talk), and in China's Dongguan factory city 90 per cent of the human workforce will be replaced by the first robot-only factory.

Roles requiring empathy, generating ideas, negotiation, thinking on your feet, assisting and caring for others are at the lowest risk. The job title Creative Director gets a 'not very likely' ranking in terms of which jobs are most threatened... the lowest at risk is a publican! So I'm probably safe... for now. Take the test here: www.bbc.co.uk/news/technology-34066941.

CREATIVE COACH

- When do you find yourself day-dreaming? How could you bring that more into your creative life?
- Where do your ideas come from?
- What do you notice about imaginative people?

Vi | Vision

Almost all creative endeavours begin with a blank canvas.

I have always marvelled at the gardener's ability on a bleak, grey December day, when the trees and the ground are bare, to envisage how a plot will look in full bloom. Or how an architect can do the same thing, seeing many years into the future. Many creative projects require a combination of ambition, vision and imagination, all demonstrated in spades by the subject of the next case study.

CASE STUDY   Building the foundations for creativity

Ambition is a form of creativity. To have the courage to think that
something is possible is a vast aspect of imaginative attention.
Thomas Heatherwick, *Wall Street Journal*, 2015

Founded back in 1994 by Thomas Heatherwick, this architectural studio has grown into a team of 180 architects, designers and makers based in London's King's Cross. The practice created the 2012 Olympic Cauldron, with its 204 flaming copper elements each representing a competing nation, which was unveiled at Danny Boyle's spectacular opening ceremony. They also updated the Routemaster London bus for the first time in 50 years, carefully blending the old features with the new.

One of the secrets behind 46-year-old Heatherwick's success is that he doesn't barge blindly in. While his vision is consistently inspiring, the ideas typically only come after extensive research: need fires the imagination. It's certainly true of the way his team approached their 'Paper House' project, which looked at something very mundane – London's newspaper kiosks – and turned them into something both practical and visually stunning.

'We set ourselves the task of designing a newspaper kiosk that could be set up in a quarter of an hour,' say the team, 'and looked for a way to make the kiosk

Figure 3.3 Heatherwick Studios award-winning design for the Bombay Sapphire distillery

secure without flat shutters or hinged panels' (Heatherwick.com, 2016). The result is drop-dead gorgeous. Fabricated from bronze with a top tier that allows daylight in and, at night, electric light to flood out, it has shaved around 45 minutes off the newspaper sellers' daily set-up times.

The team was commissioned to design the new Bombay Sapphire distillery at Laverstoke, in the south of England. Respecting the history of the buildings and the beauty of the English countryside, including the River Test, was central to the design of the new structures. The 10 exotic botanical plants that contribute to the unique flavour of the gin are grown and housed in the glasshouses, making it the world's first botanical distillery (Heatherwick.com, 2016).

In an interview with *The Guardian*, Heatherwick had an enlightening analogy for the way he approaches the creative process: 'It is more like solving a crime. The answer is there, and your job is to find it. So we go off and do bits of research that essentially eliminate suspects from the enquiry.' Then you 'follow up leads' and steadily narrow down the potential solutions. 'Ultimately what you're left with is the answer' (Wroe, 2012).

When asked if he felt under pressure to live up to the 'mad professor' tag that was starting to envelop him around 2012, Heatherwick had this to say: 'The word *invent* gets connected with the word *mad*, perhaps thanks to the British nostalgia for a bygone era of men jumping off cliffs trying to fly. I don't mind that, because there's something unpretentious in the spirit of experimentation' (Ward, 2012).

Whether it's the start-up's business plan that has to adapt to changes in technology, or the artist's canvas that hides many different versions of the same painting, visions can and should change. The creator must balance their vision with the results of the trial and error process that is so crucial to creativity. Bear in mind the old Japanese proverb: 'Vision without action is a daydream. Action without vision is a nightmare.'

CREATIVE COACH

- Think of a specific creative project you have.
  - What is your dream for it?
  - How could you share that dream?
- What inspires you? How does that relate to your vision?
- How could you fan the embers of any small fledgling ideas you have to fire up a vision?

CREATIVE EXPERIMENT

- Make a vision board in relation to your creative project – gather a stack of magazines and intuitively grab images and words that take your fancy – create a collage and use that as your inspiration.

- Imagine you were reading an article in a relevant magazine of the story of your creative success – what would it say?

- Think about your ideal scenario in relation to your creative project – if it were all going brilliantly – what would you see? What would you hear? What would you feel? What would you notice?

 # Dp Discipline

There's unquestionably magic involved in great music, songwriting, and performances – like those nights when a star athlete is totally in the zone and can't miss. But there's also work. Without the work, the magic won't come.
Jay-Z, *Decoded*, 2011

To deliver on your vision and your creative dreams requires discipline. Hemingway wrote the end to *A Farewell to Arms* 39 times before he was satisfied with it (*Paris Review*, 1958). In my experience there is a pervasive attitude from many business people that creativity is just something that will happen of its own accord. That you can do a workshop and expect that everything will change the next day, or that you can just talk about creativity and that will make everyone more creative. If you think about any area that you want to master (or you want your people to) you have to practise. Ask any musician. Nigel Kennedy, one of the world's leading violin virtuosos: 'When I was a kid I hated the practice but now, at 56, I love the discipline and practise for three hours every day' (Carpenter, 2013).

It's now pretty well-established thanks to Malcolm Gladwell's bestseller *Outliers* (2009) that the key to greatness in any field is putting in around 10,000 hours of commitment, practice, sweat and motivation. This is closely linked to the element of grit – and it casts doubt on the myth that creativity is a God-given talent bestowed on the few, suggesting rather that it is a skill that can be honed. If you read Carol Dweck's work on mindset above then you'll see this is supported by her findings.

Discipline comes up again and again in every field, from business, sports, and science to the arts. Grayson Perry has said, 'Most of the successful artists I've met are very disciplined. You know they turn up on time, they put in the hours – and that idea of us all being a bit chaotic and shaky, I think it's a myth. Artists are doers.' (BBC Radio 4, 2010).

> 'A tour requires stamina, willpower, and the ability to self-motivate, to hype yourself into game mode night after night... You're like a professional athlete, except that night after night you're the only one with the bat.' Jay-Z

The world-famous BRIT School for the performing arts busts the TV talent-show myth that musicians can get famous overnight without really working at it. Famous alumni include Amy Winehouse, Adele, FKA Twigs, Jessie J and Katie Melua and the sales and critical acclaim for these varied acts demonstrates the school is a conveyor belt for original thinking. Students follow a mix of the national curriculum and their chosen field of study (dance, music, theatre) as well as industry business essentials like copyright Law. But according to former principal Sir Nick Williams, 'they're not factory farmed. What we do is attract people into the school who are creative – that means things will happen.' The dance instructor's line from the 1980s TV show *Fame* rings true: 'You've got big dreams? You want fame? Well fame costs. And right here is where you start paying – in sweat.' (*The Independent*, 2007)

P | Passion

Our next element, *passion*, is often mentioned by prolifically creative people when they're discussing what drives them. It is related to purpose, which we explore more in Chapter 6.

It runs true that the more passionately you feel about something (work or otherwise) the more likely you are to stick with it. Researchers agree that passion is important for creativity (Amabile, 1987).

However, 'what are you passionate about?' is a pretty loaded question and one that many writers (including Pink and Gilbert) dislike because it demands too much of us. Pink invites us not to get passionate, but to get busy.

So to paraphrase Steve Jobs, how are you going to put your 'ding' in the universe?

CREATIVE COACH

- If you have passion, discipline comes easily. Where do your passions lie? What do you always find time for no matter how busy you are?

- How could you use your passion to help you creatively?

- What are your thoughts and feelings about the word passion? What is their impact? What could be the benefits of fully accessing your passionate side?

- What are your thoughts and feelings about the word discipline? How do they impact upon you? What could be the benefits of fully accessing your disciplined side?

CASE STUDY

Serial entrepreneur Michael Acton Smith first rose to fame when he helped create the Shot Glass Chess Set (in which the popular strategy game was paired up with alcohol) – and went on to form gadget retailer firebox.com. In 2004, he set up Mind Candy, which brought the online world of Moshi Monsters to tens of millions of children. He remains the company's Chairman and Creative Director.

Figure 3.4 Michael Acton Smith was named one of NESTA's 'new radicals' in 2012

How much does creativity still feature in your daily life now that you have a fair-sized company to run?

'I found that as the business got bigger my creative input got less and less – and that made me sad. A business with lots of employees around the world requires a very different kind of mindset to the one that can spark it to life in the first place. So in 2014 I had some conversations with my COO Davinia and we came to an arrangement where she would effectively run the business and I would take more of a creative role and go back to doing more of what I really loved, and that has worked out really well.'

Can you think of a time where difficulty forced you to outdo yourself creatively?

'When I was very young I used to make bookmarks and sell them outside my front door. Me and my sister would put rocks on top of the bookmarks to stop them blowing away, and someone came along and asked how much the rocks were. So we pretended we were selling these special rocks and flipped the business model. But I think the most intense, traumatic time I've been through was during the early days of Mind Candy with Perplex City, this treasure hunt we created. It was very creative but commercially it did not work at all. We were running out of money and urgently needed another idea and I think knowing that forced me to come up with the idea that was Moshi Monsters. I'm a big believer in creative constraints, whether that's time or the restrictions that you put on the idea. It's very hard to come up with an idea when you can boil an ocean and do anything.'

Are you of the opinion that everyone in your organization might have the next great idea?

'Giving people the latitude to come up with creative ideas across the organization is a healthy thing. In terms of new IP [intellectual property] we meet once a week to discuss all the new ideas that are bubbling away and develop them and debate them and at a certain point the best go on to get green-lit. Anybody in the company can come up with ideas and come and present to that team.'

What can someone do today to improve their creative output?

'Be more curious. Expose yourself to as many new things as possible. As Eleanor Roosevelt used to say, do one thing every day that scares you. Put yourself in those situations that are outside your comfort zone, and that's where you learn more about the world and how people think and tick. You can practise creativity, too – one thing I love doing is mashing up two different things and seeing what product or idea could spin off from that. Alcohol and chess is a good example of that from yesteryear.'

Do you think that failure and getting things wrong is a vital part of the creative process?

'Definitely. I think if you're afraid of failing and always stick within your comfort zone you reduce your chance of coming up with those quirky, world-beating ideas that no one else has thought of. But in order to do that you have to go to the edge a lot, and at the edge you fail a lot more than you succeed. So to be a creative person you have to be comfortable with screwing up and not beat yourself up about it and try again each time until you find the magic'.

Fe | Failure

You have to fail a lot. You have to fail early. You have to fail often and you have to fail forward.
Will Smith, 2015

Failure is the final element in this chapter. The willingness to fail is an important aspect of creativity. But failure's hard to get your head round. On the one hand, too many flops will mark you out as a failure. But as the thinking goes, to fail now and then, is absolutely essential.

But I know that 'embracing failure' is easier said than done. That horrible, shrinking feeling that comes with a flop – even a small one – can be hard to shake off. Why stick your neck out again if you know how painful it is when things go wrong? As we saw earlier, if you work in an office with a blame culture or 'fixed mindset' then it's not likely you'll be looking to add failure to your personal development plan any time soon.

What's important to remember is that failure doesn't necessarily mean total career-ending screw-up: small failures can add to understanding and doing better next time.

Fear kills creativity

During a radio interview with Zane Lowe, actor Will Smith said he believes that 'fear is the killer of creativity'.

Given his status as one of the highest-paid actors in Hollywood, you might think that Smith has had an easy ride, but as well as pushing himself physically for the likes of *Ali* – where he gained 35 lbs of muscle to pull off the look of a professional boxer – he has seen his share of flops, too; 2013's *After Earth* is a movie with an embarrassing 11 per cent 'fresh' rating on the movie critics' website Rotten Tomatoes. In the radio interview, Smith called this sci-fi disaster 'the most painful failure' of his career.

If you're wondering what Smith means by 'failing forward', he explains: 'The Monday morning after that [*After Earth*] I got right on the treadmill,' he said. 'I just got back into that mindset of being comfortable to go out there and fall on my face. If you're not willing to fall on your face you can't create at a high level.'

What he is saying is something that most experienced creative people agree on: 'Pick yourself up, dust yourself off and start all over again' (Fields and Kern, 1936).

The Museum of Failed Products

As a rule we only hear about the products that succeed, but even the big brands fail sometimes. Housed in Michigan, The Museum of Failed Products is a graveyard to consumer product failures that were withdrawn from sale owing to lack of sales. It's where you'll find Clairol's 'A Touch of Yogurt' shampoo (this followed an earlier failed launch, the 'Look of Buttermilk'), Gillette's 'For Oily Hair Only' nestling alongside Pepsi's AM Breakfast Cola which survived on shelves for less than a year (Burkeman, 2012).

CASE STUDY   Tech start-up thinking meets US federal government issues

When the status quo is the riskiest option, that means there is simply no other choice than radical disruption.
Hayley Van Dyck, 2016

Sometimes failure is the catalyst for change. Hayley Van Dyck worked in the Obama administration to bring the cutting-edge thinking of the best of Silicon Valley's tech start-ups to big government issues. In her 2016 TED talk 'How a start-up is changing business as usual' she describes how federal government spends over US $86 billion a year on IT projects alone. You read that right. That's more than the entire venture capital industry in the US.

Van Dyck describes how 96 per cent of these projects are over-budget or late, and further, 40 per cent of these are abandoned. She says: 'This is a very existentially painful moment for any organization, because it means as government continues to operate as it's programmed to do, failure is nearly inevitable. And when the status quo is the riskiest option, that means there is simply no other choice than radical disruption.' Van Dyck is part of the United States Digital Service formed in 2015 to tackle issues like the 137-day backlog a US veteran waits to receive benefits, having wrangled with over 1,000 potential websites and 900 different phone-numbers to acquire information.

The new department has hired the best talent from Facebook, Google, Amazon and Twitter in order to create a connected, digital government. These tech innovators are paired with civil servants to transfer knowledge and skills. Van Dyck adds that: 'We strategically deploy them in a targeted formation at the most mission-critical, life-changing, important services that government offers. And finally, we give them massive air cover, from the leadership inside the agencies all the way up to the President himself, to transform these services for the better.'

CREATIVE COACH

- Consider an experience you have had in your life that you consider to be a failure.
  - With hindsight, how beneficial was that experience?
  - What did you learn?
  - What were the silver linings?
- How comfortable are you with 'getting things wrong'? What if there was no such thing as failure and everything that happened to you was perfect in the sense it acted as your teacher – how would that change your relationship with experimenting?
- When you've had a knock – how do you get yourself back in the game?

REVIEW THE CHAPTER

- In this section which creative element do you most relate to?
- What wouldn't you ever compromise on?
- Which element would help to achieve your creative ambitions?
- What are you going to do to get it? List three things you can start today.
- From this chapter assess what is your greatest strength and your biggest area for development?

Table 3.1 Values

Element	Key questions	What's your greatest strength?	Which element would you most like to develop further?
Openness (O)	How open are you to doing things differently?		
Ego (E)	How much does your ego play a part in your decisions, good and bad?		
Rebellion (No)	How comfortable are you with rebelling?		
Self-belief (Sb)	To what extent do you believe this statement: 'I am creative'?		
Motivation (M)	What motivates you to create?		
Imagination (Im)	How much do you engage with your imagination?		
Vision (Vi)	To what extent do you have a vision for your projects or your people?		
Discipline (Dp)	How do you discipline your creativity?		
Passion (P)	To what extent are you driven to act by your passions?		
Failure (Fa)	How would you rate your ability to welcome and learn from failure?		

IN A NUTSHELL

The research and case studies show that a person's creative abilities aren't set in stone. They can be improved through learning from failure, applying discipline, understanding your motivation, believing in oneself and learning new skills. A fixed or growth mindset has a crucial bearing on whether you will succeed or fail in any endeavour, creative or otherwise.

DIG DEEPER

Csikszentmihalyi, M (1996) *Creativity: The psychology of discovery and invention* Harper Perennial, London

Dweck, C (2007), *Mindset: The new psychology of success* Ballantine Books, New York

David Kelley's 'Creative confidence' TED talk: http://goo.gl/BlvquI (2013)

Kelley, D, Kelley T (2013) *Creative Confidence: Unleashing the Creative Potential Within Us All*, William Collins UK

Pink, D (2011) *Drive: The surprising truth about what motivates us*, Canongate Books, London

Haley Van Dyck's 'United States digital service' TED talk http://goo.gl/c3xkkh (2016).

The creative mind 04

This chapter looks at these 10 creative elements:

Know thyself.
Ancient Greek maxim

I've always been fascinated by what's actually playing out on the hills and valleys of our three pounds of grey matter while we're generating creative ideas. Can the latest neuroscience research teach us evidence-backed ways to manage our creative state and generate better ideas?

People often ask what the secret is to getting into 'the zone'. Is there a way to switch your creativity on and off? There are three strategies that I've found to help if I'm feeling stuck on a problem. Getting physical works for me – taking a walk or playing music (something bouncy and Beyoncéish for five minutes of home-office disco). Sometimes I take a power nap. Talking it through with someone totally uninvolved can help too.

So, in this chapter I've teamed up with neuroscientist Ben Martynoga. He takes us on a whistle-stop tour of how our brains work in relation to creativity, and describes elements we can add to our mental toolkit.

Despite the recent steps forward, brain scientists are still well short of a complete and convincing account of the creative process. After all, genuine creativity doesn't happen on cue, in the sterile environment of the science lab. It happens as the poet strolls in the woods. It takes flight when the footballer squares up to his opposing defence. It unfolds as the freelancer hammers away at her laptop. It's even manifest in the toddler's first artistic scrawls.

So instead of trying to unify these disparate acts of inspiration, neuroscience is starting to unpack the psychological toolbox of creative thought. Once we've familiarized ourselves with the tools of the trade, we can start to hone the instruments we already have and to acquire the ones we lack. We can then become more focused upon our attempts at creativity. We can deliberately experiment with different activities, moods and situations. These will each activate different brain states, which will, in turn, bring distinct contributions to your creative forays. Let's see what emerges.

Thinking fast and slow

In his masterly 2011 book *Thinking, Fast and Slow*, Nobel Prize-winning psychologist Daniel Kahneman describes the two dominant modes of thought used by our brains. 'System 1' is quick and intuitive. It operates automatically, mostly outside of our awareness and control. 'System 2' is more familiar to us; it's the one we're conscious of. This (relatively) slow mode is less easily duped. It likes evidence and doesn't jump to conclusions.

When it comes to creativity, the elements described in this chapter on the brain can be broadly divided between these two systems of thought.

System 1 is the domain of the *unconscious mind* |Um|. It's where our minds *wander* |W| when we're *relaxed* |Re|. It's where we forge most *associations* |As| and it's where *emotions* come from |Em|.

Our *logical* |L| and *analytical faculties* |Am| belong to System 2. When we're being mindful, we're exercising this system and it's System 2 that keeps us on target.

The roughly equal split between System 1 and 2 indicates that neither dominates when it comes to innovation. In fact, most creativity seems to happen when the two systems bat ideas back and forth. When an insight emerges with a sudden 'aha!' |Im| it's System 2 that sees it and can choose to run with it. But it was System 1 that hatched it, brewed it and nurtured it.

As you'll see, when we're *improvising* |Ir|, we're right on the borderline between the two systems. We're consciously steering our work towards a goal, but we're totally dependent on the skills, knowledge and memories we've gathered during practice and stored in System 1.

Since its role in creativity is so crucial and often misunderstood, our first element is the unconscious mind.

Figure 4.1 The two systems of thought, System 1 ('fast') and System 2 ('slow'). Insight and improvisation exist right at the border between the two systems of thought

SOURCE: www.ecoscope.com/iceberg created by Uwe Kils (iceberg) and User:Wiska Bodo (sky)

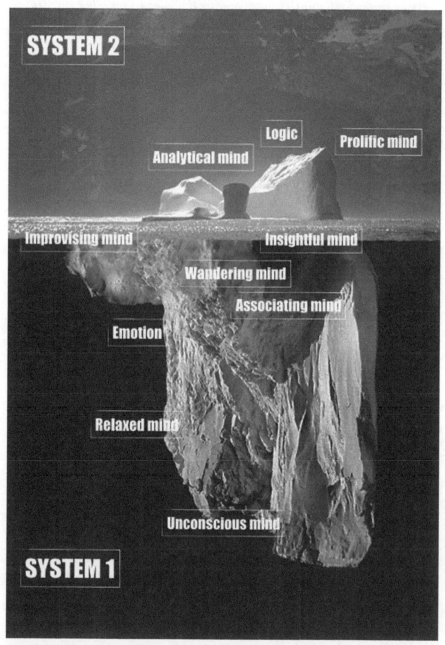

The creative elements described in this chapter can be roughly divided into 'fast' (System 1) and 'slow' (System 2) brain functions, according to Daniel Kahneman's summary of the scientific literature. Like the tip of the iceberg, we're consciously aware of System 2 elements, whereas much of the mental work of creativity goes on in the unconscious domain of System 1. Note that insight and improvisation exist right at the border between the two systems of thought.

Um The unconscious mind

At some random point, on a train or walking into a building, an idea will spring at me. Actually spring. From behind a bush or around a corner.

John Whiston, ITV's Pope of Soap, 2016

Sigmund Freud used to compare the human mind to an iceberg. Conscious thought processes – reasons, feelings, awareness – are like the iceberg's tip. Sunlight glitters impressively on this frozen peak, but the vast bulk of ice actually lies in the deep gloom beneath the waves. For Freud, this submerged and unknowable realm was the unconscious. Down there is where the crucial mental activity plays out.

More than a century on, scientific study of the brain has exploded in power and precision. Some of Freud's ideas have proved to be off-beam, but modern neuroscience fully supports his central analogy. Our self-conscious experience, which feels so dominant and powerful, is in fact often not at the heart of the brain's grand scheme. Instead it finds itself on the fringes, frantically trying to understand and influence the super-computer-like machinations of the unconscious mind (Eagleman, 2011).

Unconscious mental work plays a huge role in powering the imagination. This explains how William Blake could claim that he wrote his poem Milton 'without premeditation, even against my will'. It's why the French mathematician Henri Poincaré said one of his most famous ideas 'came to me, without anything in my former thoughts seeming to have paved the way for it'. It's perhaps why Einstein claimed to 'see' the solutions to many of his problems long before he was able to describe them.

Brain scientists have moved on from these anecdotes and are now capturing the unconscious mind in the act of creative thought.

One of the best-studied examples of the unconscious at work is the incubation effect. When you've tackled a creative problem head-on and progress slows, it often pays to back off. In 2006, psychologists Dijksterhuis and Meurs asked study participants to list as many creative uses for a brick as possible. They gave one group three minutes to consciously think about the problem before writing. Another group spent three minutes with their conscious awareness absorbed by a simple computer game. After this brief unconscious incubation period, the latter group to came up with more original uses for the brick (Dijksterhuis and Meurs, 2006).

The improved performance caused by time out is not just a passive consequence of recouping energy and attention. A recent brain imaging study showed that the unconscious mind quietly worries away at problems (Cresswell *et al*, 2013). Study participants were set a challenge and then distracted by a memory test. During the incubation period, conscious deliberation was impossible, but brain scans revealed clear task-relevant mental processing going on in the background.

CASE STUDY   ITV's 'Pope of Soap' on incubation

Nicknamed 'the Pope of Soap', John Whiston is MD for Continuing Drama and Head of ITV in the north of England. His creative remit covers new ideas and storylines for serial dramas *Coronation Street* and *Emmerdale*. He's a man with a demanding creative to-do list. John deliberately works incubation into his creative process.

He told me:

If someone wants me to come up with something, say if they send me an email about what they are looking for, I won't read it properly. I will just scan it and get the gist. And I won't start thinking about it. I'll just file away the idea behind the email and maybe a couple of phrases. That's a combination of laziness (I've got other more pleasant, easier things to do) and of pride (I don't yet have the good idea, the clever angle. I don't want to go back with a boring, sensible, perfectly satisfactory answer. I could but that wouldn't be me).

My conscious mind will know I have to reply to the email. And my inbox will nudge me whenever I'm on the computer. At some random point, on a train or walking into a building, an idea will spring at me. Actually spring. From behind a bush or around a corner.

The rest is easy. Just work outwards from the idea and then use that to reply to the email.

But whatever I do, I don't re-read the original email. I fear too much detail about what is needed will confine any idea from me, even strangle it.

Of course this sometimes means what I come up with is at a tangent to what I was meant to come up with. An interesting tangent, though. You haven't read the brief properly so this is a danger. But, in a way, you are responding to what you think the brief should have been from the few phrases you have read – the essence of brief (a heady aroma) – rather than the brief itself.

This sounds arrogant. It's not. You've come to realize and accept that you just aren't built to respond closely point by point to a detailed brief. That's not better or worse than people who are. Just different. But possibly four out of five times you are kind of on target. Or at least not so embarrassingly off target that they realize that you didn't even do them the honour of properly reading their email.

Sleep on it

Another excellent and direct way to channel the power of the unconscious is to fall asleep. Elias Howe perfected his sewing machine design during nocturnal reverie. Mendeleev's arrangement of the original periodic table was reportedly imagined during sleep (this version popped into my head while face-down and dozing during a massage following a *Breaking Bad* box-set binge). Popular culture is awash with stories of dream-inspired creativity. But once again, the brain science is right behind them. A 2009 study shows that REM sleep, the phase we dream in, is particularly conducive to creative problem solving (Cai *et al*, 2009).

By adding in stimulus, incubating the problem, wandering through daydreams and forming unexpected associations the unconscious will, with luck, dredge up pertinent insights.

CREATIVE EXPERIMENT

There is, it seems, something in the folk wisdom of sleeping on a problem. If you want to try this at home, you may find it helps to frame your question clearly before going to sleep. Writing a letter to your unconscious mind is a way to deliberately 'plant' a request for information.

You need to have engaged your *analytical mind* Am with any of the information, data or reading you want to 'sleep on' beforehand. You're going to pass the baton from the conscious to the unconscious mind. Try it for yourself.

Dear me, I am dealing with problem X. I need an answer to this chewy challenge by 9 am tomorrow morning, just after breakfast. The part I am really struggling with is how to do X, with a budget of Y, in the time that I have... and I can't quite work out how to overcome obstacle Z.

> Be as specific as you can about the problem (just as if you were briefing another person) and the time you want it solved by. Tuck the note under your pillow and head off to the land of nod. Sound bonkers? Maybe, but just think of all the times you've had that great idea in the shower, or while driving or walking. This way you are being deliberate about directing your mind. You're allowing time for incubation when you're going to be resting anyway. What's the worst that could happen? (Adapted from Michael Michalko's letter to the unconscious, creativethinking.net)

You MUST build incubation into your creative process. This is true if you work alone, but also if you're helping others to be more creative. If you are helping others, consider circulating challenges in advance, so they have time to process a problem before they step into the room. Share the ideas people arrive with at the start of the session. If you're feeling adventurous, brief everyone coming to your brainstorm to first write a letter to his or her unconscious mind. At the bare minimum give them some time for the *analytical mind* Am to think about the problem before breaking off and expecting any creative ideas to hatch out.

Re The relaxed mind

Our next element, the *relaxed mind*, is all about nurturing the unconscious mind and getting into a good state from which to create. Neuroscientists are today throwing light on what happens in your brain when you relax. In the process, they're showing why relaxed brain states can be highly creative.

Ever since Archimedes in ancient Greece, bathing has had a special place in the lore of creativity. The ubiquitous tale of the great mathematician emerging from his bath with a 'Eureka!' and an answer for his king is probably apocryphal but it contains a useful message. Who hasn't felt the unexpected blossoming of a creative idea as you savour a hot shower?

Stars of the relaxed mind are so-called alpha waves. When we're awake but relaxed, scientists can detect rhythmic waves of electrical activity lapping across the surface of the brain. These alpha waves are slower than the brainwaves typical of alert, focused mindsets; yet faster than the slow waves of deep sleep.

In the 1970s American psychologist Colin Martindale made the first links between alpha waves and creativity (Martindale and Hines, 1975). His research didn't make much impact, but neuroscientists have recently picked up his baton again. Today alpha waves appear to be one of the most reliable brain-based features of creative processes (Fink and Benedek, 2014). They're crucial for the *insightful mind* |In|, for example, but they are also turned on when we try to come up with creative ideas. People judged to be more creative have more alpha waves. Moreover, their best ideas are often preceded by a burst of alpha activity.

Even so, an important question remains. Do alpha waves themselves enhance creativity, or do they just happen to show up at about the same time? In 2015 neuroscientists in North Carolina provided a first answer (Lustenberger *et al*, 2015). They applied electrodes to people's foreheads and ran an alternating current across the frontal part of the brain. The electricity triggered alpha waves; which in turn caused significant improvements in creativity test scores.

Don't try this at home

It sounds so simple – a tickle of electricity to get your brain into a creative state. But ignore the webpages full of homebrew electrical brain stimulation recipes. The experimenters used specialist equipment and low currents. It's too early to tell if this kind of stimulation is completely risk-free.

It's still not totally clear what alpha waves actually are, or why they can boost aspects of creativity. The best guess at the moment is that they shut out incoming sensory stimuli and block off task thoughts (Fink and Benedek, 2014). Free from these noisy interrupters, the mind quietens and starts to hear the timid voices of growing hunches and tentative new ideas.

Watch out though – the relaxed mind won't fix all your creative problems. There's no point in asking your boss if you can wallow in the bath while you work. Your (distinctly unrelaxed) *analytical mind* |Am| must put in the legwork first, and iron out the kinks later on. And often you'll need the busy-ness of the *prolific mind* |Pm| to press on through lean spells. The real knack lies in knowing when to push and when to kick back and let the relaxed mind take over.

Figure 4.2 Main types of normal adult brainwaves, with the associated creative mind elements

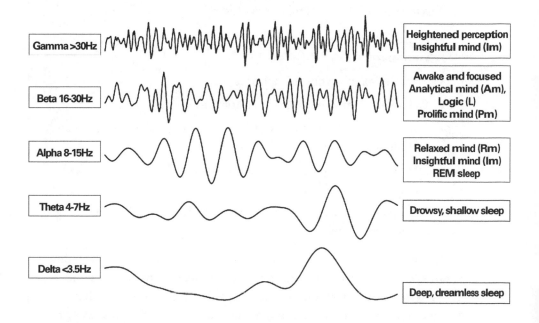

So how do you tap into your relaxed mind at your desk or in a brainstorm?

Given that group brainstorming is the default setting for many organizations, it may not always be easy to nurture alpha waves in an office setting. Ben Martynoga suspects that alpha waves come on more readily during quieter, less pressured times.

Nevertheless if you're facilitating, it's still a great idea to aim to make group sessions as relaxed as possible. Many people joke about their local pub being where the ideas flow. Perhaps a more relaxed atmosphere and a glass of something helps the process. I've worked with teams where we've all lazed on the grass on a sunny, spring day looking up at the clouds and allowing our minds to relax and wander. It's not for everyone, but to help make people feel less stressed see IDEO's rules in Chapter 5.

CREATIVE EXPERIMENT

Tap into your relaxed mind at the office:

- Switch your phone to airplane mode, quit your mail app, close your diary.
- Try to relax, put your headphones in.
- Get away from your desk – even for 15 minutes.
- Get your lunch from somewhere different and take a physical and mental detour.
- Step outside and find a bench and just sit on it for a while. Take a metaphorical mini-break.
- Stop planning and let your mind unfurl and explore the bigger challenges in a more organic way.

If you're at home, indulge yourself with a warm bath or shower. But you could also listen to your favourite music, meditate, take some exercise or quietly savour a delicious meal. In fact, anything that takes you away from social interactions and out of the pressures of the day is good. With planning (and luck) your mind will unwind and start to turn on the alpha waves.

Sometimes when our minds relax, they amble off to interesting places. This is the focus of the next element.

 The wandering mind

You get ideas from daydreaming. You get ideas from being bored.
You get ideas all the time. The only difference between writers and
other people is we notice when we're doing it.
Neil Gaiman, 1997

After this paragraph, stop reading. Close your eyes. Do your best to stop thinking. Stay in the here and now. Keep it up for two minutes.

How did you get on? Most likely you experienced a moment or two of serenity. But then a thought bubbled up, uninvited. Even if you evicted that one, another soon took its place.

The human mind is a squirming, itchy thing

In fact, psychologists estimate that we each spend an average of 46.9 per cent of every waking day in a distracted, mind-wandering state (Killingsworth and Gilbert, 2010).

Neuroscientists, meanwhile, have pinpointed a set of brain regions that flare into action whenever our thoughts meander away from the task at hand. So reliable and common is this pattern of brain activity that they call it the brain's *default network*.

Many, perhaps most, of the thoughts emerging from the default network are mundane musings, focused on the minutiae of everyday life. You dwell on the embarrassing noise your tummy made in in the coffee queue, you think about what you might have for lunch, or you fret about the presentation you've got to give next week.

Occasionally though, our thought patterns loosen and we link ideas in wholly unexpected ways. We consider how things *could be,* rather than how they *are* (influencing the *vision* $\boxed{v}$ element, in Chapter 3). Sometimes our wandering trains of thought blossom into elaborate, creative daydreams.

However until recently, there was little hard evidence that mind wandering could help ordinary people with everyday acts of creativity. Most of the data from psychology focused on the negative effects wreaked by distraction and rumination.

In 2012 cognitive scientists at the University of California, Santa Barbara started to change this (Baird *et al*, 2012). Their experiment was simple. They asked 145 students to complete a classic in-lab test of creativity. They had to think of as many uses as possible for familiar objects like paperclips, newspapers or bricks. The students then had a short break, just 12 minutes, before having another crack at the creativity task.

During the interval one group of students were given an unrelated exercise that demanded their full attention. Another group completed an easy, repetitive task (they had to simply indicate whether a bright arrow appeared on the right of left of a computer screen). A third group waited idly.

The students who did the undemanding task didn't spend their 12 minutes thinking about the problem, but they reported much more mind wandering than the other groups. They also came up with many more creative uses for their bricks and paperclips.

We can learn from this experiment. When faced with a creative problem, tackle it head-on first, do what you can. Then stop. Do something else, preferably something boring. Wash up all the coffee cups in the office, pick the longest queue at the supermarket checkout or sit in on an irrelevant seminar. Inevitably, your mind will start to wander. With luck the idling capacity of your default network will subconsciously chew away at your creative problem.

It's not always an exact science, but given time, and some initial grit to consider, the wandering mind can quietly generate beautiful pearls of insight.

CREATIVE EXPERIMENT

TAKE A CREATIVE SAFARI

We don't know where we get our ideas from. What we do know is that we do not get them from our laptops.
John Cleese, 1991

We spend so much time looking at our devices that historian Simon Schama has called us the '*look down*' generation. Just as we're connected to friends, family and colleagues around the globe, we can become disconnected from sources of inspiration and stimulation that surround us. So 'look up' and use the place where you live or work to help find answers to your problems. Try this:

- Get clear in your mind the problem that you're trying to solve. What's your specific question? Repeat it a few times to yourself.

- The first time you do this you'll need to be really deliberate about carving out a space in which to think, but as you gain more experience you can do it any time you like. You just have to commit to 'looking up' and noticing.

- Go outside. Turn off your phone. Take a pen and paper to make notes.

- Allow yourself to drift. Be open to whatever happens and whatever you see; don't censor yourself. Have a conversation with a stranger, take pictures, and make connections as you go.

- Don't force any answers, just meander and allow your thoughts to percolate. Be content with not knowing. You can take pictures or pick up random stimuli, postcards, a leaf or a flyer to act as prompts later.

- If you can, persuade one of your colleagues or a friend to do it with you. Wander alone, then collaborate, compare notes and build on each other's ideas.

What did you notice?

- Did you pick up any items or take any images? Did these help you make connections – see the next element, associating mind (Am) – and generate ideas for your problem?

- What new questions, themes, ideas or answers come to mind? Use these and build. If you got stuck or couldn't make connections, consider why that might be – is the problem well formed? What don't you know that you need to? Do you need more time?

- What do you know now that you didn't know before – about your challenge or about your own process?

23 Am The associating mind

Think left and think right and think low and think high. Oh, the thinks you can think up if only you try.
Dr Seuss, 1975

Inside our skulls we each carry an incredibly powerful internal search engine: a Google made from grey jelly. Feed your brain an idea, a feeling, a smell or a memory and it will instantly and effortlessly start hunting for links. It even works for a single word.

Avocado.

What just happened in your brain? What came to you? *Pear, stone, smooth, fruit, green, yuck, unripe*, perhaps?

The word entered your mind like a drop of ink into water. Within milliseconds a cloud of associations appeared, bloomed outwards, then faded. Your brain's associative memory system is tuned to categorize, describe and call up relevant memories. It can even activate physical sensations and emotional reactions. You weren't consciously aware of most of the connections, but they were made.

Figure 4.3 A tiny fragment of a possible associative memory cloud, showing the dense web of associations we rapidly and automatically form when we think of a word like 'avocado'

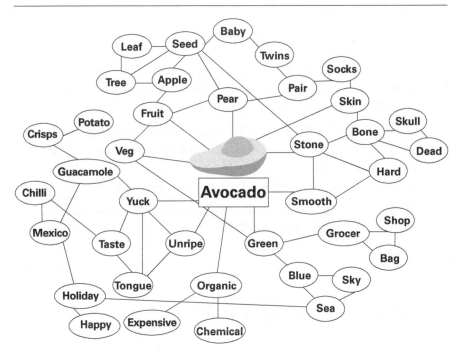

Tiny fragment of a possible associative memory cloud, showing the dense web of associations we rapidly and automatically form when we encounter a new word like 'avocado'. These memory webs are highly personal and have the potential to throw up unexpected and creative links between disparate thoughts, ideas, concepts and memories.

In the early 1960s pioneering psychologist Sarnoff Mednick proposed that the associative memory is at the core of the creative process (Mednick, 1962). He argued that more creative ideas tap more unexpected associations. They connect the seemingly unconnectable. Crucially, they do it in ways that we recognize as 'making sense', being useful, beautiful or thought provoking.

A recent neuroscience study supports Mednick's idea. Brain scientists at Bar-Ilan University in Israel gave 144 volunteers a list of 96 prompt words. They then gave them a minute per word to list all the associations they could think of (Kenett *et al*, 2014). From the long lists of words, they reconstructed each participant's 'associative cloud'. In effect, they took snapshots of people's associative memories.

As predicted by Mednick, less creative individuals had relatively diffuse, wispy memory clouds. The more creative types, by contrast, produced densely interconnected webs of association. This is exactly what one needs for remixing surprising associations into fresh ideas.

The Kenett study homed in on inbuilt differences between the brain function of more and less creative individuals. But what can we all do right now to free up the power of our associative minds?

Several recent psychology experiments offer evidence-backed suggestions. Moving abroad seems to help (Maddux and Galinsky, 2009). For most of us that's not a workable suggestion. Luckily, mental travel appears to be good enough. Researchers in Indiana asked people to come up with as many different modes of transport as they could. When they told people that researchers in faraway Greece posed the question, they came up with more creative suggestions (Jia *et al*, 2009).

There's a clear message here. If you want to think out of the box, try to frame your creative challenges in unexpected ways (see tools in Chapter 8 to help you do this). By forcing yourself to access the vast search space of your associative memory from a new perspective, you should summon up more creative connections.

34 En Emotion

If your job calls on your creative powers, it's easy to forget that how you *feel* has a huge impact on how you *think*.

It might seem as if you get to work and simply turn your imagination on. But of course it's not as simple as that. Did you have run-in with a disgruntled commuter on the bus? A tiff with a partner over breakfast? Did your book make you laugh this morning?

When it comes to creativity, your emotional backdrop matters. Brain scientists are starting to illustrate why. Positive moods seem to have an especially clear effect on creative thought. Psychologists have suspected this for some time. In 1987 researchers at the University of Maryland (Isen *et al*, 1987) showed people five-minute film clips that were either funny (a set of bloopers from TV westerns) or boringly neutral (maths tuition). Those who'd had a chuckle performed better on a set of lab creativity tests. An unexpected gift of a chocolate bar had the same effect too.

Just as being happy can make you more creative, the reverse is also true. Making imaginative associations makes you measurably more cheerful (Brunyé *et al*, 2013). With luck a virtuous cycle starts to emerge as you get into the creative zone: good ideas are pleasing and clear the path for even more.

But why the link between positive emotions and inspiration? The researchers believe it's all about attention. When you're anxious and uncomfortable your attention narrows. You zoom in on the details. You flip into 'survival mode', where you focus on practicalities and realities. Sometimes this can be helpful. But when you're feeling positive you broaden your scope and entertain speculative ideas.

Apply this brain science back at work:

CREATIVE EXPERIMENT

- Make creative sessions *fun* F .
- Look for opportunities to play and laugh.
- Introduce an element of competition.
- Reward successes and help your team shrug off failures.
- Intersperse your session with five-minute comedy clips.

Once everyone is happy and receptive, the room will start to fizz with ideas and insights.

A final important note on emotion: As well as getting in the right emotional state to create, think hard about how your work will make your audience feel. It will have a huge impact on how they act (see the Institute of Practitioners in Advertising (IPA) study that follows).

A quick word of warning: sadly, the happy bubble won't solve all creative challenges, as we shall see in the next element, Logic.

L Logic

It is an old maxim of mine that when you have excluded the impossible, whatever remains, however improbable, must be the truth.
Sherlock Holmes in *The Adventure of the Beryl Coronet*

Back in Chapter 3 you considered the characteristics of creative geniuses, perhaps sketching a picture of a freethinking maverick: playful, unconventional, irrational, perhaps even a little bit mad.

If we ask you to name some creative geniuses your list will most likely include several scientists in your top 10: Albert Einstein, Charles Darwin, Stephen Hawking and Isaac Newton, perhaps?

These scientists are, by necessity, champions of rationality and logical ninjas. This mismatch shows that even though we all know that logic is a crucial pillar of the creative process, we tend to overlook it. And it doesn't just stop with the scientists. Without logical, mathematical patterns, music is just noise. Most good poems are built around a clear structure. Shakespeare's plots unfold in a way that 'makes sense', even if the twists and turns are hard to predict.

As well as providing a scaffold to build ideas around, logical thought can help you dare to think differently.

I'll be more enthusiastic about encouraging thinking outside the box when there's evidence of any thinking going on inside it.
Terry Pratchett, 2016

Take Nobel Prize winners Barry Marshall and Robin Warren. They proved that bacteria cause most stomach ulcers. At the time most other medics ridiculed them: they said that bacteria couldn't possibly live in the stomach. Stress, diet and excess acid cause ulcers.

But the facts didn't quite add up so Marshall drank a petri dish full of the bacteria in question giving himself terrible ulcers in the process. Marshall and Warren eradicated all the dogma and false assumptions from their minds. In its place they re-built an accurate but more creative, explanation.

The easy path usually leads back to habitual and socially accepted ways of thinking. A measure of logical thought can help you take a different fork in the road, spot the gap in the market, or the hole in the theory. It can also help you hone ideas that you and others have generated.

Brain scientists have gathered some clues that may help us tune into this way of thinking. Australian psychologist Joe Forgas argues that a negative mood can help. According to him, as well as improving your memory and persistence, being a bit sad can help you think more logically. It can improve your judgment, help you avoid psychological biases and make you less gullible (Forgas, 2013). You don't even have to be genuinely miserable; simply frowning can sometimes help you think more clearly and avoid common mistakes (Kahneman, 2011).

So consider keeping the jollity for the idea generation sessions (see emotion, above). When it comes to strategy and evaluation it can pay to make things a bit more serious, challenging even. Use our evaluation tools (Chapter 8) to draw up rational plans, including thinking about the emotional effect of your work on your target audience. When the mood is more downbeat, you can rein your freewheeling (but distraction-prone) attention back in and be more analytical in your thoughts. The nitty-gritty work of creativity can then start in earnest.

CASE STUDY   Emotion trumps reason in marketing and beyond

Think about the last time you responded to a TV or radio ad, or a direct mailer dropping on the doormat. What made you pay attention and take action?

Chances are that it was an emotional response. The best adverts don't have a rational message; they don't try to persuade us to buy anything. Instead they induce a warm glow, a welling tear, a dropped jaw or a butterfly flicker of excitement.

Leading marketers have known this instinctively for decades. It also happens to be the rational conclusion of an influential report published by the UK-based Institute of Practitioners in Advertising (IPA) (Binet and Fields, 2013). They analysed the effectiveness of hundreds of ads that have aired over the last 30 years.

They found that:

- Emotional advertising delivers nearly twice the profit of rational campaigns.

- The effects of emotional campaigns build over several years, steadily increasing profits (by up to over 20 per cent difference between emotional and rational campaigns over 3+ years).

- Long-term brand preferences are associated with System 1, while rational product and pricing messages that drive response in the short term are associated with System 2.

- The advice is to balance the heart and the head (Binet and Fields, 2013).

Research from one of the world's biggest advertisers, Procter & Gamble (P&G), found that even in low-interest, everyday item categories such as washing up liquid, emotional content lifts sales. US brand, Dawn dish soap was used by volunteers to clean oil from birds after the Exxon Valdez spill crisis in 1985. The brand used an association with protecting wildlife to make an emotional connection and build a strong brand. Pete Carter, marketing director/creative strategist at P&G is clear that 'indifference is the killer here. And that's what you want to avoid' (Whiteside, 2015).

This finding won't surprise many neuroscientists. They've long known that the emotional and memory systems of our brains are closely intertwined. If we experience strong emotions, we're much more likely to lay down strong memories (LeDoux, 2007).

When trying to choose between two competing brands, frequently the products are very similar. We rarely weigh up the pros and cons. Usually one product ignites a dim flicker of recognition. That memory will be more strongly activated if it's an emotional one.

So if you're trying to sell soap powder don't set out to prove that your product shifts the toughest stains. Instead convince buyers that doing the family laundry is an act of love.

This message is not simply for marketeers. If the goal of your creative endeavours is to persuade someone, change behaviour, educate, build a brand or attract followers, first hook people with their hearts. Only once you've got their full attention, should you start to deliver your other, more nuanced message.

See Chapter 8 for a creativity tool that uses emotions as to trigger fresh ideas.

Am The analytical mind

Most creative projects leave a trail of carnage in their wake. Thousands of tiny changes, invisible in the final draft, but tracked by your computer's writing app, dozens of rejected sketches and musical scores obscured by scribbling. The 17 discarded takes needed to nail a single film scene.

Copious amounts of conscious striving are required to unearth, refine and perfect most new ideas. Much of this is unglamorous and mind numbing, but it's absolutely essential.

Predominantly the majority of this work at the coalface of creativity takes place in your brain's working memory. This crucial brain system has its main home in your prefrontal cortex; the area at the front of your brain that drives many of your more complex mental operations.

Figure 4.4 Analytical mind: key brain circuits of working memory, crucial for much analytical thinking, operate in the prefrontal cortex

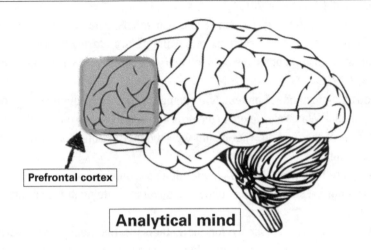

Prefrontal cortex

Analytical mind

Play with your mental Lego

You can think of working memory as a play-space where ephemeral ideas, concepts and chunks of information take on more tangible forms. They temporarily become Lego blocks that your mind can consciously rotate, combine, break apart and *experiment* with.

Your working memory is powerful, but limited in its capacity. Neuroscientists estimate that most of us can only handle a few chunks of information at a time: usually around four, depending on how they measure it (Cowan, 2001). While in working memory mental 'objects' are shielded from distractions and less relevant thoughts. For these reasons the new links forged within working memory are usually incremental and often pleasingly logical. They don't feel mysterious, like the leaps made by the *insightful mind* In (see below).

It's easy to see how this mental faculty is useful in problem solving, troubleshooting and conscious planning. But initially it is harder to grasp how it serves creative thought.

In a 2012 study, psychologists at the University of Amsterdam took a straight-faced look at how working memory relates to creativity (De Dreu *et al*, 2012). They observed that loading working memory with unnecessary thoughts made solving creative word puzzles much harder. They also studied a group of semi-professional cellists, asking them to improvise new melodies. With each round of practice, only the musicians with larger working memory capacities generated more creative tunes. Meanwhile, in brainstorming sessions, participants with bigger working memories generated more original ideas. They achieved this by staying on-task and persisting (see the element of *Grit* Gr in Chapter 1 and the *prolific mind* Pm (below) until they had devised novel contributions.

In many ways the analytical mind is the opposite of the *wandering mind* Wm and the *insightful mind* In. It's no less creative, but it creates in a different way. The analytical mind sifts through the hunches and brainwaves that enter your brain's working memory circuits. If it likes a fragile new idea it pushes on and refines it, until it can survive on its own in the big, bad world.

Given the limited capacity of our individual working memories, it makes sense to pool your resources. Work together to enhance your combined processing power. And since the analytical mind demands effort and concentration, don't try to bring it to bear when you're tired, hungry or open to other distractions.

But most of all, knowing the generative power of the analytical mind reminds us that creativity isn't just about 'waiting for the wild summer lightning strikes of inspiration' (Kreider, 2012). Most of creativity is hard work and requires *grit* Gr. Set to it.

Pm **The prolific mind**

Hard work is a feature of our next element, *the prolific mind*. Many of humanity's most imaginative and successful creators have also been the busiest. Pablo Picasso is estimated to have produced over 13,000 paintings, 300 sculptures, 34,000 bookplates and 100,000 prints. Miles Davis recorded 138 albums. Meanwhile, Australian inventor Kia Silverbrook has more than 4,500 patents to his name.

Productivity doesn't always predict creativity – remember your last brainstorm and the reams of flipchart paper covered in ideas with none of them fitting the bill?

During the last 50 years of his career, Nobel-winning physicist Peter Higgs of Higgs boson fame only published 10 articles. But often volume does seem to help.

Brain scientists have now begun to clothe this anecdotal impression in hard data. The most recent experiments come from neuroscientist Rex Jung at the University of New Mexico (Jung *et al*, 2015). Using a simple and easily scored laboratory test of creativity, they looked at how the *quantity* of ideas related to the *quality* of ideas.

They showed a large group of 246 students a series of simple graphic designs (a wiggly yellow line on a black background, for example). They asked them to write down all the things the image 'makes you think of, looks like, reminds you of, or suggests to you'. An independent panel of judges then rated the ideas for their originality.

When they plotted the data, the scientists discovered an exciting association, as the students with the most ideas, also produced more creative ideas.

Jung and colleagues then used brain scans to search for physical differences in the brains of the more prolific, and hence more creative, students. They found a relative thickening of the left frontal pole. This is the part of the brain crammed up against the left side of your forehead, which is implicated in thinking about oneself in the future. Hopefully, further research will flesh out what role that this brain region plays in creative thinking.

Figure 4.5 Prolific mind

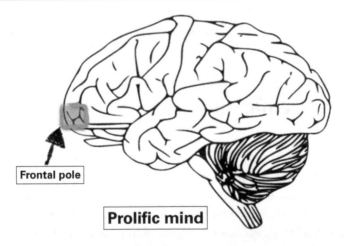

The correlation between the number and originality of ideas meshes with another well-established finding. According to the serial order effect, when given a creativity test like devising unusual uses for a brick, your later responses tend to be the more creative ones (Beaty and Silvia, 2012). Most of us spew out our most obvious ideas first. If we want to reach more ingenious suggestions, we have to push on and invest in a bit more mental work.

In other words, we tend to pick the low hanging fruit first, even if the more inaccessible harvest has been better ripened by the sun.

Now, it may seem a big leap to go from thinking about wiggly lines and bricks to real-world creativity. Even so, there is empirical evidence that the quantity as a prerequisite for quality rule does apply. Psychologist Dean Keith Simonton, for example, looked at the career spans of 2,026 scientists and inventors (Simonton, 1997). Those who produced the most influential research also produced the biggest volume of research (they also published some of the most ignored and unimaginative studies).

Apologies if this brute-force approach to creative idea generation shatters your romantic vision of the economical, perfectionist genius. But take heart, as this research indicates that if you need a lot of good ideas, try starting with the less intimidating goal of having *lots* of ideas. As we've seen *failure* F is a crucial part of the creative process. To find nuggets of gold you've got to sift through an awful lot of worthless gravel.

Being prolific can also increase your self-belief. The more ideas you have, the more options you have. If one idea doesn't work you have other avenues to follow.

Tip

Set yourself a target number of ideas for your next project. Don't stop until you've reached your quota. If you have eight people and each person brings four with them to the meeting, challenge everyone to double their ideas.

One of the most frequent questions in our workshops is: 'How do I get into a perfect mental state for creativity'?: our next element – the *improvising mind* Ir offers some clues.

The improvising mind

Bad improvisers block action, often with a high degree of skill. Good improvisers develop action.
Malcolm Gladwell, 2016

To date, most scientific research into the creative process has focused on watered-down acts of inspiration. Instead of going out into the real world, brain scientists have used simple word puzzles and mundane idea-generation tasks. They've studied these minor feats of creation with tests that are simple to deploy and that can be assessed creativity somewhat objectively. They can be completed within the confines of state-of-the-art brain scanners.

Useful nuggets of wisdom have emerged from this work, but nagging doubts remain. Realistically how creative can one be in inventing alternative uses for a paperclip? Can solving an anagram really call on the same brain circuits as composing a symphony or dreaming up a brand identity? And what does word play actually have in common with designing a webpage or painting a picture?

Recently neuroscientists have developed working relationships with writers, designers, musicians, poets and other creative individuals (Beatty, 2015). They're peering into these fertile brains and catching unprecedented glimpses of genuinely creative thought unfolding in real time. Surprisingly consistent patterns, and some useful lessons, are emerging from this new wave of studies.

In 2012 US researchers teamed up with 12 professional rappers (Liu *et al*, 2012). They ushered them into the brain scanner and asked them to do what they do best: improvise to an 8-bar beat. Interestingly, '[looking] at the brains of these verbal wizards, the headline finding wasn't a specific turning on, it was a turning off' (Liu *et al*, 2012).

As the lyrics started to flow, the dorso-lateral prefrontal cortex quietened down. This busy region right at the front of the brain plays many roles but most relevant here is it's contribution to the so-called executive control network. This system drives focused attention, analytical thought and self-control.

As the self-restrained dorso-lateral cortex hushed, the medial prefrontal region fired up. This is a key hub of the default network, the brain system that drives daydreaming |w| and allows thoughts to bubble up freely from within.

Put your inner critic on ice

The rappers had taught themselves to silence their inner critic and give free rein to their stream of consciousness. In trying to cough out our best ideas, this is a brain state that with practice we can all aim to achieve (see how in the creative experiment below).

Even so, the brain's self-censor still plays a crucial role in most creative processes. In a follow-up to the rap study, the largely same team of researchers probed the brains of poets at work (Liu *et al*, 2015). During the early, freeform stages of poetic composition the poet's brains looked reassuringly like the freestyle rappers. They were then asked to review and edit their creations. Instead of the default network ON, executive control network OFF state of free improvisation, both of these central brain systems flared up in synchrony.

This makes sense. The poets were still generating new ideas, but now they were also bringing their *analytical minds* |Am| to bear. They were scrutinizing, error-checking and chiselling their stanzas to fit their creative goals. When neuroscientists imaged the brains of pianists constraining their improvisations to specific emotional cues the pattern was identical (Pinho *et al*, 2015).

These new brain-imaging studies are revealing remarkable similarities between the brains of rappers, poets, writers and artists. But they're also highlighting crucial differences.

In short, there is no such thing as a 'creative brain' or an all-purpose 'creative-brain state'. All of our brains are capable of radically creative thought. To get the best ideas out into the world, our brains flit between a wide range of different mental states.

CREATIVE EXPERIMENT

Are you familiar with your inner critic? I certainly am – the harsh voice that makes you doubt yourself, calls you names and questions your decisions, saying things like: 'Who do you think you are? That idea is rubbish. What do you know anyway? No one cares what you think'.

If only for a moment or so, this is the part of the brain that the rappers had temporarily silenced.

Author and artist Julia Cameron has an exercise called 'morning pages' which is a great way to think in an unrestricted way. Cameron encourages you to write three pages of completely unedited, stream-of-consciousness thoughts the moment you wake up. She writes (2016):

> [Morning pages] are not high art. They are not even 'writing'. They are about anything and everything that crosses your mind – and they are for your eyes only. Morning Pages provoke, clarify, comfort, cajole, prioritize and synchronize the day at hand. Do not over-think Morning Pages: just put three pages of anything on the page... and then do three more pages tomorrow.

Escape The City's Matt Trinetti, from whom we heard in Chapter 1 finds morning pages helpful.

> I tried many times to keep up with a journal but never succeeded past a day or two. Daily word limits don't work for me either. Morning pages work because there is no word limit – it's just three pages. Also, the output of morning pages doesn't matter at all. Some gold may come from my morning pages, but that's not the point. The point is just to write. To get the muck out of the front of your head and just put it onto the page.

Fundamentally many of the elements described here relate to laying the foundations for creativity. Our conscious struggles and periods of unconscious incubation generate ideas, options and connections. Often what we're really working towards is that priceless moment when the pieces of the puzzle fall into place and we see the whole picture at last.

This is the work of our next element, the insightful mind.

In The insightful mind

It is not easy to convey, unless one has experienced it, the dramatic feeling of sudden enlightenment that floods the mind when the right idea finally clicks into place... It now seems so obvious. Yet before, everything was in a fog.
Biologist Francis Crick, 1990

Marsha and Marjorie were born on the same day of the same month of the same year to the same mother and the same father yet they are not twins. How is that possible?

At first this question might not make much sense. Turn it over in your mind and see what emerges?

If the solution comes, it's usually a sudden and slightly unexpected arrival. Once you've got it, it seems obvious.

In this case the answer is not very creative, it's no epiphany (they are triplets). Even so, many neuroscientists trust that you can draw meaningful parallels between this kind of minor moment of insight and the more seismic jolts of revelation that have sculpted the history of science, art and technology. (Think Fleming's unexpected discovery of penicillin; Mahler unexpectedly 'hearing' the elusive theme for his Seventh Symphony in the splashing of oars in a lake; Descartes translating the movement of flies on his bedroom ceiling into a unified system of geometry.)

But unlike the more headline-grabbing breakthroughs, scientists can pin down the lesser insights required to solve word puzzles. Useful lessons are already emerging from their detailed lab studies of the insight-generating mind.

In a landmark investigation Mark Beeman and colleagues watched insights bubble up in the brain in real time (Jung-Beeman *et al*, 2004). They first recorded a wave of neural firing in the right visual cortex at the back of the brain. Next came a rapid flurry of action in the right temporal lobe, the bulge of brain above your right ear. The telltale action all took place long before the solution popped into awareness, confirming the crucial behind-the-scenes work of the *unconscious mind* Um.

The left-brain, right-brain myth

The other thing that stands out from Beeman's work is that most of the relevant brain activity takes place in the right hemisphere of the brain. This plays directly into the popular notion that creative thought is a unique property of the right brain. As Jarrett (2012) explains, this is a myth. It's one that is particularly erroneous and potentially damaging when used to typecast people as 'right-brained creative types' or 'unimaginative left-brainers' (Jarrett, 2012).

Figure 4.6 Insightful mind

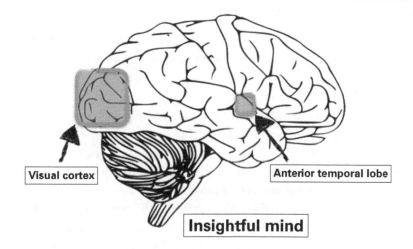

Still, Beeman's findings stand up. They add to decades of research showing that the two halves of your brain process information in distinct ways. To a broad approximation, the left-brain tends to deal in specifics and precise meanings. The right half, by contrast, is more inclined to paint with a broad brush. It's better at forging the less obvious links needed to solve insight problems – and to have 'eureka' or 'aha' moments in the real world.

> *You can't decide to use the right side of your brain any more than you can decide to breathe only with your right lung.*
> **Ben Martynoga, 2014**

So what can we learn from this research that will help us at work and at play?

In fact, the scientists have unearthed some useful tips that can help nudge mental activity into a more insightful mode. First up, there is no sense in waiting for inspiration until you've cemented the key question and your *analytical mind* Am has had a go at your creative problem.

Then pull back and try not to worry about your challenge: anxiety is the enemy of insight. Stay positive, relaxed and, if possible, happy En (Subramaniam *et al*, 2009) and see if you can invoke the powers of your relaxed or wandering mind (take a Creative Safari). Then, if you have a sense that the solution is near at hand, it might help to close your eyes, or stare at a bare wall. We often do this intuitively, but psychologists reinforce the idea that it is has a positive outcome (Salvi *et al*, 2015).

The mysterious art of summoning up insights out of the blue is just one element within the creative process. Not all projects rely on insights, but when they finally shimmer into plain sight, they can make all the difference.

Mindfulness for creativity

A key aim of this chapter is to describe the main brain processes that underpin creative thought. But often it's very hard to get a clear view of what's going on inside your own skull. An ancient practice, but one currently seen as 'on trend' might just help.

Don't panic if the word 'mindfulness' triggers images of sandal-wearing mystics 'finding themselves' in healing fields. You don't even have to sit cross-legged to be mindful. In fact, we all can and do spend some part of every day in a state of mindfulness. Mindfulness training programmes are all about beefing up this universal human ability.

To be mindful is to sit quietly like a stone in the stream of consciousness. It is acknowledging thoughts, emotions, mental patterns and incoming sensory information as they happen. Mindfulness is proving to be an effective system to help some people understand and manage their most intimate mental worlds. Such is its power, mainstream neuroscientists are getting interested in the mindful brain.

Brain scans show that consistent mindfulness practice can drive marked physical and functional alterations in the brain, in particular, in areas that contribute to emotional regulation, control of attention and self-awareness (Tang *et al*, 2015). These changes help people deal with stress and mental turmoil. They also appear to foster aspects of creativity.

A key mindfulness skill is observing and paying attention to mental events, without passing judgment. According to two recent studies, this boosts the capacity to generate new ideas (Baas *et al*, 2014, Colzato *et al*, 2012). Ostafin and Kassman (2012) used tricky word puzzles to prove that mindfulness expertise can also help with creative problem solving. For them, the key skill taught by mindfulness was the ability to fully inhabit the present. If you can master that, you can avoid falling back into yesterday's bad habits and stop worrying about what might go wrong tomorrow. Free of these blocks, your imagination can work more creatively, with less inhibition.

CREATIVE EXPERIMENT

Practise mindfulness for a week and see, if and how, it affects your creativity. Download one of the most popular free apps, a so-called 'gym membership for the mind', at www.headspace.com

---

If you still doubt the value of mindfulness, consider this quote from the film-maker David Lynch (2006). He's one of a growing number of high-profile creative types devoted to meditative practices:

> Ideas are like fish. If you want to catch little fish, you can stay in the shallow water. But if you want to catch the big fish, you've got to go deeper. Down deep, the fish are more powerful and more pure. They're huge and abstract. And they're very beautiful.

Tempted to dive in?

REVIEW THE CHAPTER

- Next time you have a creative problem, try to keep tabs on the mental processes you used in solving it. Does your workflow tap into any of the elements we've identified in this chapter? Do you have a natural preference for any particular mode of thinking over another?

- It may feel lazy to be 'incubating' a problem in your unconscious mind. It's not. Carve out time for it. It could make a world of difference.

- If you find yourself always drawn to a particular style of thinking, try to shake things up. If you're usually very focused and logical, try loosening your grip. If, on the other hand, your mind wanders too readily, see if it helps to force yourself to put in a bit more analytical graft first.

Table 4.1 The creative mind

Element	Key take-out for creativity
Unconscious mind (Um)	So easy to forget, but crucial: make time, lots of it, for unconscious incubation.
Relaxed mind (Re)	When the mind unwinds, tentative ideas and growing hunches bubble up to the surface.
Wandering mind (W)	Be distracted. Sometimes daydreams throw up sticks of creative dynamite.
Associating mind (As)	Frame questions in unexpected ways to connect the seemingly unconnectable.
Emotion (E)	Mood matters. Feeling good helps you to explore the outer reaches of what's possible.
Logic (L)	When the time comes to plan, evaluate and plot, be serious, challenge yourself and others. That way you focus like a laser and make the right calls.
Analytical mind (Am)	Play with your 'mental Lego' and build something new and dazzling, block-by-block.
Prolific mind (Pm)	Don't worry about having good ideas, just have *lots* of ideas. Some will fly.
Improvising mind (Ir)	Once you've put in the hours of practice, you can learn to put your inner critic on ice and get into the creative flow.
Insightful mind (In)	Do the legwork first, cement your problem, then back off and wait for the lightning strike of sudden inspiration.

IN A NUTSHELL

Creative minds are messy minds (Kaufman, 2014). The idea of a creative brain or even a single creative brain state is an illusion. Instead, to be creative is to explore every corner and crevice of your brain. It's to switch smoothly between completely different, often contradictory modes of thought. Creativity is knowing when to put in conscious, effortful mental work. Creativity is also changing tack, letting the mind perambulate and giving in to the powerful workings of the unconscious mind.

With practice it will become second nature to structure your day so that it incorporates a range of activities, environments, moods and constraints. Each will call on a different device from your mental toolbox. And if you see your mind falling back on the same reassuring habits, trapping you in non-creative ruts, fear not. Our brains are much more malleable than earlier generations of neuroscientists had us believe. This science of neuroplasticity has attracted more than its fair share of hype (Martynoga, 2014), but with time and determination it seems we can the re-route many of the neuronal highways and byways of our brains. In doing so we can master dramatically new thinking styles. We can learn to be comfortable with the messiness of creative minds.

DIG DEEPER

Scott Barry Kaufman's informative blog – http://blogs. scientificamerican.com/beautiful-minds/

On the unconscious brain – Eagleman, D (2011) *Incognito*, Canongate Books, London

System 1 and 2 thinking – Kahneman, D (2011) *Thinking, Fast and Slow*, Penguin Books, London

Building a creative culture

This chapter looks at these eight creative elements:

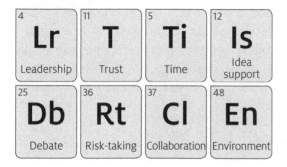

4 **Lr** Leadership	11 **T** Trust	5 **Ti** Time	12 **Is** Idea support
25 **Db** Debate	36 **Rt** Risk-taking	37 **Cl** Collaboration	48 **En** Environment

> *Lewis Thomas said: 'If you want a bee to make honey, you do not issue memoranda on solar navigation nor protocols on carbohydrate chemistry. You do what you can to arrange the environment around the hive. And when the air is right, the science will come.' Make sure the air and the soil are right. The creativity will come.*
> **Keith Reinhard, Chairman Emeritus DDB, 2015**

What do creative companies do differently from those that stagnate or, even worse, die? Explore how to create an environment where creativity can thrive.

We've explored what contributes to individual creativity in Chapters 3 and 4. Now we're going to address the question I'm most regularly asked: 'How do you build a creative culture? What's the "secret sauce"?'

If you're reading this with your team or company in mind, and want to understand more about how to deliberately, consistently and successfully nourish the best creative conditions in your hive for creativity, then you're in the right place. This chapter explores research around what makes one company creative while another flounders, and the eight elements that you can adopt to harness your organization's creative potential.

We're going to look at distributed leadership in the NHS, see how book-maker Paddy Power ripped up the corporate rulebook via its Mischief Department, and hear about creative leadership from the copywriter who climbed the ranks to CEO at one of the world's biggest ad agencies.

This chapter owes much to the work of the eminent Swedish researcher Göran Ekvall (1996) and his work on the factors that support and inhibit creative working. There are a number of creative coaching questions and experiments to enable you to evaluate where you are now and practical tips that you can incorporate into your working practices immediately.

This is the chapter that would have helped me most when I began in my role as creative director in a 100-strong global PR agency. How do you make the leap from being someone who has been considered personally 'creative' to someone who has to lead creativity and nurture it in others?

Initially I focused on up-skilling myself and familiarizing the whole agency with a range of creativity tools and techniques (see Chapter 8). These had a positive impact on the way ideas were generated, enabling us to produce better ideas more quickly. But I quickly realized that skills were only part of the equation.

I had so many issues to wrestle with, but I didn't know the answers or where to go to find them:

- How could I carve out the time to think that I, (and my teams), needed to really deliver against the problems we were facing?

- How could I allow people to take risks and make mistakes that might result in game-changing ideas for clients, but equally might end up in a lost pitch or a failed campaign?

- How could I harness diverse points of view and manage conflicts in a way that helped creative thought and allowed us to break out of our silos?

- Was sitting behind a desk from nine to five the right way to get inspiration?

I now know from my studies and work with organizations both large and small, that these are common challenges for those tasked with leading the creative charge in their business. The elements in this chapter offer insights and practical ways as how to make creativity part of your business DNA.

Ideas need time to emerge, and once they are out in the world, they need to be supported. Creators need a safe environment to allow for risk-taking, healthy debate and a way to manage conflict (which can be a great source of ideas).

Trust is one of the core elements needed to build a creative culture and building trust requires leadership, which is the first element in this chapter.

Lr Leadership

Creativity is a step, sometimes a leap, into the unknown. It requires strong and confident leadership. And leaders need followers.

Why would anyone want to follow you?

This is the question Keith Reinhard asks of all aspiring leaders. Keith is Chairman Emeritus of DDB Worldwide – one of the world's biggest advertising agencies – and a founding director of The Berlin School of Creative Leadership. He rose through the ranks from copywriter to CEO, leading one of the world's largest and most creative advertising agency networks for 16 years. He points out that you may have the title or you may be the boss but that doesn't make you a leader and adds:

'People will follow you if you excite them with a vision. Antoine De Saint-Exupery who wrote *The Little Prince* said: "If you want to build a ship, don't drum up the people to gather wood, divide the work and give orders. Instead, teach them to yearn for the vast and endless sea." In our case, the vision was clear: bring the insights of Bill Bernbach to life in the service of deserving clients around the world.

People will follow you if you represent values they can embrace and share. Our core values were those that Bill espoused – creativity and humanity – values that reflected Bernbach's criterion for hiring. 'To work at DDB,' he had said, 'you have to be both talented and nice. If you are nice but not talented, you may become our friend but you won't work here. If you are talented but not nice, you'll have to work elsewhere, because life is too short to spend with bastards.'

People will follow you if they see that you are not just about money, but also about meaning.

People will follow you if they believe that by doing so they can be part of a winning team, one where the leader sees achievement as a team effort in which every member will be given both responsibility and recognition.

People will follow you if they are made to feel important, and at the same time have the opportunity to achieve personal and professional growth and have fun doing it.

People will follow you if you inspire them. (Keith Reinhard, 2015)

So, why would anyone want to follow you?

Perhaps you are already confidently leading people for creativity and innovation, with your company values established to underpin the direction. If not, revisit Chapter 2 for to find out which values support creativity or read on and explore how other companies lead the creative charge.

CASE STUDY   Leaders everywhere – NHS Change Day

Without followers you are not a leader, but enabling others to lead is an even greater achievement. (Lynton, 2016)

'NHS Change Day' invited staff to make a public pledge to improve patient care. This grassroots movement follows the principle that there is not one leader – rather that hundreds, even thousands of people can be part of a creative charge in pursuit of a common purpose – known as distributed leadership.

As former head of transformation in the NHS, Jackie Lynton talked to me about mobilizing a grassroots movement for change within an organization like the NHS, which typically has a 'top-down' leadership style.

She told me: 'Fostering a creative culture is all about building relationships, giving permission and enabling rather than gate-keeping. People are creative when they have freedom to express. Hope overcomes fear, so if we hold hope, inspire hope and give hope back to people they can create change (and things) we never thought possible.'

You can be creative, get things done, be a driver of change but not actually bring your people with you. One of the greatest characteristics of a creative leader is one who can master building positive relationships while having great delivery and results. We have all seen or experienced the results of 'on-point delivery' but an aftermath of destroyed relationships and staff trampled in the process. So understanding the mindset of your people, how they understand change, what drives them and what their purpose is, is critical.

When you are not directly responsible for people or they do not report to you the concept of 'management' is nigh on impossible. You can't lead a social movement from the top of an organization but you can support it especially as the movement might want to go in the opposite direction to you. So letting go of control and letting come what wants to be born is a creative act.

I think ultimately creativity produces collaboration. If as a leader you can't work with other people, build positive relationships and foster a spirit of partnership, while respecting difference it's questionable if you are an effective leader. 'Leaders don't just get the job done; they enable others to achieve purpose,' Jackie says.

Engaging the heart and the head – leadership through storytelling

> *'Change Day is a joint effort full of real people working in the NHS telling their stories.'*

'Recognizing I had a story, and learning to share my story, profoundly changed my outlook on all my years of learning about leadership and my work,' says Jackie Lynton. I trained as a community organizer with Marshall Ganz (senior lecturer in public policy at the Kennedy School of Government) including the public narrative approach, which is that your public story, or narrative, contains three pieces: a story of self, a story of us, and a story of now. This combines why you were called to leadership, asking your community to join you and a call to action.

'This, and coaching others to develop their narrative was, central to the success of Change Day.

'Telling your own story also gives others the confidence and courage to tell their stories and it becomes about finding shared values in our stories and co-creation that is immensely powerful.' (Lynton, 2016)

CREATIVE COACH

- If you are a creative leader, why would anyone follow you?
- What vision are you creating and sharing with your people?
- What meaning or purpose are you creating for people to believe in?
- Do you have set goals for creativity or innovation?
- What funds and time have been allocated to drive creative capabilities?
- Based on what you've read so far, how can you improve the creative conditions in your hive?

T | Trust

Our next element – *Trust* – is essential for creative leadership.

The way to make people trustworthy is to trust them.
Ernest Hemingway, writer, 1953

Trust is key as it has the power to unlock the potential of many of the other elements particularly self-belief, collaboration, motivation, courage, freedom and openness.

A high degree of management trust is *the most* important factor for innovation, according to senior management at FTSE 100 companies, surveyed by PricewaterhouseCoopers (Milton and Brown). Innovators require the belief in their own abilities and the trust of their colleagues and paymasters to pursue their ideas. Often it is a self-fulfilling prophecy; the person with the idea must be able to show that there is a high possibility of converting a fledgling idea into a commercial reality, which becomes the basis for further trust. The innovators must also have permission to fail, and for there to be trust on both sides. Building acceptance for ideas also requires trust.

Based on his work with Volvo and other companies, trust is 1 of 10 key dimensions that Swedish researcher Göran Ekvall (1996) identified as central to inhibiting or supporting creative working. He writes, 'when there is a strong level of trust, everyone in the organization dares to put forward ideas and opinions... Where trust is missing, people are suspicious of each other and are wary of making expensive mistakes' (Ekvall, 1996).

Ekvall refers to the climate, or 'weather' in an organization. It is 'an attribute of the organization, a conglomerate of attitudes, feelings and behaviours which characterizes life in the organization, and exists independently of the perceptions and understandings of the members of the organization' (Ekvall, 1996).

Ekvall's work formed the basis of an audit – the Situational Outlook Questionnaire (SOQ) – as a way to evaluate how well an organization is doing in terms of the 10 dimensions – and to identify where changes could be made to improve innovation and creativity. It was applied in a range of businesses in different countries and disciplines, and the findings compared in 10 'innovative' and 5 'stagnated' organizations with between 100–200 employees. The companies were defined thus: 'The 10 innovative organizations have been successful in developing new, profitable products and thereby secure their survival in the market. The five stagnated organizations needed renewal of their product programmes but had not tried or tried in a lame or futile manner' (Ekvall, 1996).

> **KEY FINDINGS**
>
> In innovative companies trust/openness was higher than in the stagnated companies, as were other factors including challenge, freedom, idea support, dynamism, playfulness, debates, risk-taking and idea time.
>
> In the stagnated companies risk-taking in particular had a very low score and conflict was higher. The elements of freedom, debate and risk-taking are particularly important if big leaps forward rather than small changes are required (Ekvall, 1996).

Trust is also a key in successful collaborations

Felix Barrett is founder and Artistic Director at Punchdrunk, one of the world's leading immersive theatre companies. Brands are keen to partner with those shaping culture, and to harness the emotion and excitement that the Punchdrunk experience inspires.

Felix told me about a recent project. 'Trust is crucial. You have to take chances – we are at our most successful in brand partnerships when we are able to take creative risks and the edges don't get smoothed off. Take our work with Absolut UK – a digital research and development experiment launched to celebrate the Absolut Andy Warhol limited edition bottle. Absolut were thoroughly involved in each decision, but were also happy to step back and let us get on with it. They trusted us to develop an exciting and innovative way to reconnect their brand to London's taste makers, and I think we succeeded.

'The project revolved around a Match 3 game. As players matched the symbols, they received small snippets of narrative which they had to piece together bit by bit. As they progressed the story behind the game gradually began to infiltrate the real world, coming to life in spaces across London. People were engaging with the game for 6–10 hours at a time, which is pretty amazing for a brand experience. The collaboration feels like it's blazing a trail in terms of merging the digital and live arts.'

CREATIVE COACH

- Can you recall a personal experience where trust (or lack of it) has positively or negatively impacted your creativity or that of your company?

- Can you see any current examples of where lack of trust is negatively impacting creativity?

- Consider your most collaborative creative partners or teams, to what extent is there a correlation between the trust they have and the creativity they deliver?

- If there were one thing that would enable your business to increase trust, what would it be?

CREATIVE EXPERIMENT

> Without trust you cannot lead. Without trust you cannot get extraordinary things done.
> Kouzes and Posner, leadership experts (2003)

They suggest the following ways to develop trust. Be the first to:

- 'Disclose information about who you are and what you believe.'
- 'Admit mistakes.'
- 'Acknowledge the need for personal improvement.'
- 'Ask for feedback – positive and negative.'
- 'Listen attentively.'
- 'Share information.'
- 'Show that you're willing to change your mind.'
- 'Say, "We can trust them" and mean it.'

What impact do you think adopting any of these behaviours would have on the creative output in your business?

CASE STUDY   Award-winning agency Unity on what it takes to build a creative culture

Worth an estimated US$13.5 billion (Holmes Report, 2015), the global PR industry is fiercely competitive and companies rely heavily on ideas for sheer survival. In the US and UK there are many mature brands in an increasingly saturated space. Every year many start-ups emerge to compete with the established players on price, service and ideas. Independent firms must quickly prove their creative mettle in a brutal competitive environment or die. Named the most Creative PR Agency in the world in 2015 and 2016 in the Global Creative Index by industry bellwether *The Holmes Report*, Unity won over 52 industry awards in 2016 alone.

Figure 5.1 Launched 10 years ago by founders Nik Done and Gerry Hopkinson, Unity is a new kind of creative agency.

The world of work is changing as people seek more meaning from their jobs. Gerry talked to me about how this nimble East London based agency leads for creativity and creates an environment where ideas can flourish.

Gerry says: 'We exist to increase human happiness.' That purpose informs Unity's hiring policies, rewards and client work for brands including Nissan, Hyundai, Ben & Jerry's and Marks and Spencer.

Unity is not staffed like a typical PR agency. They are the only UK PR agency to have ethnographers, design-thinking experts, a social psychologist, human-centred new graduates, planners, digital experts and traditional PR people – media experts and publicists – all under one roof. They further collaborate with and employ art directors, filmmakers, journalists, researchers, data crunchers and craftspeople. The decision to create a diverse workforce was deliberate.

Gerry told me:

We went to design schools and scooped up the best graduates (who were from Goldsmiths) to form a design team. We just started with two guys and kind of incubated them and said 'yes there are practical skills you guys have, but really what we want is for you to come with your different attitude and your approach and we'll come with ours, and we'll see where we get to'.

The big thing that they brought to the table was a design-led, product-led approach. Before then we could riff on or what would be completely novel but we would only see it in a context of communication and PR. And what they got us to do was to think, 'you've got to start by observing'.

Blending the skills of the diverse team, Unity explored how to uncover actionable insights, and how to test their hypotheses. Demonstrating the principles of taking small steps to mitigate risk, and experimentation, Unity built themselves a lab (something common to tech-companies but still quite rare in marketing agencies) to test ideas.

Gerry explained that the idea of a lab is both physical and a metaphor for how ideas are born.

It's about physical environment, and it's also how you operate. Ideas don't just generally pop out. Good thinking, which is really a better way to talk about things, than ideas is a flow, it's a continually evolving flow, a progression and a combination of things and stuff has to be out there for a while. If you look at anybody's decent workshop, it's messy. I don't trust a workshop that isn't messy. And by that I mean, there are lots of half-baked ideas everywhere, there are lots of building blocks and starting things and projects that were dead ends and experiments and there's just a bunch of stuff around and there's a way for people to mess around.

Messing about and play inspired Unity's Pocket Playground for GSK brand Ribena Plus and focused on an issue to resonate with cash-strapped mums – low-cost play. The free box could be converted into a boat, rocket or puppet theatre and it's a great example of how Unity's purpose 'to increase human happiness' coupled with design thinking comes to life.

Figure 5.2 Ribena cardboard box, part of the Ribena Plus Play campaign showing the value of imagination and open play.

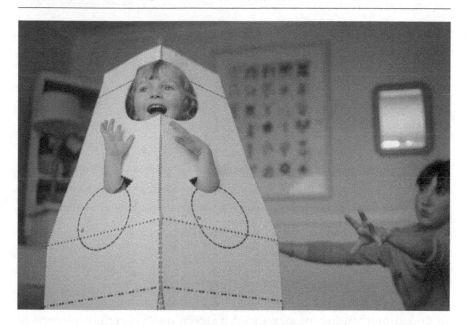

Gerry goes on to extend this 'making' principle to proposals. He told me:

> *Some people used to call them draft proposals. But it's a prototype and the reason why it's a prototype is, this is the 21st century. No one really knows exactly how brands should engage with people and if they tell you they do they are probably lying. In the really early days we'd say to clients, if you want to test stuff with us we'll do it at half rates and we'll learn together and do it out of the glare of the public eye. As we get confident then we'll have proof of concept, and then we can develop it.*

Many of Unity's core creative principles are informed by design thinking and we'll explore IDEO – one of leaders in this field – a bit later on.

Think like Unity

- Be human.
- Experiment and make a mess.
- Find your purpose and use it as a lens for every decision.

- Fight for your ideas.
- Everyone can screw up.
- Trust your instincts.
- Stay stupid.

Time

My ideas usually come not at my desk writing but in the midst of living.
Anaïs Nin, writer, 1971

In my day-to-day work with a diverse range of companies, lack of time to think is one of the most cited perceived barriers to creativity. 75 per cent of people say that they are under pressure to be productive rather than creative and only one in four people believe they are living up to their creative potential (Adobe, 2012).

The 'always on' culture means that there is little downtime to daydream, think and ponder on a problem. Many businesses have no formal structures in place to allow employees time to generate ideas.

Ekvall (1996) explains: 'In the high idea-time situation, possibilities exist to discuss and test impulses and fresh suggestions that are not planned or included in the task assignment… In the reverse case, every minute is booked and specified. The time pressure makes thinking outside the instructions and planned routines impossible.'

We explored the role of the *unconscious mind* Um in the previous chapter, and the research is clear that people need time in order to daydream, incubate and generate new ideas.

In my experience idea time is a concept that managers pay lip service to, but initiatives that have been put in place to support it are instantly put on the back burner when the pressures of day-to-day work creep in or billable hours take priority. But it's a downward spiral because the lack of time to think means that the ideas being generated are not good enough – to win competitive new business pitches, to find truly creative solutions to big problems or to keep existing customers happy.

Contemporary and friend of Ernest Hemingway, American writer Gertrude Stein found writing for long periods of time difficult but said 'if you write a half-hour a day, it makes a lot of writing year by year' (Currey, 2013). Writer Elizabeth Gilbert's (2014) advice on this topic? Buy an egg-timer and use it daily.

Google's '20 per cent time' is well-known – employees spend 20 per cent of their time working on any innovation project that inspires them with the aim that some of these ideas become big money-spinners for the company tomorrow. Products born out of this model famously include Gmail and Google Earth. Anecdotally there is debate about how 20 per cent time works in practice (it has been referred to as 120 per cent time by former employee Marisa Mayer (Business Insider, 2015) but the principle acknowledges that idea time must be baked-in.

CASE STUDY   Twitter's hack week

It's just taking the pause from the things that we think we need to do to get on with the job of thinking and imagining.
Bruce Daisley, 2016

Making idea time work in the real world requires a practical approach. Twitter's business relies on a constant stream of ideas and improvements and UK MD Bruce Daisley talked to me about some of the ways that Twitter makes time to innovate. Constraint is built into the DNA of Twitter and the company deliberately applies this concept to the creative process too.

From my observations and experience, almost without exception, companies that stay creative achieve it because they make time for ideas. What we do here is something called hack week.

We recognize that the day-to-day, urgent requirements in anyone's life always push out creativity – it's the thing that suffers.

So our hack week brings a constraint to it. It has to be on one of three topics but it's where anyone in the company can stop what they're doing and work on a labour of love, or they can work on a project they are interested in. We have two of those a year – the first week after Christmas when everyone is just getting going after the break and a week in the middle of the summer.

What you find is that people organize themselves very quickly into tribes because people realise 'if I do this on my own the impact that it's going to have is going to be far smaller than if I find people who've got an adjacent interest'. So you tend to find that the first day or the week before there is this horse-trading with people saying 'I've got this idea would anyone like to join forces with me? Anyone across the company can do it whether you work as an engineer or as an illustrator. The interesting thing is that some of the best hack week ideas come from teams like the accounts department. Most of the new stuff that Twitter launches comes from those hack sessions.

Twitter's Bruce Daisley – how to be more creative in 140 characters

- have purpose
- hold a hack week
- get stimulus
- be flexible

- don't get comfortable
- interpret the world fresh every day
- filter noise from signal

CREATIVE COACH

- Does your business have built-in processes and structures that give employees realistic amounts of idea time?
- What difference would more idea time mean for you personally and for your company?
- Is there something you've promised yourself you'd do for fun, enjoyment or inspiration but haven't got round to yet? How could you make it happen?
- Could you find just one hour a week to focus on creativity?

CREATIVE EXPERIMENT

- Review your weekly tasks – create a specific time in your next week to 'perfect your inventions' and explore a pet creative project. Think less about a specific outcome and invest some time in the exploration.
- For your next team meeting – allocate a portion (or all) of the agenda to exploring ideas together – use some of the exercises from Chapter 8.
- Buy an egg timer and set aside 30 minutes a day for creativity.
- Next time you're developing ideas think about how you could play around with your time and budgets using the 70:20:10 rule.

Is | Idea support

¹²

> Ideas are like little furry creatures coming out of the undergrowth... and you've got to be nice to the first one... be non-judgmental about it... and then suddenly that ridiculous idea that you're having, that's like your next ten years of really serious money-making work.
> **Grayson Perry, artist, 2013**

Once you've generated something new, the next challenge relates to how those ideas are treated out in the world – *idea support*. How ideas are handled in the early stages can make the difference between them being designated to the bin or seeing the light of day. For individuals, getting idea support is linked to many of the other elements – courage and self-belief in particular, and grit for when faced with hurdles.

> *They initially said no, it's a silly project to work on, it's too gimmicky, it's not a real computer science test, and we probably can't do it anyway.*
> **Paul Horn, IBM**

Watson is IBM's supercomputer, combining artificial intelligence (AI) and analytical software, developed over many years by teams as part of one of IBM's 'grand challenges' – man against machine competitions. Deep Blue, the first-ever machine to defeat a grand chess master in a match was a result of one of an earlier challenge. Paul Horn, then Director IBM Research was keen to try and create a machine that would pass the Turing test – to convince a person that they were conversing with another person instead of a machine. The idea was to create a machine that could win the US game show *Jeopardy* (which Watson did in 2011). But the team didn't get support at the start. Having proved Watson's abilities, the team focused on healthcare where Watson's capabilities are being applied to ground-breaking oncology projects (Best, 2016).

CASE STUDY   How global design firm Gensler nurtures ideas

Gensler is responsible for creating buildings all over the world including the world's second-tallest building, The Shanghai Tower. The company relies on ideas from its 5,000 staff in 43 offices globally. To stay at the top of its creative game, Gensler has many scalable processes that support ideas:

- Weekly and bi-weekly video calls with different members of the company to share ideas beyond their own regions.

- The leadership team feature the best ideas within the wider company quarterly.
- The annual Gensler Design Excellence internal awards encourage competition amongst the whole company with entries judged by an outside panel that includes clients, designers and journalists (Fast Company, 2015).

CREATIVE COACH

- How do you currently support ideas in your business – especially the silly, gimmicky and seemingly ridiculous?
- How could you give 'fledgling' ideas more room to breathe?
- What do you think stops people from supporting ideas in your business?
- How could you change that?

CREATIVE EXPERIMENT

- Encourage your team to suspend judgment for the idea generation part of the creative process. Make a game of it and create a penalty (like a swear box) for the use of 'yes, buts', 'we've already tried that', 'we don't have the budget', raised eyebrows, or sneers.
- Create a conscious approach to brainstorming ideas (see IDEO rules later in this chapter).
- Complete a creative session by asking 'what idea that came from someone else did you like most?'
- How could you reward the best ideas in your business?

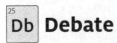 **Debate**

Every team needs a deviant, someone who can help the team by challenging the tendency to want too much homogeneity, which can stifle creativity and learning. Deviants are the ones who stand back and say, 'Well, wait a minute, why are we even doing this at all?'

J Richard Hackman, Professor of Social and Organizational Psychology at Harvard University, 2009

The debate element is concerned with deliberately questioning what exists and challenging the status quo. Actively encouraging deviancy of thought is to be encouraged at times when creativity is required. In 'Why teams don't work' team expert Hackman said '... the deviant opens up more ideas, and that gets you a lot more originality. In our research, we've looked carefully at both teams that produced something original and those that were merely average, where nothing really sparkled. It turned out that the teams with deviants outperformed teams without them' (Hackman, 2009).

Pixar's Ed Catmull (2014): 'This principle eludes most people, but it is critical: You are not your idea, and if you identify too closely with your ideas, you will take offence when challenged.'

There are many different personality diagnostic assessments for individuals that can help the management of conflict and debate.

The VIEW is a problem-solving assessment that focuses on style, asking '*how* am I creative?' rather than '*how much* creativity do I have?', which is an important distinction (Treffinger *et al*, 2007). When I took the VIEW it was a real 'scales falling from the eyes' moment, instantly clarifying why I had a more productive creative relationship with some people over others. Things to think about include whether you like the big picture or prefer detail, whether your preferred process is social or solitary and whether you're task- or people-focused. If you're a big-picture, process-challenging, task-focused extrovert (as I am) working with, say, a process-loving, people person you can see how you may have differing opinions about creative ideas!

In 'Putting Your Company's Whole Brain to Work' (1997) Harvard Business School's Dorothy Leonard and Susan Straus suggest using a psychometric assessment like the VIEW to identify different thinking styles and harness the company's 'whole brain' for creative advantage.

They warn of 'comfortable clone syndrome' – an enemy of creativity where '... managers who dislike conflict – or value only their own approach – actively avoid the clash of ideas. They hire and reward people of a particular stripe, usually people like themselves'. Leonard and Straus (1997) suggest trying to 'depersonalize conflict when it does arise. Acknowledge that other approaches are not wrongheaded, just different'. This is one insight that I really wish I'd understood better when I was leading creative teams as I think it would have changed our work for the better.

How an organization manages conflict is key to whether those disagreements can be productive, useful and open up opportunities and discussions to move the company forward or whether they become all out wars that undermine creativity.

When debate becomes conflict

Social activist Jackie Lynton, whom we met earlier in the chapter, on managing conflict:

> For me this manifested itself in managing cynics and sceptics and we had lots! Some people were obsessed with justifying every cynical question. I was less bothered; I do not see my role as trying to convince you as a cynic.
>
> I accept from a social activist lens that conflict and resistance is inevitable because we are looking to make profound social changes in the status quo. I never think it's OK just to say, 'well that's your opinion' because I think that can sound defensive. I see debate and conflict as part of the creative act, and it can dissipate energy or fuel energy for a cause, on the other hand you have the choice to ignore them too.

THINK LIKE IDEO

We happen to think idea generation is an art form. It's about setting a safe, creative space for people to feel like they can say anything, be wild, not be judged – so that new ideas can be born.
Open IDEO, 2015

Global design and innovation company IDEO work with everyone from Coca-Cola to GE to solve big problems. IDEO are masters of the creative process and have seven ground rules to get high creative performance in teams and to manage debate. They are:

- defer judgement
- encourage wild ideas
- build on the ideas of others
- stay focused on the topic
- one conversation at a time
- be visual
- go for quantity

(openideo.com 2015)

Remind people of the rules whenever you run a creative session – IDEO have them emblazoned all over their offices. It helps to be able to drive the relevant conversations and manage problems if things get off track.

CREATIVE COACH

- Who could you bring into your team or business to offer an alternative perspective?
- How could you make it easier for people to disagree and actively want to hear the lone deviant voice?
- As a creative leader – how open are you to modelling the way and actively seeking debate and dissent?

CREATIVE EXPERIMENT

- Evaluate your hiring policies and actively recruit to recognize the benefit of different thinking styles.
- Check out how to create the optimum environment for equality and diversity in the book the *Time to Think* by Nancy Kline (2002) – an approach that allows for everyone to have their (differing) views in a safe environment.
- Introduce the IDEO rules, or create your own to improve collaboration and manage debate.

 Rt Risk-taking

Management's job is not to prevent risk but to build the capability to recover when failures occur.
Ed Catmull, President Pixar and Disney Studios, 2008

When talking about business creativity, the maxim of taking risks versus playing it safe is a cliché. It relates to 'the tolerance of uncertainty in the organization' (Ekvall 1996). As we've identified, a key factor to being creative both for businesses and individuals is the desire, ability and the support to take risks, particularly where big breakthroughs are required. But risk can be a toxic word, particularly in relation to not-for-profit organizations and governments. Even for fast-moving consumer brands, there is an inherent tension. If coming up with breakthrough ideas involves taking risks how can that be operationalized in a business without wasting money, upsetting shareholders and damaging the core brand?

Innovators need to be able to perform a complex balancing act, juxtaposing freedom with structure and risk with safety.

The 70:20:10 rule (with its origins as a teaching model) is a way to experiment and mitigate the risks involved in trialling new ideas and ways of working. Think of the 70 per cent as the business bread and butter – not to be messed with, working well, delivering returns and low risk. The 20 per cent is middle risk and the 10 per cent is high-risk, possible high return in the future, but with the risk of failure too. Both Coca-Cola and Google have used this model to test out new areas and experimentation.

With its origins in Silicon Valley and tech start-ups, Eric Ries' *The Lean Startup* (2012) is all about learning fast from mistakes, without betting the farm. It challenges conventional business models and approaches to creativity with its ethos of launching concepts fast, promptly responding to feedback, and rapidly changing course when needed, using a 'build, measure, learn, loop'.

Adobe's innovation in a box

Kickbox is Adobe's open-source innovation process, honed over 30 years and developed for individuals and teams. The red innovator Kickbox starter kit includes everything a person or team needs to start an innovation project without the need for lengthy approvals, internal red tape and process. They just get on and do it. It contains:

- money – a pre-paid credit card for US $1,000 to be spent pursuing the idea;
- instructions and a process checklist;
- innovation tools;
- coffee and chocolate to fuel the ideas!

The company takes a balanced risk by allowing employees to spend time and a (limited) amount of money on projects of interest, with the potential for big gains. Empowering teams and encouraging ideas from everyone, over 1,000 boxes have been distributed to Adobe employees worldwide. The kit is available to download free at https://kickbox.adobe.com

---

How to structure your business to manage risk

Do you need completely separate teams of people for creative research and implementation? In *The Other Side of Innovation, Solving the Execution Challenge*', Govindarajan and Trimble (2010) suggest that ongoing business as usual is run by what they call 'performance engines'.

The authors discuss the importance of learning from experiments. 'Companies launch innovation initiatives when predicted outcomes justify the investment. But these predictions are based on assumptions. They are guesses in some cases, and frequently they are wild guesses. As you learn, you convert assumptions into knowledge. Wild guesses become informed estimates, and informed estimates become reliable forecasts' (Govindarajan and Trimble, 2010).

They argue that to be successful the dedicated innovation centre must be strongly connected to the 'performance engine' as a partnership, although there are inherent tensions between the two inextricably linked components. They explore six models for innovation in practice:

1 Innovation = ideas

2 Innovation = ideas + execution

3 Innovation = ideas + motivation

4 Innovation = ideas + process

5 Innovation = ideas + leaders

6 Innovation = ideas + leaders + team + plan

(Govindarajan and Trimble, 2010)

What models are you currently adopting?

CASE STUDY

A creative company is a co-operative and you have to show leadership.
Harry Dromey, former Mischief Maker, Paddy Power, 2015

Harry Dromey was bookmaker Paddy Power's Mischief Maker and under his tenure, in order to drive bets, the brand hijacked sporting events creating headlines across the world's media. Stunts and pranks spared no one and involved Stephen Hawking, the Vatican, illegal immigrants and the Amazon rainforest. Despite being a listed company the brand admits to a 'tongue-in-cheek attitude' to marketing. Harry is now Group Marketing Manager at Channel 4. I spoke to him about provoking controversy, tearing up the rulebook and taking risks. He says: 'The riskiest thing is to be boring. You need an element of risk to make great creative work. You also need to foster a culture, the right atmosphere and the attitude. Things get lost to consumers if messaging is bland.'

'The Mischief Department was originally set up by Ken Robertson, [now Director of Brand Engagement at Paddy Power] 15 years ago with the aim of getting the media and people talking. In the early days it was scrappy, guerrilla, with minimum investment, maximum noise. The idea of making mischief grew organically and it worked. There was sponsorship at the top from the founders, it wasn't a case of doing it without the suits knowing, having a little guerrilla organization within the firm, no, the people at the top get it and love it. I fear for anyone who wants to 'Paddy Powerify' their brand and push barriers without buy-in from the top team.'

Harry has strong views, too, on the next element – collaboration. 'A creative company is a co-operative and you have to show leadership. Don't go around saying "it's my idea" – the idea came from a culture with others and the right circumstances. You can't make it "all about me" otherwise people think "if I'm not part of this, I'm not going to bust a gut." Once you have a great idea I'm a great fan of sharing it. Bring in other experts and put wings on it and take a solid idea to a great one. Ask how can you make it bigger and better? Bring others in for constructive criticism and build. But it can't be done by committee, ultimately someone has to be the creative lead and retain the right to give an idea the thumbs up or down'. (Dromey, 2015)

Figure 5.3 Nigel Farage unveiled as Paddy Power's Ambassador for Europe at the 2014 Ryder Cup

Damon Statt is Creative Director at Mischief PR, who enjoyed a working relationship with Dromey during his tenure at the company, and who now works with the current in-house Paddy Power team. Mischief created the 'Farage Swings for Europe' campaign ahead of the 2014 Ryder Cup. He told me: 'Brave ideas are par for the course with Paddy Power but the difference between a good idea and a game-changing one is earning attention for the right reasons. In this case, we used an insight about what the Ryder Cup means to people whether they're golf fans or not and used it to create an idea and supporting content strategy that not only grabbed headlines and dominated conversation but drove the best-ever Ryder Cup revenue.' (Statt, 2016)

CREATIVE COACH

- How do you or your company approach taking risks to move the company forward?

- How could you apply the 70:20:10 rule to a current project you're working on? What difference might that approach make to your confidence in selling a new idea or experimenting?

- When you have projects that don't quite deliver, how could you review the mistakes and identify what could you learn from them?

CREATIVE EXPERIMENT

- Make a list of your past projects where you took risks. Reflect on them: Were they successes or failures?

- What did you learn? Was what you learned worth the experience?

- Take a small bet. Do something new or different with low stakes and notice what happens, what impact it has and how you feel about it.

Cl Collaboration

*Collaboration is fundamental to the needs of a creative business.
There is not one person that can outthink the whole. As a creative
leader, I'm not interested in single, shiny stars, I want a whole
constellation of people really working on a business opportunity.
Our breakthrough ideas and moments are found when we build
on each other's thinking and work deeply together.*
Wendy Clark, Chief Executive Officer, DDB North America, 2016

Collaboration can mean anything from a pair to a group brainstorm, and
now technology can mean harnessing the ideas of thousands.

Buddy Up

Ad agency creative teams typically work in pairs incorporating the skills of
a copywriter and an art director, and they're often paired for their whole
careers, even moving jobs together.

Joshua Wolf Shenk, author of *The Powers of Two: Finding the essence
of innovation in creative pairs* (2015) writes that 'two people can basically
make their own society on the go. Pairs naturally arouse engagement, even
intensity. In a larger group an individual may lie low, phone it in. But no one
can hide in a pair.' Shenk challenges the idea of a lone genius and explores
the idea of the dyad in depth as the key to creative brilliance looking at the
chemistry of legendary pairings such as Lennon and McCartney. His research
shows that working in pairs can use triggers such as conflict, turn-taking,
opposites and sparring.

Setting up a creative buddy system for yourself or for your teams is one
way to energize the dynamics of your creative process.

Group creativity

Alex Osborn was the 'O' in legendary New York advertising agency BBDO,
reputedly the inspiration for the TV series *Mad Men*. Sometimes called the
grandfather of brainstorming, he wrote some of the first highly influential
books about the creative process.

Osborn was way ahead of his time in the 1950s, but in my experience the
group brainstorm is still the default setting for idea generation. We discuss
this in more detail in Chapter 7, The creative process.

Collaboration is a core principle at Pixar.

CASE STUDY   Pixar: fostering a culture of creativity to infinity and beyond!

The mighty Pixar demonstrates every one of the elements in this chapter – in fact the whole book could be brought to life by examples from the animation company. No doubt you will be familiar with some of its practices. How do Pixar create an environment where ideas and creativity are a constant and what can we mere mortals learn? The leadership constantly seeks, encourages and provokes change. As Ed Catmull, President of Pixar and Disney Animation states: 'Things never stay the same, they are supposed to change. We are not trying to freeze anything in time' (Catmull, 2008).

Collaboration is central to Pixar and the linchpin of their philosophy is to foster a culture of trust and openness to encourage debate with many peer-review processes along the way, such as:

1 *'Giving notes'* – every person involved in a production from top to bottom is encouraged to give feedback. The senior team including Catmull and John Lasseter, Pixar's Chief Creative Offer, give notes but do not override the Director who makes the final decision.

2 *The Braintrust* – an oft-referenced (and highly respected) Pixar concept. When a producer runs into difficulties they can request assistance and a small group of the most trusted and respected brains is convened – not necessarily the most senior. They spend two hours candidly debating and discussing the work in progress.

3 *'Dailies'* – Pixar works hard to avoid silos, isolated individuals and self-censorship with its 'dailies' – the idea that work is opened up every day to scrutiny regardless of what stage it is at or even how the producer feels about it. In this way there are more opportunities for improvement.

4 *Freedom* to communicate with anyone is a highly organized part of the communications structure. When Pixar talks of an open-door policy they literally mean that all doors are open (Catmull, 2008).

At Pixar, all types of creative approaches are considered equal. Employees are encouraged to work and learn together. Pixar has its own university whose motto is *Alienus non diutius*, Latin for 'alone no longer'. 'It's the heart of our model, giving people opportunities to fail together and to recover from mistakes together,' says Dean Randy Nelson. Everyone from accountants to chefs learn how to draw as well as having the opportunity to enrol on hundreds of other courses. They share their work at each stage in the same way as the 'dailies' in order to continue the open culture of feedback and improvement.

Pixar has embedded these deliberate processes throughout the organization to creatively empower every employee via high levels of trust, collaboration, diversity and autonomy.

Think like Pixar

- Set up your own version of the Braintrust.
- Accept failure is a key part of the creative process.
- Have an emotional core at the heart of your ideas.
- Find ways to play and learn together.
- Be ambidextrous – balance risk-taking (original movies) with safe bets (sequels).

CREATIVE COACH

- Think about a current project that would benefit from a collaboration:
  - With whom could you collaborate?
  - What communities could you collaborate with?
  - Is there a way to work with your customers?
- What's the unlikeliest collaboration you can think of?
- Do you have a sparring partner, someone to kick ideas around with?
- Could you apply any of Shenk's triggers like turn-taking and sparring to improve your ideas?

48 En Environment

An effective way to encourage collaboration involves the final element in this chapter, environment.

According to Google HQ architect Clive Wilkinson, one of the most common client requests is: 'How do we encourage creativity?' (2014).

I've worked in some truly terrible office environments – a particular low was running a creative workshop in a poky room in a government building with peeling, grey paint and an unpleasant odour.

But do grey rooms produce grey ideas?

The biggest single question of the past decade or so in relation to this topic seems to be: how do we encourage serendipitous encounters between different members of staff?

Chance encounters with other employees has been regarded as a key element of the creative workspace since Steve Jobs engineered the placement of the bathrooms at Pixar, ensuring that people would bump into each other frequently.

Most organizations now accept the idea that chance encounters and the collaboration they encourage is vital if you want creativity to flourish. When online clothing retailer Zappos kitted out their Las Vegas headquarters, they closed down a sky bridge between the office and its car park so that people would have to walk through the city to enter via the front door (*Business Insider*, 2013). Not only would this force them to observe and interact with the outside world, it would also increase the likelihood of random encounters with other employees on the way in. Author Adam Alter visited Google's New York City campus and discovered that no part of the office was more than 150 feet from food explaining how this encourages employees to 'snack constantly' and bump into co-workers from different teams across the company.

While the office environment is often a high priority for companies wanting to boost their creativity (and makes it *look* as though it's being paid attention to) no amount of gimmicks will make up for a lack of leadership or trust.

Five tips to boost office creativity

1 Follow the lead of Pixar, Google and Apple (whose new HQ in Cupertino is a never-ending loop where people will stumble across new people every single day) and figure out how to encourage interactions between members of the team who don't currently meet. And put effort into working out which teams should meet (and where) for maximum effect.

2 During the ideation phase, aim to create a space where people can interact with each other and ideas. Your stimuli and ideas need to be there in front of the team, not on a locked file on the MD's laptop or packed away in a cupboard.

3 Always allow quiet time and space for reflective thinking and for introverts who might be intimidated by 'forced' interactions. A way to do this is to create designated work zones. At broadcaster Sky's West London campus the vibe is more akin to a relaxed private members club than an office, with cafés, a restaurant, high-backed chairs offering privacy and circular meeting booths offering spaces to think, meet and work. For the Googleplex Campus project the building was zoned into 'hot' areas – public and active zones, while 'cold' zones are more private.

4 Add black (or white) boards. Big ones. I introduced this to great effect during an office redesign, and found it was a great silo-busting way to share problems and showed that ideas can come from anywhere. It went from being 'my' problem to a shared issue and good ideas came from everywhere including the HR department as well as the account teams. It's very levelling. And comparatively cheap.

When Racepoint Global moved in April 2015, they made sure that there was creative space in various areas of the new office. The meeting rooms and MD's office have dry-wipe walls to make brainstorming in meetings quick and easy. There are also two big walls painted in chalkboard paint which are used for both more permanent displays as well as specific brainstorming activities. As a PR agency, they regularly run creative sessions to develop innovative ideas for their clients and the ability to quickly capture those thoughts wherever they are in the office is a priority. Art Director Haruka designed one of their chalkboard walls to reflect two key components of the Racepoint world. The first component is somewhere to track the weekly 'Brucie Bonus' awards (where staff nominate others for recognition for a job extremely well done; a monthly winner receives a £50 reward). The second comprises an annual networking calendar – a visual representation of what events are coming up throughout the year, as well as a way to reflect on what events have happened so far (Middleton, 2016).

5 If you're still using individual offices, think about how you can encourage more collaboration. Mother London is one of the world's most respected creative agencies, with a client roster of household names. Their head of strategy Chris Gallery told me:

> Our office space is a living breathing example of our entire working ethos. It encourages collaboration, sharing and transparency in all of our working lives. Most creative companies talk about these kinds of principles, but our office space ensures this isn't just talk, at Mother it's how we do things... no hiding, no baton passing, no egos, everyone in it together trying to help make the best ideas live.

Figure 5.4 Blackboards offer a simple and effective way to share information at Racepoint Global

Figure 5.5 Designed by Clive Wilkinson architects, Mother London has a vast (250 feet) concrete table that snakes through the space like a racetrack

REVIEW THE CHAPTER

Look and reflect on the eight Creative Elements in this chapter and rank your business out of 10 for each of them. Try to be honest and objective about how the company actually is, rather than how you want it to be.

For example, are there really high levels of trust or does this need work? Do people feel free to debate, dissent and discuss their ideas? Is there really an open-door policy?

Once you've scored the different areas, rank them in order of the highest to lowest so you can see your strengths and areas for development.

- What one thing could you do *today* that would have the biggest impact on your team and business?
- Can you identify your biggest barrier to creativity at play in your team or company right now based on the elements in this chapter?
- What would your creative formula for success be made up of if you had to choose three elements to focus on from this chapter?

Table 5.1 creative culture

Element	Key questions	What's your organization's biggest strength on a scale of 1–10 in relation to the elements here?	What's your biggest area for development?
Leadership (Lp)	To what extent are leaders aligned and modelling the way on creativity?		
Trust (T)	How high is the level of trust in your business?		
Time (Ti)	To what extent is time allocated for ideas?		
Idea Support (Is)	How supportive are people of each other's ideas?		
Debate (De)	How much to you encourage debate and dissent with your own point of view?		
Risk-taking (Rt)	To what extent do you encourage risk-taking and learning from mistakes?		
Collaboration (Cb)	How prepared are you to collaborate?		
Environment (En)	Is your office space conducive to creativity? What could you change to improve things?		

IN A NUTSHELL

There are many ways to stack the creative chips in your favour, 'un-level' the playing field and establish the ideal conditions to create truly original work.

We've seen examples of the eight elements at play in companies that deliberately and consistently create the optimum climate for creativity. If you were to focus on just one element in this chapter then it must be addressing how leadership can work to harness your organization's creative potential.

DIG DEEPER

On climate – Ekvall, G (1996) Organizational climate for creativity and innovation, *European Journal of Work and Organizational Psychology*, 5 (1), 105–123

Catmull, Ed (2014) *Creativity Inc: Overcoming the unseen forces that stand in the way of true inspiration*, Bantam Press, London

Purpose 06

This chapter looks at these five creative elements:

Humans, by their nature, seek purpose – a cause greater and more enduring than themselves.
Dan Pink, author and motivation expert, 2011

What's your purpose?

For individuals this can be a big and scary question and, for many, hard to pin down, particularly when you work for a big corporation. Why do we do what we do? And what does that mean for creativity? For companies the question is increasingly relevant – one you must answer if you want to hire or target millennials who care as much about this as getting a salary.

Purpose is about meaning, and what drives us to get out of bed in the morning. Creativity and motivation experts Amabile and Kramer write that 'people need to know what problem they're trying to solve, and why it matters; they can't be intrinsically motivated unless their work has meaning. That requires clear strategic direction toward a worthy purpose – whether it's curing a disease or providing a new form of entertainment that will enhance consumers' lives' (Amabile and Kramer, 2012).

We read earlier how creative agency Unity's purpose is 'to increase human happiness'. It's a mission that informs their hiring policies, rewards and client work for household-name brands. Keith Reinhard, Chairman Emeritus of advertising agency DDB Worldwide told us back in Chapter 5 that purpose is a key part of leadership. He said: 'People will follow you if they see that you are not just about money, but also about meaning.'

> *To have a sense of purpose about where you are going is really*
> *important to get you through bumps in the creative process.*
> **Bruce Daisley**

Twitter UK MD Bruce Daisley has first-hand experience of this connection between purpose and creativity. He told me:

> We've had cases where you have to rip up months of work. People have built something, dedicated themselves to it for six months and they're convinced about it, they really buy into the dream and you think it's going to happen. Then maybe at the end of six months someone says either we tested it and users hated it, or we've changed our mind and that version of the future we were painting, we don't believe in it any more.
>
> Whether you're a recording artist and you destroy an album, or whether you're an author and you start again, that can be incredibly demoralizing. The sense of purpose is important to remind you that 'OK we knew there were going to be difficult times but here's why we're doing this is'. Purpose is what you draw upon to remind you that you're doing things for the right reasons because otherwise most people can't sustain defeats like that'.

We live in changing times

For this chapter I've teamed up with business journalist Kate Magee, who has spent the past decade covering brands, creativity and marketing for titles including *Campaign* and *Marketing*. In particular, she has observed the growing trend for creativity for social good.

People want more meaning from their work and consumers have higher expectations of transparency and social responsibility from the corporate world. In response, marketing for brands in many cases has moved from 'building brands to taking stands' (TED 2013).

Brands as well as non-profits can make a real contribution to improving and even saving lives, while working to enhance their own reputations and delivering profit. '#Like A Girl', a campaign for P&G feminine hygiene brand Always, sparked global conversations about the unconscious prejudices inflicted on girls. It led to a 50 per cent lift in intent to purchase *and* a UN award for supporting female empowerment. When I first started in PR 20 years ago work like this would have been part of a corporate social responsibility campaign. Now it *is* consumer brand marketing.

Our first two elements are love and joy.

L J **Love and joy**

You've got to find what you love... Your work is going to fill a large part of your life, and the only way to be truly satisfied is to do what you believe is great work. And the only way to do great work is to love what you do. If you haven't found it yet, keep looking. Don't settle.
Apple founder Steve Jobs, 2005

The premise of this book is that we are all creative. Some of us are lucky enough to have to choose careers that allow and demand of us, to apply that creativity at work. We love experimenting, making, puzzling, even obsessing over finding the answer, expressing ourselves and filling the blank page. Sometimes (back in the good old days when print ruled the world) I'd set my alarm for 4 am to pick up the first edition of a newspaper if I knew I had a story for a client running. The *joy* J of seeing my carefully crafted press release appearing in the editorial made all the hard graft that often went with the job worth it.

Of course the thrills we get from our creative efforts vary wildly. Creative director Kelly Finnegan says he gets his kicks from 'loving design, and creating design, that makes me want to lick the page.' John Wardley, the designer behind Nemesis at Alton Towers said simply: 'I love what I do and get great pleasure out of it.'

Many artists, writers and creatives feel compelled to create and do it because they must. *Metamorphosis* author Franz Kafka had to relegate his writing to the evening as he worked in insurance by day. Singer-songwriter Adele said of the four-year hiatus between making her best-selling albums, 'it was that thing of, do I or don't I want to go back to my music? Obviously I do... I can't do anything else' (Percival, 2015).

E Paul Torrance (1998) has spent decades researching creativity and he concludes that '... the essence of the creative person is being in love with what one is doing, I have had a growing awareness that this characteristic makes possible all other personality characteristics of the creative person: courage, independence of thought and judgment, honesty, perseverance, curiosity, willingness to take risks and the like.' It's a finding echoed by Harvard Business School Professor Theresa Amabile (1986) who says that 'it's the "labor of love" aspect that determines creativity.'

Even one of history's most respected scientists recognized the importance of love. Evolutionary systems scientist David Loye discovered that Darwin mentioned love 95 times in *The Descent of Man* but only twice mentioned 'survival of the fittest' – his famous phrase on evolutionary theory.

I think it's a lot easier for entrepreneurs to talk about doing what they love because they have deliberately created their own business and way of working, aligned with their personal values rather than working for 'the man'. I've worked for just one company in my 20-year career where I think that any common sense of purpose *beyond* making money would emerge. Until my early thirties making money was my main purpose, but I became increasingly unhappy and unfulfilled with that existence, which ultimately led to me jumping off the corporate hamster wheel. I'm far from alone as the Escape the City team have discovered.

> We have tapped into a groundswell of disillusionment: people want more from life than a meaningless pay cheque and 40, 50 60? – years of drudgery, subordination and purposelessness. Time is running out for today's status quo. (Dom Jackman, 2015)

In their 2015 'Diagnosing job satisfaction' report they found three major trends marking a fundamental shift in the way people want to work today:

- Advances in technology have revolutionized the concept of work in the 21st century (you can work from a Bali beach).
- Employee trust was at an all-time low for big institutions in the aftermath of the recession.
- People entering the workforce now have differing aspirations for their working lives than their parents.

Escape the City aim to help people find meaning and say that 'millions of individuals doing work they love will change the world.' ('Escape the City', 2015). See the interview with The Escape School's Matt Trinetti in Chapter 2.

CREATIVE COACH

- What do you love? What brings you joy? (reflect on and allow yourself to answer intuitively – could be anything from coding, to shoes, to coffee to your nana). How could you bring that love more into your creative process?
- When have you done really brilliant work where you just forgot about time?
- What conditions were present?
- What do you always find time for, no matter how little time you have? How could this play more of a part in your creative process?

²⁷ Mn Money

Money is of course often a key driver for creativity, for both individuals and businesses. Using creativity to advance a commercial purpose, or 'applied creativity' is what the marketing industry specialises in, and was the focus for most of my 20 years spent working in consumer PR.

A strong brand or communications campaign can create more emotional engagement with customers, make a product more memorable and shareable, increase someone's propensity to buy, and ultimately drive sales. You might not be able to outspend your rivals, but you can outsmart them, with a more creative sales and marketing approach.

The business case for creativity

In *The Case for Creativity* James Hurman (2011) explains why more creative campaigns lead to higher sales. More creative ads attract more attention from consumers, are more memorable and are more likely to generate conversations.

In 2011, the Institute of Practitioners in Advertising (IPA) found that between 2003 and 2010, creatively-awarded campaigns were 12 times more effective at increasing a brand's market share than those that did not win creative awards.

This is because more creative campaigns tend to elicit a more emotional connection with people, and generate more buzz and talkability amongst opinion formers, consumers and media. This has become increasingly important in a more fractured media landscape where it's ever more difficult to reach a mass audience, but fame can help you achieve this.

> The goal is not just to sell to people who need what you have; the goal is to sell to people who believe what you believe... if you hire people just because they can do a job, they'll work for your money, but if they believe what you believe, they'll work for you with blood and sweat and tears. (Simon Sinek, Leadership expert, 2009)

In his book and TED talk, Simon Sinek's *Start With Why* uses examples from Apple to Martin Luther King to argue that 'people don't buy what you do, they buy why you do it' (Sinek, Tedx, 2009). He argues that money is a *result*, it is not a *reason why*.

He has a three-question process he calls the golden circle: beginning with why, then how, then what. He argues that many companies can clearly articulate the what and the how of what they do, but not the why.

CREATIVE COACH

- To what extent do you think money motivates you to be creative?
- How could you measure your creative output and put a number against it?
- What could be a personal motivating purpose for you in your job – irrespective of the organization's purpose?

If thinking differently can be challenging in the commercial sector where profits and competitive advantage are the prize, imagine trying to mobilize a grassroots movement for change within an institution like England's National Health Service – the fifth biggest employer in the world. That's exactly what a group of change makers including Jackie Lynton did.

CASE STUDY   From Zero to 189,000 Pledges – a personal tale of purpose in the NHS from social change activist Jackie Lynton

To reveal who you really are you have to show the 'working out' like a maths exam; you don't just give the answer. It's in the working out you find the answers.

Jackie Lynton

New radical' creative leader Jackie was one of the key people behind the development of 'NHS Change Day', a grassroots movement with staff invited to make a public pledge to improve patient care. Described as a game changer that has since spread to 10 provinces globally, NHS Change Day challenged the status quo.

Jackie told me how purpose is central to her story and her success.

Jackie started out as a mental health nurse in the NHS following a strong sense of purpose to help others and her hopes to change the world. She credits Blanche – her first ever patient – as her inspiration for understanding the power of relationships and says that Blanche taught her to listen.

Figure 6.1 Jackie Lynton

However, her career was not plain sailing. Showing an early streak of rebel thinking Jackie had to choose whether to challenge the status quo when she was faced with a difficult situation. She became a whistleblower when she refused to cover for a colleague. But the experience left her feeling powerless and let down by her profession.

'I learned inner strength, to fight for change and to speak out from my early experiences as a child. My family migrated to the UK in the early 1950s and endured oppression. But like many people who lose their way I began to "check out" and question what I was doing, which seriously impacted my productivity. Along my journey I had to dig deep and ask searching questions, the main one for me: "How can I address my yearning for greater creativity and autonomy?".'

Jackie used the feeling of being powerless in a creative way and her experiences drove her to positions where she could influence change in the system.

Thirty years later Jackie was engaged to tackle some of the serious issues in the NHS in the aftermath of the failings at the Mid Staffordshire Hospital and she observed many of the same failings in the system that she had experienced, with 'lack of permission' a key issue.

Jackie told me the point she realized her purpose was no longer clear:

During the last interview (that was about the 10th) for a director position, in response to what should have been a dream question, I completely froze. I could not utter anything sensible. I felt like I was in a white tunnel and that everyone had left the room except for me and the person who had asked the question. That was the moment I realized I had actually lost my purpose.

I had got lost in the sea of corporate noise, distracted by the sounds of organizational position and power. Following the interview I travelled to Scotland for a short break, I cried for five days, not only feeling the pain of the interview but the deep sense of loss of myself and that I had been sabotaging myself, not doing what I want to do, what I love.

Following a period of deep reflection and recognizing my own vulnerability, I took a role I was really passionate about that was way below my current level (it wasn't about money), but that I believed in it and it met with my values.

I learnt when you work with purpose you achieve more because you are doing what's natural to you, and stop unconsciously sabotaging yourself. When you align your own purpose with others or an organization's purpose that's when it can be even more cogent. Organizations start with their purpose and then invite you to align your purpose with them. Change Day on the other hand aligned people's individual purpose with the organizational purpose, which is subtly different but intensely more creative and engaging.

When I started my journey to finding my purpose again, I recognized the significance that I was seeking wasn't about a badge or label but meaningful work, so I could do my best work. I'm a creative and spiritual person and when I'm not exercising that creativity I'm dead inside.

Jackie's inspiring story shows how purpose connects with creativity directly. It can provide the courage to take risks, to dig deep and find grit, and to have the self-belief to do something radical that has never been done before.

Jackie's tips on how to find your purpose

For individuals:

- 'Start with finding your own story of who you are and know your values. When you live your values it builds resilience by reminding you *why* you do what you do.'

- Find your superpower! 'What is important to me is the 'power of connection' – connecting people to people. The real problem was that, it is not a key quality found in any job description or title; Chief Connector! This is what I call my superpower.'

- What's yours? What are you (un)consciously great at? Ask your three biggest supporters to tell you what they think your greatest strength is.

- Show grit. 'I realised I had a choice – to stay where I was or lean into my own discomfort.'

For organizations:

- 'The place to start is with co-creating a powerful shared purpose. The NHS team were influenced by the work of Marshall Ganz (Senior Lecturer in public policy at the Kennedy School of Government) and his teachings on social movement (which were the organizing principles in the Obama for America election campaign). These chimed so clearly with my own work and personal values.'

- When people understand the purpose of the change, they don't need permission to take the next step; they can just do it – not because they *have to* but because they *want to*.

- Do the 'work before the work', relentlessly connecting with people to enable the human spirit to flourish and achieve purpose.

- Create a burning ambition that moves people from fear to hope, focusing on intrinsic motivation and energy, with a specific ask of others, measurable goals and practical change. When you generate this source of social energy, it will tip a project or idea into a movement, not mandated but inspired.

- Give hope not fear. When hope germinates it's powerful, when power is divided it multiplies, when hope is restored and people connect who share a common purpose it's possible to create a movement for change. I am in hope of people. What are you in hope of?'

Of course, doing what we love (whether at work or play) contributes to our wellbeing and our happiness. As we've seen, an important motivator for creativity for businesses and individuals is to live a more meaningful life. And what better way to find meaning than by helping to make the world a better place?

In business, love and money intersect at the next of our elements – social good.

Sg Social good

*It is society that gives us the right to be active, our licence to operate.
A business leader has to think about how to solve the societal challenges
of today, because if we don't solve them, we will not have a business.*
Peter Brabeck-Letmathe, Chairman of the Board, Nestlé, 2016

Over the past few years, the idea that companies can have a positive impact
on society, and can deliver this alongside making profit, has become increasingly accepted by the corporate world. Of course, the idea that a company
has a responsibility to its employees, customers and the broader world in
which it operates is not a new concept. The Cadbury family created progres-
sive working conditions for their employees and later Henry Ford treated
his workers well, because he realized it would improve productivity and
longevity of service and 'incidentally to make money'.

The principle of self-interest and the 'greed is good' philosophy, epitomized
by the fictional Gordon Gekko character in the 1987 film *Wall Street* was
the prevailing business ideology during the eighties.

Today, doing good is good business

*The days when companies regarded sustainability as a bit of window-
dressing (or, worse, a profit-sapping distraction) are long gone. Today's
business leaders understand that social responsibility goes hand-in-hand
with sustained growth and profitability. Doing good is good business.*
Sir Martin Sorrell, Chief Executive, WPP, 2014

Jim Stengel, the former chief marketing officer at the world's biggest adver-
tiser Procter & Gamble and author of *Grow*, conducted a 10-year growth
study with research company Millward Brown looking at the performance
of 50,000 brands. He found that brands who put the purpose of improving
people's lives at their heart created stronger connections with consumers
and financially outperformed their rivals.

His research showed that an investment in 'The Stengel 50' – the companies he identified as being the fastest-growing brands with ideals at their
core – would have been 400 times more profitable between 2001–2011,
than an investment in the broader S&P Index (Stengel, 2011).

Shift in consumer thinking

Consumers are more empowered than ever, with easy access to information and they are able to quickly mobilize support online to shame a company. Transparency has become an increasingly important behaviour for companies. The *Edelman Trust Barometer* 2016 found that 80 per cent of those it surveyed (more than 33,000 people across 28 countries) expect businesses can take actions to both increase profits and improve economic and social conditions in their communities.

It also found that if a business or leader actively engaged in addressing social issues, an employee's motivation to perform, stay at the company and recommend it to others increased (Edelman, 2016).

In an oversaturated marketplace, having a positive social impact can be a good point of differentiation. A relationship that is based around shared values is deeper and can create more loyal customers. It can also attract more motivated employees.

The B Corporation movement

Figure 6.2

Companies like Patagonia, Warby Parker and Cook are part of a growing ethical certification for companies: the B Corporation movement. The key requirement to become certified is that a company 'must create value for society, not just shareholders' and use their business as a force for good? (bcorporation.net, 2016). The founders of Warby Parker set out to offer an alternative to expensive and bland prescription eyewear. For every pair of glasses sold, the company donates a pair to someone in need.

Meanwhile outdoor company Patagonia famously encouraged its customers not to buy its clothes if they did not need them. For Black Friday in 2011, the company ran the ad below in *The New York Times,* which stated: 'Don't buy this jacket' and explained the environmental impact of manufacturing its products. Worn Wear is the company's programme to encourage consumers to repair their garments, reuse them and recycle them when required.

Rose Marcario, CEO of Patagonia writes in her missive on patagonia. com (2016) that 'repair is a radical act' and that 'the B Corp movement is one of the most important of our lifetime, built on the simple fact that business impacts and serves more than just shareholders – it has an equal responsibility to the community and to the planet'.

UK-based frozen food retailer Cook has a range of initiatives including donating leftovers to charity, a 'Dream Academy' for staff and a school meal donation programme in Malawi. They say that becoming certified as a B Corporation has provided them 'with a 'no bullshit' stamp that proves we mean what we say. To be certified we had to pass a rigorous assessment to prove we meet tough standards of social and environmental performance, accountability and transparency' (cookfood.net, 2016).

There are over 1,700 certified B Corps, spanning 130 industries. In 2016 Natura, Brazil's leading cosmetics company, became the first publicly traded company to attain B Corp status. It is also the largest, giving a major boost to the movement. Ben & Jerry's ice cream brand became B Corp-certified in 2012 and 'was one of the first companies in the world to place a social mission in equal importance to its product and economic missions' (www.benjerry.com 2016). Chief Executive of Ben of Jerry, Jostein Solheim, has been in discussions with B Corps on behalf of Unilever, which bought the company in 2001, to explore how the multinational could become certified. A surefire sign that the movement is gaining major support and momentum (Confino, 2015).

Figure 6.3 B Corps Patagonia's 'Don't buy this jacket' advert

DON'T BUY THIS JACKET

It's Black Friday, the day in the year retail turns from red to black and starts to make real money. But Black Friday, and the culture of consumption it reflects, puts the economy of natural systems that support all life firmly in the red. We're now using the resources of one-and-a-half planets on our one and only planet.

Because Patagonia wants to be in business for a good long time – and leave a world inhabitable for our kids – we want to do the opposite of every other business today. We ask you to buy less and to reflect before you spend a dime on this jacket or anything else.

Environmental bankruptcy, as with corporate bankruptcy, can happen very slowly, then all of a sudden. This is what we face unless we slow down, then reverse the damage. We're running short on fresh water, topsoil, fisheries, wetlands – all our planet's natural systems and resources that support business, and life, including our own.

The environmental cost of everything we make is astonishing. Consider the R2® Jacket shown, one of our best sellers. To make it required 135 liters of

COMMON THREADS INITIATIVE

REDUCE
WE make useful gear that lasts a long time
YOU don't buy what you don't need

REPAIR
WE help you repair your Patagonia gear
YOU pledge to fix what's broken

REUSE
WE help find a home for Patagonia gear
you no longer need
YOU sell or pass it on*

RECYCLE
WE will take back your Patagonia gear
that is worn out
YOU pledge to keep your stuff out of
the landfill and incinerator

REIMAGINE
TOGETHER we reimagine a world where we take
only what nature can replace

water, enough to meet the daily needs (three glasses a day) of 45 people. Its journey from its origin as 60% recycled polyester to our Reno warehouse generated nearly 20 pounds of carbon dioxide, 24 times the weight of the finished product. This jacket left behind, on its way to Reno, two-thirds its weight in waste.

And this is a 60% recycled polyester jacket, knit and sewn to a high standard; it is exceptionally durable, so you won't have to replace it as often. And when it comes to the end of its useful life we'll take it back to recycle into a product of equal value. But, as is true of all the things we can make and you can buy, this jacket comes with an environmental cost higher than its price.

There is much to be done and plenty for us all to do. Don't buy what you don't need. Think twice before you buy anything. Go to patagonia.com/CommonThreads or scan the QR code below. Take the Common Threads Initiative pledge, and join us in the fifth "R," to reimagine a world where we take only what nature can replace.

patagonia®
patagonia.com

* If you sell your used Patagonia product on eBay® and take the Common Threads Initiative pledge, we will co-list your product on patagonia.com for no additional charge.   TAKE THE PLEDGE

CASE STUDY

Cindy Gallop was one of the founders of creative advertising agency Bartle Bogle Hegarty's New York office and the founder of MakeLoveNotPorn, a video sharing site that promotes healthier attitudes to sex. She believes that 'the future of business is doing good and making money simultaneously'. She spoke to Kate Magee about her views.

'I started IfWeRanTheWorld (an online platform that helps people turn good intentions into action) because I believe the business model of the future is 'shared values plus shared action equals social profit and financial profit'.

Why don't more companies already do this?

'One of the huge barriers to more businesses doing good is that they are not structured in the right way. There are silos between sales/marketing and corporate social responsibility (CSR). They operate a model which is: "We make money here and write cheques to clear our conscience over there". There's a mindset in leadership about CSR, which is that "those are the chaps who give our PR folks something to talk about". You don't change until you bring them together. The future is making money because you are doing good and integrating it into the way you do business on a day-to-day basis. It's a key driver of future growth.'

Why should businesses be interested in creating social good?

'Because you will make more money and sell more product. There's still a ridiculous mindset that you only do it for altruistic reasons. Fuck altruism. I want people to see how much money they can make. That is the way you will convince everyone to adopt this model. Having shared values and jointly creating positive social impact will help lock consumers into a relationship with you. You make money because you do good. I am absolutely championing the business model of the future.'

Where does creativity fit in?

'Everything in life and business starts with you and your values. This is as true for companies as it is for people. What are your values? What do you stand for? What do you believe you are about?

'That is what drives the type of CSR you should be taking. It should be a direct result of what business you operate or your personal values. When you adopt that route, you have the ability to bring a different approach and creativity in a way that can affect real change. The world really needs a whole lot more creativity applied to doing good.'

C Culture

Culture is what makes us who we are. It gives us strength; it is a wellspring of innovation and creativity; and it provides answers to many of the challenges we face today.
Irina Bokova, Director General of UNESCO, 2012

Having an impact in popular culture can inspire an original idea, extend its shelf life, generate business success and secure genuine social and behaviour change. However long-term impact is not always achievable depending on how tied to the cultural moment the ideas are. Do you remember who sponsored the London 2012 Games ($1.1 billion raised) or which advertisement 'won' the Superbowl ad battle this year? Both huge cultural moments with billions of marketing dollars spent but it's unlikely that however impactful at the time, these campaigns will be referred to 20 years from now.

Social good is definitely having a cultural moment at the time of writing when Facebook's Marc Zuckerberg pledged to give away 99 per cent of the company's shares worth $45 billion to good causes in 2015.

This ties into a broader discussion about creativity and culture. Csikszentmihalyi (1998) writes that creativity 'exists only in specific social and historical contexts'. He uses the analogy of a good fake painting versus an original work of art – if you only saw the fake you might say it was highly creative but compared with the original it is not creative at all.

Howard Gardner (1998) writes that Sigmund Freud was a product of fin de siècle Vienna – his education, social circle, peer group, critics and the prevailing ideas of that moment in time all influenced his ideas and his work. How could it not?

The most important creative figures of any historical period – the ones that leave a legacy – shape and challenge the prevailing ideas of that time. They affect culture, and are born of that culture.

CASE STUDY   Making a dent in popular culture

Vicki Maguire is an Executive Creative Director at Grey London. The creative advertising agency has produced a stream of award-winning work 'for good' for both commercial and not-for-profit organizations in recent years.

One of Maguire's most impactful and effective pieces of work was the 2012 advertisement for the British Heart Foundation, which featured Vinnie Jones showing people how to give hands-only CPR to the timing of the Bee Gees' tune 'Stayin' Alive'.

'Vinnie' for the British Heart Foundation tackled a serious issue. How can creativity help deliver this kind of message?

I've got to admit 'Vinnie' is one of the hardest briefs I've ever worked on: 'Show the British public how to save a life. In 40 seconds.' We knew that a straight public service announcement wouldn't cut through. We asked around and found that, actually, most people don't actually want the responsibility of knowing how to save a life. People are fearful of being sued. And they don't want to give the kiss of life to anyone with a beard... so if you have a cardiac arrest in Shoreditch you're fucked. We knew we needed something that was a million miles away from your standard 'bloke in a white coat' charity ad but still deliver some hard-hitting instructions in a way that would be memorable. To perform CPR correctly you have to push hard on the chest to the beat of something like 100 beats per minute. Vinnie Jones is

Figure 6.4   Vinnie Jones showing people how to give hands-only CPR in Grey London's award-winning ad for the British Heart Foundation

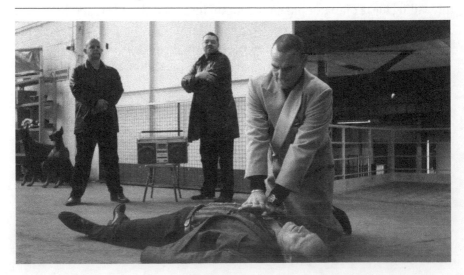

your archetypal hard man. If he tells you to inflict GBH [grievous bodily harm] on someone you'll listen. To perform CPR correctly you have to push on the ribcage just under the chest (where you'd wear a medallion). And the song Stayin' Alive just happens to be 100 BPM. Weave these together in a sketch and you not only have a funny spot people will talk about and share (5 million views) but you'll remember 'Push hard and fast on the sovereign to the beat of staying alive'. To date 40 people are alive today because someone 'did a Vinnie on their chest.' The NHS use the ad in training and Mini Vinnie, the training film we made for kids under 16, is regularly shown in schools. I think every brand should examine their role within culture. If they have the means to do something good for society they should be encouraged.

How do you persuade clients to use their ad budget for social good?

I don't buy jumping on the bandwagon. I think consumers can spot self-service masquerading as social good a mile off. A car marque with a social conscience could easily fall into that category but Volvo are special. Their social purpose is at the heart of company. They have a company vision 'no one should be killed or seriously injured in a new Volvo by 2020'. That's an incredibly powerful statement for a car manufacturer to make. But these are the guys who invented the safely belt then opened up the intellectual property for every manufacturer to use. So Life Paint, the invisible/visible reflective spray for cyclists is right up Volvo's street. It took safety out of the car and onto the road. Sure, no one wants to die behind the wheel, but you don't want to kill anyone either. Life Paint is now sold in over 500 dealerships and independent bike shops around the country. We've sold half a million cans to date.'

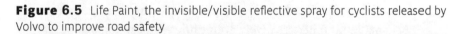

Figure 6.5 Life Paint, the invisible/visible reflective spray for cyclists released by Volvo to improve road safety

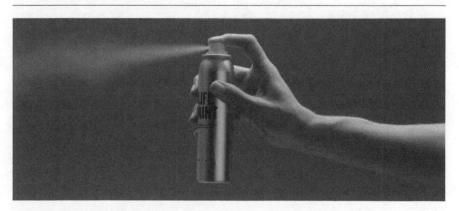

CREATIVE COACH

- How could you clarify and increase your commitment to social good as a motivating purpose in your organization?

- Where do you/your business share values with your clients and consumers, how could you align these more to your creative process?

- What good have you always wanted to see happen in the world? How could you engage others in your organization towards that cause?

CREATIVE EXPERIMENT

EXPLORE YOUR PERSONAL OR COMPANY PURPOSE

- What would you be willing to stand up, stand out and stand firm for?

- In their book *On Purpose: Delivering a branded customer experience people love* (2015), authors Milligan and Smith say that companies with purpose do three things: they stand up, stand out and stand firm. They have a great free online toolkit with a step-by-step process to help you and your company establish your purpose here www.smithcoconsultancy.com/the-cem-toolkit.

- Come up with one thing you or your company can do differently today that will help advance your purpose. It can be something very small, but think creatively about how you can make a positive change.

Table 6.1

Element	Key questions	Greatest strength and your score 0–10	Biggest development area and your score 0–10
Love (L)	Do you do anything related to work for the love of it?		
Joy (J)	What aspect of your work gives you joy?		
Money (M)	How well do you demonstrate the connection between creativity and financial return on your work?		
Social good (Sg)	How important or relevant is creating a sense of meaning and purpose for social good in your business?		
Culture (C)	To what extent do you or could you tap into popular culture to add purpose and relevance to your creative ideas?		

REVIEW THE CHAPTER

Purpose gives us reason and meaning, the answer to the question: why get out of bed in the morning? Reflect on your own:

- What issues get you fired up?

- What are you passionate about?

- Where do you think you can make a difference? (You may want to use the thinking you did in Chapter 1 about values as this will definitely impact your purpose).

- How could you bring any of these into your work?

- Review the chapter elements in turn – where do you think your greatest strength lies?

- Where are your blind spots?

- Give yourself a score out of 10 for both.

IN A NUTSHELL

The world of work is changing fast. People want to find more meaning from their work. As we've seen this is driving more creativity applied to 'doing good' and to tackle difficult issues like female inequality championed for UN Women. It's driving the rise of mission-driven businesses like TOMS combining purpose and profit. Helping to create a better world can be a great motivator, and can help inspire people to do their best work if they feel they are contributing to something worthwhile.

A sense of purpose as an individual enables us to have the grit to deal with setbacks, the ability to stay focused and the determination to complete the task in hand. It can make the difference between mediocre and award-winning.

For companies, making money and offering benefit to others are not mutually exclusive. Creativity that advances social good can be a great motivator, provide meaning, forge stronger relationships with customers, and increase profits.

DIG DEEPER

Sinek, S (2009) Start with Why; How Great Leaders Inspire Action
on TED.com for his talk on the same subject.
A free World Economic Forum guide to help companies embed social
innovation practices into their business strategy and operations
www3.weforum.org/docs/WEF_Social_Innovation_Guide.pdf
Milligan A, Smith S (2015) *On Purpose: Delivering a branded
customer experience people love*. Kogan Page. London.

The creative process 07

This chapter looks at these 13 creative elements:

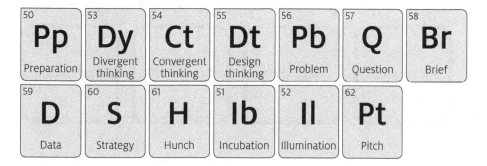

Pp Preparation

In the fields of observation chance favours only the prepared mind.
Louis Pasteur, scientist, 1854

The idea that we can deliberately shape and influence our personal creativity is a relatively modern one. This chapter shares different ways to approach creative challenges and to add structure. The word process suggests that there's a clear step-by-step approach, which some methodologies support, but it's often a non-linear, messy business.

Graham Wallas (founder of the London School of Economics) proposed an early four-stage creativity process based on his studies of creative people in *The Art of Thought* (1926). Three of the stages contribute three elements in this chapter:

- *Preparation* Pp – a 'hard, conscious, systematic and fruitless analysis of the problem'.

- *Incubation* `Ib` – the work of *the unconscious mind* `Um`.
- *Illumination* `Il` – 'the appearance of the "happy idea" together with the psychological events which immediately preceded and accompanied that appearance'.
- *Verification* – the validity of the 'happy idea' is explored and tested.

Figure 7.1 The Wallas model of the creative process

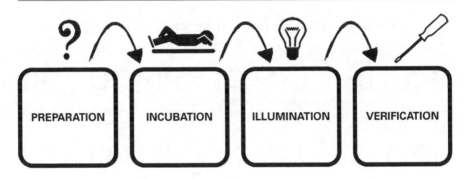

Verification is not a new element as it is covered by *evaluation* `Ev`, which we explored in Chapter 1, with practical tools to follow in the next chapter.

The Osborn-Parnes Creative Problem Solving (CPS) process was developed by pioneers in creativity research – initially by Alex Osborn then notably Sidney J Parnes and Ruth Noller, who founded the International Centre for Studies in Creativity at Buffalo State University in New York. At Now Go Create we regularly use the CPS framework and tools in our day-to-day consultancy and training work. The stages of the CPS process are:

- objective finding
- fact finding
- data finding
- problem finding
- idea finding
- solution finding
- acceptance finding

Adapted from www.creativeproblemsolving.com, 2016.

Figure 7.2 You can think of different parts of the creative process as building blocks or 'mental Lego'

The tools that follow in the next chapter are separated to reflect some of the various phases of the creative process, and the different types of thinking required.

Models that rely on individual and team creativity, and involve intuition are typically described as psychologically based.

 Divergent and convergent thinking

The model (like many others) is influenced by Guilford's (1967) notion of two further elements. The first, divergent thinking, opens things out and explores how to devise many, varied options while convergent thinking requires prioritization and selection of the most promising ideas to take forward. We all do this flexing between options and narrowing them down numerous times every day. In the early stages of idea generation the art is deferring judgment and not closing anything down too early.

Figure 7.3 Divergent and convergent thinking

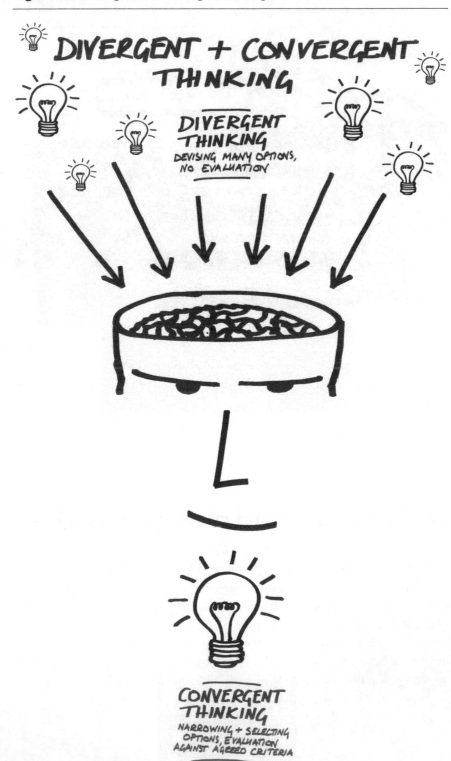

Dt Design thinking

'The Squiggle' is a brilliant representation of the messiness of the creative process. Ex-IDEO designer Damien Newman, now of Central, is an expert in design thinking and teaches a graduate class at the School of Engineering at Stanford. His work focuses on large-scale, complex systems, which are difficult to explain.

Damien writes (2010): 'Years ago I dropped a simple illustration into a proposal to convey the design process to a client. It was meant to illustrate the characteristics of the process we were to embark on, making it clear to them that it might be uncertain in the beginning, but in the end we'd focus on a single point of clarity. It seemed to work. And from then on, I've used it since. Many, many times.

Figure 7.4 'The Squiggle' by Damien Newman

Noise / Uncertainty / Patterns / Insights   Clarity / Focus

Research & Synthesis   Concept / Prototype   Design

'Even years before this, I had the fortune to work at Xerox Europarc as an illustrator. I'd help convey the scenarios the researchers worked on in cartoon form. My father, a principal scientist there, told me that for them the design process started with the abstract, moved to the concept and then finally the design. So I used to use these three words, back in the day, to convey the process of design to my unsuspecting clients. It wasn't as effective – even if I knew what it meant. So I found myself saying, "Here, it looks like this......" and drawing the squiggle. It particularly helped with my then Japanese client to convey the uncertainty in the ethnographic approach we used for our program.'

CASE STUDY   Think like IDEO

Global design firm IDEO's CEO Tim Brown defines how they work like this: 'Design thinking is a human-centred approach to innovation that draws from the designer's toolkit to integrate the needs of people, the possibilities of technology and the requirements for business success' (2008).

Experts suggest that there are five steps that need to be implemented to apply design thinking to any problem: empathize, define, ideate, prototype and test.

Are you a natural-born design thinker?

According to Brown the qualities you need are:

- *Empathy* – 'They can imagine the world from multiple perspectives,' Brown told the *Harvard Business Review*. He says that great designers observe the world in small detail and notice things that others don't. By being able to empathize with others, you can better assess how different people see the world.

- *Optimism* – Says Brown: 'Design thinkers assume that no matter how challenging the constraints of a given problem, at least one potential solution is better than the existing alternatives.'

- *Experimentalism* – 'The next big idea isn't just an extension of what's gone before', says Brown, 'it's more of a leap than that. Design thinkers pose questions and explore constraints in creative ways.'

- *Collaboration* – Brown says that because modern problems can be so complex, the lone creative genius idea doesn't really work any more. At IDEO, he points out, they have people who are engineers *and* marketers. Architects *and* psychologists (IDEO.com, 2015).

Balancing efficiency and experimentation

Models like Six Sigma use statistical analysis to produce 'unambiguous data that help produce better quality, lower costs, and more efficiency' (Hindo, 2007). Typically used by large manufacturing companies like GE and 3M to systematically eliminate errors, Six Sigma originated at Motorola in the 1980s and is now widely used in the corporate world. Employees train as 'green belts' and with experience progress to 'black-belt' status.

On finding the balance between efficiency and experimentation, former 3M CEO George Buckley said 'you can't put a Six Sigma process into that area and say, well, I'm getting behind on invention, so I'm going to schedule myself for three good ideas on Wednesday and two on Friday. That's not how creativity works' (Hindo, 2007). As we've seen in previous chapters 'while process excellence demands precision, consistency, and repetition, innovation calls for variation, failure, and serendipity' (Hindo, 2007).

Based on analysis of over 3 million Russian patents, the theory of inventive problem solving, commonly known as the TRIZ process assumes that your problem has been encountered and solved somewhere else before. It 'relies on the study of the patterns of problems and solutions, not on the spontaneous and intuitive creativity of individuals or groups' and 'provides repeatability, predictability, and reliability due to its structure and algorithmic approach' (triz-journal.com, 2016). The process uses comparison to transfer a solution from another domain or problem to solve your particular problem.

56 Pb | 57 Q **Problem and question**

Whatever process you choose to follow there are elements that are common to most; the first of these being the problem, which will probably involve starting with a question.

Defining the problem is an aspect common to most models and different creativity tools can be useful for different problems – see the toolkit in Chapter 8.

The master problem-solvers at the CIA have advice about the importance of this first stage: 'It is also essential that the analyst think the problem through, going beyond a mere statement of the question. Although such an analysis may appear premature, it is imperative that the problem be mulled over thoroughly for disclosure of its implications and ramifications and that these be formulated in the shape of a preliminary outline of what is desired to be known about the subject' (Drell, 1993).

If the problem is not framed correctly then the end results tend to 'veer away from purposeful, sharply focused research to fuzzy shotgun collection characterized by uneven coverage and inefficient allocation of time' (cia.gov, 2016).

See the toolkit in Chapter 8 for ways to think about the issues, frame the problem statement and formulate great questions to get off to a flying creative start.

Junk in, junk out

Brief

The brief is the blueprint for the ideas you'll generate and will determine the quality of creative output. It must contain the criteria against which the ideas will be judged. So if you're responsible for writing the brief that others will respond to, be clear about what your evaluation criteria are upfront. If you're responding, then ensure that you know what these are.

If you are presenting your ideas to others make sure that the person who wrote the brief and the decision-makers are in the room, otherwise from the outset you may be at cross-purposes. I've been in meetings where the key decision-maker has turned up for the pitch, but clearly didn't write the brief, and it's been painfully apparent from early on that his criteria didn't make it into the briefing. In those circumstances (sadly more than I wish to recount) I have never won the business.

Data

> *Data and creativity are the Montagues and Capulets of advertising. They are seen as polar opposites, yet when they combine they create something profound, like Romeo and Juliet.*
> **Ogilvy and Mather Worldwide Chief Creative Officer Tham Khai Meng, 2014**

We saw in Chapter 1 how the data relating to the difference in the cost per word 'meerkat' and 'market' drove the highly creative strategy for comparethemarket.com. There are myriad sources of data that can feed into the preparation stage – personal experience, market research, focus groups, social media monitoring, customer feedback, trends, experiments, failures and accidents for starters. You will no doubt have your favourite go-to resources. Data feeds into what I call 'the detective phase' and is closely linked with *knowledge* K .

> *The combination of imagination and maths is going to be extremely important... it is great to be a wordsmith and it is great to be able to create beautiful images but you need to be able to count as well.*
> **Sarah Wood, Unruly, 2016**

Unruly is a fast-growing ad tech company creating videos that are watched online. With publishing clients including *The New York Post* and the *Mail*, the company operates in the new frontier where video, social and mobile intersect. In a great interview about how data and creativity go hand in hand, Unruly founder and COO Sarah Wood said: 'We take big data and our data powers data-driven creativity. So we are helping the brands to create shareable content that will be watched, shared and distributed at scale.'

HOW DATA DRIVES CREATIVITY

As part of Unilever Dove's ongoing 'Campaign for Real Beauty' the 2013 Dove Beauty Sketches garnered nearly 135 million views online and challenged women's perceptions of their own looks using an FBI sketch artist. According to Ogilvy and Mather, the ad agency behind the work, 'the key insight from which the creativity sprung came from the data gatherers. Unilever researched global attitudes towards beauty, and found that just 4 per cent of women considered themselves beautiful' (Worldwide Chief Creative Officer, Tham Khai Meng, 2014).

However some people wholeheartedly reject the idea of using data. Oliviero Toscani, is an Italian photographer best-known for his often controversial adverts for clothing retailer Benetton. He says: 'We try to make our ads personal. If you do research you get yesterday's results. If they did research 500 years ago, they never would have discovered America. They would have found the world is flat. You have to have the courage to make mistakes. Everything we do is about impulse, about guts. That's what built Benetton' (Gogatz and Mondejar, 2005).

Data is often the key to our next element – strategy.

S | Strategy

Everyone has a plan until they get punched in the mouth.
Mike Tyson, boxer, 2012

The word 'strategy' has the power to intimidate and confuse the hell out of people and I cannot possibly do justice to strategy development here. One of my favourite books on the subject is *Strategy, a History by* Lawrence

Freedman who writes: 'Having a strategy suggests an ability to look up from the short terms and the trivial to view the long term and the essential, to address causes rather than symptoms, to see woods rather than trees. Without a strategy, facing up to any problem or striving for any objective would be considered negligent' (Freedman, 2013). Although the word is overused Freedman adds that '... strategy remains the best word for expressing attempts to think about actions in advance, in the light of our goals and capacities' (Freedman, 2013).

Suffice to say here that for complex challenges, while it's tempting to dive straight into generating ideas, they often won't stack up without rigorous thinking and interrogation of the problem at hand.

H Hunch

Where in a conversation about strategy and process do you allow for the hunch? This may be the initial thoughts, feelings or guesses we have about a problem (or it may precede even this part) the hunch being the thing that propels us to tackle the problem in the first place.

While we might assume that science is the domain of reason, evidence and facts, hunches have been part of many major scientific breakthroughs. In one study of chemists, 83 per cent reported that they had 'assistance from a scientific revelation or hunch in the solution of an important problem' (Rothenburg and Hausman, 1976).

Founder of the Webby Awards and filmmaker Tiffany Shlain has created a series of brilliant short films on technology, creativity and much besides for AOL. *The Future Starts Here* has had over 40 million views. Shlain says: 'Any project starts with a hunch, and you have to act on it. It's a total risk because you're just about to jump off a cliff, and you have to go for it if you believe in it' (Shlain, 2013).

This element exemplifies the mysteries of the creative process.

Our next element is incubation.

Ib Incubation

James Webb Young wrote *A Technique for Producing Ideas* in 1965 and it has become a classic reference for the creative process. He describes incubation as 'the mental digestive process', the part that follows the fact-finding and information search. 'What you do is to take the different bits of material you have gathered and feel them all over, as it were, with the tentacles of the mind. You take one fact, turn it this way and that, look at it in different lights, and feel for the meaning of it. You bring two facts together and see how they fit' (Webb Young, 2003).

Some of the most famous occurrences of the 'happy idea' have happened during incubation. Archimedes' 'Eureka!' moment happened while he was stepping into the bath and displaced a volume of water, Henri Poincaré (who Wallas studied) was boarding a bus when he had his revelation about a fundamental mathematics problem and in 1865 Friedrich Von Kekulé's insights about Benzine happened during a fireside doze (Boden, 2004).

In Chapter 4 Ben Martynoga offers fascinating insights from neuro-science into what is actually going on unconsciously in our grey matter during incubation. Our self-conscious experience, which feels so dominant and powerful, is in fact often not at the heart of the brain's grand scheme. Instead it finds itself on the fringes, frantically trying to understand and influence the super-computer-like machinations of the unconscious mind (Eagleman, 2011).

Our next element is illumination which results in the idea.

Figure 7.5 The four stages of the Wallas model of the creative process, overlaid with the brain-related elements from Chapter 4, indicating the stage where they contribute most to creative thought. Note that some elements contribute to several stages (Martynoga, 2016)

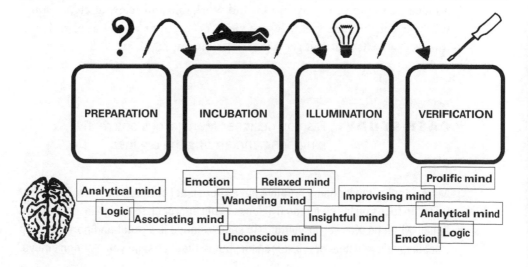

52 | Illumination

An important commentator on the dilemmas of the 20th century, Arthur Koestler describes illumination as 'the moment of truth, the sudden emergence of a new insight, is an act of intuition. Such intuitions give the appearance of miraculous flashes, or short circuits of reasoning. In fact they may be likened to an immersed chain, of which only the beginning and the end are visible above the surface of consciousness. The diver vanishes at one end of the chain and comes up at the other end, guided by invisible links' (Boden, 2004).

Clarence Birdseye (founder of the frozen food company) had his illumination about how to flash-freeze food as he observed local Eskimo fishermen fishing under ice and noticed that their catch froze almost instantly. His insight and subsequent innovation revolutionized his business.

But what makes an idea [I] brilliant and creative rather than ordinary or mundane? We explored this back in the definitions chapter where the concepts of novelty, value and surprise were common to highly creative ideas or innovations.

ITV's 'Pope of Soap' John Whiston (Creative Director of serial dramas, responsible for *Coronation Street* and *Emmerdale*) told me: 'In terms of a "Good Idea" – for me it's heart. In that, when you hear it, it has the same effect on you as a good joke. It's out there. It makes you gasp a bit because it's so wrong and so beyond the pale. And deep down I know you can drag an idea like that back inside the pale by the application of intellect and craft skill. Far harder (I would say impossible) would be to push a so-so idea, an idea that your brain says is OK and workable and relevant etc, to somewhere it can become great. In my view, no amount of the application of intellect or craft skill will get it there.' (Whiston, 2016)

CASE STUDY   Fashion designer Marc Jacobs on creative ping-pong and finding the big idea

Marc Jacobs, the longtime creative powerhouse at Louis Vuitton, until 2013 when he left to focus on his own brand, discusses his approach to design in an interview filmed when he was still at Vuitton. He said: 'Change is a great and horrible thing. People love it and hate at the same time, but without change you just don't move.'

'First, there's the idea,' he says, 'but the road to that idea is not always so clear. The clarity comes from doing and making, trying and retrying. I really believe that it's the process, not the initial idea, which creates the end result.'
Jacobs, 2011

During Jacobs' tenure as Creative Director, the French luxury brand grew from strength to strength (parent company LVMH's annual revenue today is north of £20 billion), though not every day resulted in creative breakthroughs. Jacobs admits that 'there are days I feel paralysed and think, "Oh, there's no big idea," but sometimes a little idea gains momentum.' He adds that it is important to 'get out to see other things', explaining that a creative environment – be that movies, art or dance – can 'nourish your creative soul.'

As for the day-to-day process that he put in place at Vuitton, the designer paints a picture of an open, highly collaborative approach and 'cross pollination' which he describes as 'ping-pong, back and forth.' He says 'we all feed off of each other's ideas and we all work on all the things together. A shoe can inspire a dress and a dress can inspire a bag and vice versa. When we do our job the best, it's because there is a connection between all of the things and there's a constant re-looking at each one of the products.' (Jacobs, 2011)

Ideas must be tested and validated to ascertain how novel, valuable and surprising they are, and evaluation is discussed in the toolkit in the next chapter.

So you've got your big idea. Now what? Last up in this chapter is the Pitch element.

Figure 7.6 Selling your idea is the acceptance finding aspect to the CPS process

Pt Pitch

At some point in your business life you will have to present your ideas in a formal environment – perhaps a job interview, board presentation or new business pitch. The inimitable Wendy Clark is Chief Executive Officer DDB North America – if you're not familiar with the advertising agency's name you'll no doubt know their work for brands including IKEA, McDonald's, Skittles and John Lewis amongst many others. An accomplished public speaker herself, Wendy has seen hundreds of presentations over the course of her stellar career including 12 years working in marketing client-side at Coca-Cola and AT&T. Here are her 11 tips on how to persuade, influence and sell your ideas to your audience:

1 *If you're doing more 'sell' than 'great work,' take note.* Great work, the right work and solution, should not require Herculean effort to sell in.

2 *Know the business case.* Current performance, desired performance, business challenge and opportunity are all your responsibility to understand. After all, if you don't know the business, how can you possibly offer creative solutions that will work to change it?

3 *Plan well; timing can be everything.* Do everything in your power to schedule meetings outside of distracting or challenging timeframes – eg quarterly earnings reports.

4 *Prepare a tight, cogent rationale.* Make sure it's really good. Again, if you cannot express in a compelling, articulate manner why your idea and work are right, why would your audience be able to?

5 *Be realistic.* Often our brilliant ideas simply challenge some core fundamental to what's possible either through timing, budget, legalities, etc. It's always worth sharing all on-strategy ideas, but don't be crestfallen if a magical idea, which presses against a fundamental, doesn't get sold in.

6 *Be passionate.* 'Some of the most powerful presenters I've seen have levitated me out of my chair with their passion. To sell an idea you need to show your belief in it,' says Wendy.

7 *Consider your non-verbals, everything communicates.* This includes things like looking at your phone during the presentation, other open windows on your computer as you present and appropriate attire for their meeting environment.

8 *If you use them, make great visuals and support materials.* 'The best creative presenters I've seen require no visuals and simply use the imagery in your mind,' says Wendy.

9 *Rehearse. Rehearse. Rehearse.* While they make it look effortless, the best presenters in the world rehearse aggressively. Nothing in your presentation should surprise you. Make it a point never to say, 'Oh, I didn't know that slide was next.'

10 *Have empathy.* Wendy believes the ability to empathize is perhaps the most underleveraged skill in helping to sell great work. Letting your audience know your understanding of their situation, their needs, their challenge and your matched excitement/concern/optimism, etc, for their situation is one of the most powerful connections you can make.

11 *Be resilient.* 'In our business, you have to believe that a "no" is just a "yes" waiting to happen. If I don't succeed this time, what can I do differently or better to convince you this is the right path? You have to be relentless in this belief'. Wendy believes that to be resilient you also need to stand up to your inner critic – the voice in your head that makes you question yourself – often called 'imposter syndrome'. Her advice: 'You have to shut that bitch up! Have confidence that you've prepared, in every sense, for success in this moment.'

Show runner, artist or neophtye? What's your pitch style?

Professor of Organizational Behavior at the University of California, Kimberly D Elsbach worked with 50 Hollywood executives to determine what made them greenlight a movie pitch. Was the quality of the story always at the heart of a successful pitch, or was there was more to it?

She found that the person on the receiving end of the pitch – 'the catcher' – tends to gauge the *pitcher's creativity as well as the proposal itself*. Elsbach concluded that a pitcher quickly left an impression on the exec as to whether or not they were able to come up with workable ideas, and that this tended to 'quickly and permanently overshadow' the catcher's feelings about the idea's worth. In other words, they weren't just pitching their script, they were pitching themselves, too (Elsbach, 2003).

She discovered 'catchers' subconsciously place successful pitchers into one of three distinct categories:

- show runners – smooth and professional;
- artists – quirky types, a dash of the unpolished about them;
- neophytes – people who came across as inexperienced and a little naïve.

She concluded a successful pitcher must portray themselves as one of the three creative types and be a 'likeable collaborator' so that the decision-maker is able to feel some of the love for the development of the idea too (Elsbach, 2003).

CREATIVE EXPERIMENT

To wrap this chapter up, here's a useful exercise adapted from CPS to visually explore and map your natural creative process (Isaksen *et al* 2011).

- Take a large sheet of paper, the bigger the better, and a pen. Lay the paper landscape style.

- Think of a time you had a real-life problem to solve, whether at work or at play; one where you achieved a successful outcome.

- Now using a nice chunky pen, take 5–10 minutes to try and draw or illustrate your creative process. This is not about creating a beautiful image, just capturing the essence of your thought process.

- Now reflect on your drawing. What did you do? Was anyone else involved? Or were you alone? Did you find the answer straight away or did you step back? Did you use words, symbols or pictures? Does it feature emotional and/or rational responses?

- You can do this exercise alone or with a group – compare your drawings and explore any similarities or differences and share your findings. What do you notice? Can you identify any of the elements outlined in this chapter – for example the incubation or verification stages – do you notice if you prefer or lean towards spending more time in any of the stages?

REVIEW THE CHAPTER

- Does your workflow tap into any of the process elements we've identified in this chapter? If you identify with any of the processes, do you have a natural preference for any of the stages over another?

- It may feel lazy to be 'incubating' a problem in your unconscious mind. It's not. Carve out time for it. It could make a world of difference to the end result.

- What do you think you could do differently to improve either your own creative process or that of your team or company following this chapter? If you don't have one do you think your business would benefit from a formal process?

Table 7.1

Element	Key questions	Assess yourself or your team on your current process. Are there clear areas of strength and those for development?
Preparation (Pp)	Do you feel sufficiently well-prepared to tackle any creative challenges?	
Incubation (Ib)	Do you allow for incubation in your creative efforts at work, personally or for your team?	
Illumination (Il)	Can you identify what happens when you get your 'happy idea'?	
Divergent thinking (Dy)	Are you naturally more comfortable in one or the other of these different thinking styles?	

Table 7.1 *continued*

Element	Key questions	Assess yourself or your team on your current process. Are there clear areas of strength and those for development?
Convergent thinking (Ct)	Are you naturally more comfortable in one or the other of these different thinking styles?	
Design thinking (Dt)	Could you apply any of this process to your work?	
Problem (Pb)	How well do you think you currently define the problem?	
Question (Q)	How much time do you spend thinking about useful questions?	
Brief (Br)	How much do you interrogate the brief?	
Data	Are there gaps in your knowledge in relation to your information-gathering process?	
Strategy (S)	Are you confident in your ability to understand and devise strategy?	
Hunch (H)	What role do hunches play in your creative process?	
Pitch (Pi)	How confident are you in your ability to sell your ideas?	

IN A NUTSHELL

We all have a natural creative process. Researchers over centuries have tried to understand and pin down what is going on in our grey matter so we might add structure and discipline around our creative thinking. Advances in neuroscience now reveal more about what is going on during the different phases, yet this still remains one of the most unexplained aspects of creativity. What I do know is that if you rely on your personal muse then you may well be in for a long wait. Better to understand your natural creative process and add structure where you can, and to be deliberate about your approach. It's helpful for individuals, critical for teams and organizations.

DIG DEEPER

For a full understanding of the CPS process, read Isaksen, SG, Dorval, KB and Treffinger DJ (2011) *Creative Approaches to Problem Solving*, 3rd edn, Sage, London

Prepare for a big, juicy, informative read and order Lawrence Freedman's *Strategy, a History*, Oxford University Press, 2013

Watch AOL's *The Future Starts Here* http://on.aol.com/shows/the-future-starts-here-shw517951318

See the full Marc Jacobs interview at https://vimeo.com/27007803

The creative toolkit

Tackling the blank page

In a global study 40 per cent of people said that it's essential to have tools to create and yet 'one in three people say they need training to learn and use creative tools' (Adobe, 2012). Being faced with the blank page can be daunting. Although I have worked in PR for nearly 20 years, for the first 15, learning creative techniques was not on the agenda – even though ideas are the lifeblood of the business. When I became a creative director I decided I needed more ammunition, so I taught myself a host of techniques in order to have a more structured approach to problem solving.

This practical chapter is a shortcut through the thousands of techniques out there. There is both an art and craft to choosing creativity tools, particularly if you are facilitating others. What follows is my 'go-to' selection, based on years of personal trial and error. I've added research where it's relevant to explain a bit more about why the tools work. You'll notice that many of them are part of the processes introduced previously – a smorgasbord of options including those from Creative Problem Solving (CPS), Design Thinking and my own adaptations.

This chapter is slightly different from the others. There are no new elements as the tools build on existing components addressed in other chapters – for example *convergent* [Ct] and *divergent thinking* [Di] from process or *emotion* [E] from the neuroscience chapter.

The tools are split into three sections depending on the task – problem finding, idea finding or solution finding. I've given each tool a difficulty rating from creative rookie to a ninja. This is as much a mindset as your years of experience.

I'm going to share tools that can be applied to a diverse range of problems – from 'I need an idea for a simple problem right now' to how to tackle more complex challenges.

Before we dive in, some factors to consider when thinking about which tool(s) would best fit your challenge:

- Where are you in the creative process?
- Do you want divergent or convergent thinking?
- Do you want analytical thinking or a more intuitive method (remember the different types of thinking preferences from the Creative Mind chapter?)
- How much time do you have to prepare, generate and evaluate ideas?
- Will your tool appeal to introverts and extroverts?
- What are your personal preferences versus what you think the group needs?
- What's your level of expertise in facilitating tools and workshops?
- What kind of physical environment will you be working in?
- What is the size of your group?

Since it's the default setting for many organizations when creative ideas are required, the first tool here is the brainstorm.

What is it? I've referred to the founder of CPS, 'father' of brainstorming and real-life 'Mad Man' Alex Osborn elsewhere in the book and his influence cannot be understated. Osborn formalized the brainstorming process to the one that we all know, which even today is still the default setting for many companies.

How to do it: I've run (and participated in) hundreds of brainstorms, with varying levels of success and I've come to the conclusion that there isn't one fail-safe way to run a brainstorm.

We all know the excitement and optimism that comes from a dynamic, successful session, and conversely the disappointment (and anxiety for the facilitator) induced by a session that's not working.

Research shows that unless they're properly planned and facilitated that brainstorms can be a waste of time. At their worst they are what the former head of the creative problem-solving unit at media planning agency Manning Gottlieb OMD and my fellow trainer Anahita describes as 'the untrained, leading the unwilling, to do the unnecessary' (Milligan, 2016).

One of the most frequently asked questions in workshops is whether there is an ideal number of people in a session. This is tricky because there are so many variables – we've successfully run them for 150 and had bad experiences with 5 people. Anahita says 'airtime' is a crucial consideration. If you have 1 hour and 10 people, and you subscribe to the 'shout out your ideas to the group method' (not one we advocate), then at absolute best, everyone will only have 6 minutes' airtime. However, not all personalities are equal! It's all in the planning, the exercises and the facilitation.

Why it works (or doesn't): As we've seen, companies like Pixar who have high creative output take advantage of collaboration. So what are the pros and cons of a standard group brainstorm and what are some alternatives?

All of the tools that follow can be used for group or individual ideation. I am assuming that as part of your process you will have done whatever aspects of the objective, fact and data finding from the CPS process and will feed that information when using these tools.

Figure 8.1

Table 8.1 Brainstorm pros and cons

Pros	Cons	Try this instead
Can harness diversity of thought.	Can lead to what psychologists call 'groupthink', where the group strives for consensus and harmony rather than disagreement, diluting ideas. Can lead to 'social loafing', where people make less effort or opt out in a group setting.	Include individual exercises. Work in creative pairs then bring a bigger group together to discuss the ideas generated.
Good for extroverts.	Harder for introverts unless good process is followed.	Have a 'silent' brainstorm (allocate individual exercises from the selection above) and allow some quiet time in the room. Or ask people to spend time beforehand and bring ideas to the brainstorm.

Table 8.1 *Continued*

Pros	Cons	Try this instead
An individual's ideas can be supported and developed by others.	Can damage an individual's confidence if badly managed.	Train people in facilitation skills to manage the process. Use IDEO rules.
Can generate ideas quickly and be done at short-notice.	Hard to allow for the crucial incubation phase.	Circulate your well-formed problem statement in advance or do a stand-up briefing at the end of the day then regroup in the morning.
Can generate lots of ideas.	Can be left with reams of flipchart paper that remain unsorted, unevaluated and, ultimately, lost.	Make sure the session is structured to allow for evaluation at key stages throughout. Use tech tools to collate and share information.
Getting people together in the office is quick and cost-free.	Some office spaces are uninspiring and drab.	Get out of the office and take a creative safari.

Problem-finding tools

Always the beautiful answer who asks a more beautiful question.
E E Cummings, poet, 1938

Great *questions* Q are at the heart of great ideas. The art of questioning is often a game of mental ping-pong between divergent and convergent thinking.

You're trying to open up and explore options, and to get the questions or problem statement right well before you start to try and generate ideas. You might want to generate lots of problem statements before you focus on those that look the most promising.

Asking the wrong questions can lead you down blind alleys, waste time and further confuse the issue. Often business briefings are filled with marketing jargon that, to quote ad agency stalwart and marketing expert Jeremy Bullmore, 'kills thought, strangles speculation, anaesthetizes the imagination' (2004).

Problem-finding tool 1: Generating an effective problem statement (Isaksen et al, 2011)

What is it? A CPS tool that helps to generate useful problem statements to open up ideas. With inexperienced facilitators I sometimes find that a brainstorm topic has not been written as a question, but as a statement or an objective. For example: stunt ideas for the World Cup or get more 'likes' on Facebook. This tool helps to overcome that.

How to do it: Follow this format to create potential problem statements. These may be informed by insight or data.

Write down your initial problem as you see it. Here's a working example of a challenge that I see every time I take a commuter train. The problem is that people often fall asleep on the train without having their ticket on display for the guard. How can we make people leave their ticket out?

1 *Start with an invitational stem* – this is a way of asking questions that 'opens up, or invites, many possible responses'. There are three suggested stems:

- How to...
- How might...
- In what ways might...

2 *Identify an owner* – This might be a specific person responsible for the problem or a company, for example: How might Loco Trains corporate communications team... In what ways might Loco Trains staff... In what ways might Loco Trains guards... How to encourage commuters to...

   By playing with the ownership you give yourself options. You can change the gender, the demographic, the age, to give you different (divergent) avenues.

3 *Have an action verb* – 'Identify a specific and positive course envisioned by the statement' (Isaksen *et al*, 2011).

   For example: 'In what ways might Loco Trains guard force/encourage/cajole/provoke/avoid/reward/persuade...

4 *An objective* – 'Identify the target or desired outcome and direction for your problem-solving activity' (Isaksen *et al*, 2011).

- In what ways might the Loco Train guard reward customers for showing their tickets, thus avoiding awkward customer interactions on the train?'
- How might the Loco Trains design team create a ticket holder that people actually want to have on display?

- How might female commuters on Loco Trains be persuaded to leave their ticket on display to avoid being woken up?
- How might you engage with Claire on the 6.05 am Loco train to London Waterloo and encourage her to display her ticket without prompting?

Changing the owner, the verb and the outcome (being specific and general) gives you different creative options and opens up different routes.

Forming a 'central question'

You can ask yourself whether from all the options you generate whether there is a 'central question?' One that takes priority over all the others and that gives you a clear way into your problem.

Who it's for? Anyone at the start of the creative process.

Good for: Ensuring that you're asking the right question. Checking that you have a well-formed problem if you're having difficulty generating ideas (often due to a poor question).

Not so good for: There's really no occasion when having a well-formed question will hinder your creative efforts!

Experience required: Creative rookie.

Problem finding tool 2: User empathy map

What is it? A widely used tool from design thinking and the world of user experience (UX). A structured way to plot what your target audience currently thinks, feels and does in relation to your problem or challenge on one page in order to highlight where you might be able to affect change.

How to do it: Do this before or in an ideas session to better get an idea of the consumer or customer. Simply split a piece of paper into four with a cross that runs from corner to corner.

In each of the four segments write one of the following: 'Say, do, think, feel. The idea is to spend a little time thinking about the customer's or consumer's world and writing things down in each segment.

- For 'say', that could be some quotes and defining words about him/her (ie 'confident').
- 'Do' is all about what actions you want them to do as a result of your activity or what they currently do.
- 'Think' is what your consumer might be thinking. What are the underlying beliefs?

- 'Feel' – what emotions they might feel now in relation to you problem. What do you want them to feel?

The next part is to think about what the target audience's 'pain points' might be – what is annoying, irritating or upsetting for them about the subject, product or area you're working in? You consider these pain points in order to generate 'gains' – where can your product or service or idea help?

Why it works: it's based on real needs and empathy, a deep understanding of the person for whom you are designing your product or service. It's a brilliantly simple way of trying to get into the consumer's head before trying to think up an idea intended to target a real need.

Who it's for: groups or individuals trying to find a place to start from in order to generate creative ideas, or a way to hone ideas you already have. One of our favourite ways to start devising strategy for campaigns.

Good for: plotting a lot of disparate customer data, using insights, getting into your customer or target audience's head. Finding an emotional trigger or genuine need. Can be done alone or in a group.

Not so good for: speedy idea generation (unless done before a workshop). Crunching massive amounts of data.

Experience required: Creative middleweight.

Problem-finding tool 3: one word

What is it? Distillation of your problem or challenge into a single word.

Back to Jeremy Bullmore, who says that: 'other people's imaginations need to be engaged, excited, signed on as accomplices' (2004). This isn't likely with a ubiquitous word like 'sales' or 'awareness'. But the word 'desire' or 'headline-grabbing' would begin to stimulate the creative juices better.

How to do it: Take a look at your problem statement(s).

- See if you can distil it/them down to just one word. You want what I would describe as a 'juicy', interesting word, so get the thesaurus out and play around with it.
- Does your word begin to get the heart of the matter?
- Ask your team-mates to do the same exercise ahead of a brainstorm or meeting. See what your collection of words is. It's often surprising how the same brief to a team of six reveals six very different words/themes.
- If you're working with any third parties, ask them to do the same thing or sanity check it with them *before* you head off into that territory.

Figure 8.2 User empathy map example

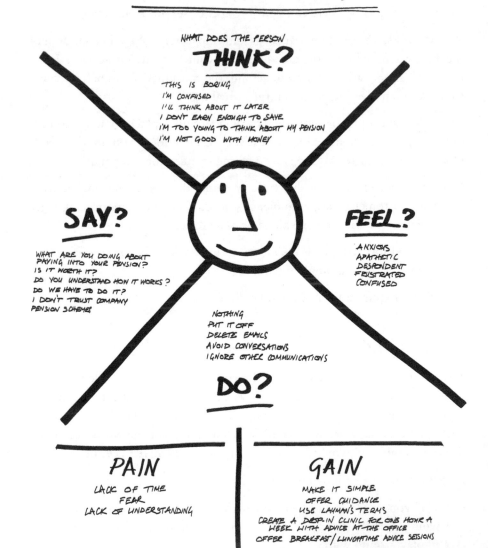

Why it works: Working in conjunction with your problem statement, what this tool does is make it really easy to dip into a 'related world' (see tool below) and find out how someone else – another brand, person or institution has dealt with your problem in the past. It focuses thinking and ensures you are targeting the right issue or highlights where a group is not in alignment.

Who it's for: Anyone who wants to get clarity on a given topic.

Good for: getting new perspective, developing strategy, focus and creative direction.

Not so good for: idea generation at speed.

Experience required: Creative middleweight (rookies just need to practise!).

Note: I have not been able to source the origins of this technique. I have adapted it over many years and believe that it was originally referenced by creativity expert Michael Michalko but is no longer available online.

Simplicity in practice

The Saatchis are probably the most famous names in UK advertising. Their agency, M&C Saatchi, uses the creative philosophy 'Brutal Simplicity of Thought' to inform everything it creates. Charles Saatchi explains: 'the phrase expresses our distaste for waffle and vagueness and a strong preference to get to the point... It separates the intellectual wheat from the chaff... simplicity is the outcome of technical subtlety; it is the goal, not the starting point. Now more than ever, because people are busier than ever, a precis is a modern form of good manners' (*The Guardian*, 2010).

If you try one word in conjunction with the empathy map or using your data, you might find that your word comes from that research. So the key emotion you want the audience to feel might be summarized by the one word 'happiness', or if it's to target a problem the word may be 'convenience'. Using the internal comms pension problem above the challenge could be summarized as perhaps 'fear' or 'apathy'. The comparethemarket.com meerkat campaign could be summarized into 'love'.

'Happiness' was the one-word strategy for Coca-Cola's marketing between 2009 and 2015, which was the filter for all its creative work, like the 'happiness vending machine' that gives you a hug. 'Convenience' is the jump-off point for Domino's' award-winning pizza emoji ordering system on Twitter which won the Titanium Grand Prix at Cannes Lions Festival of Creativity in 2015. Give it a try!

Here are some problem statements distilled into one word, and the ideas they sparked from real briefs:

1 Consumer brand problem statement: how do we start to make our marketing communications a dialogue with our customers, rather than a one-way flow of information from us to them?

- *Distilled into one word:* reciprocity.

- *Leading to creative ideas* about how give to and receive from one other, rather than just asking customers to give us what we want – leading to ideas about loyalty programmes; personalized products; a random act of kindness day for customers; tickets to events in exchange for participation; customer ideas published on our blog; our advertising airtime donated to a good cause; an ideas swap shop; 'ask us anything' days.

2 B2B business problem statement: how do we get our foot back in the door with lapsed customers?

Some of the issues that came up in discussion were relevance, price, forgotten, laziness, outdated, reinvigoration, love, ignorance, scale and trust.

- We distilled the challenge into one word: *love*. The problem was then restated as – how can we get our customers to love us again?

- This led to creative ideas that focused on the company making a big effort to woo customers back, as if they had fallen out of them with them or were in the early stages of a romance! We imagined what a dating ad would look like from both the brand and the customer's point of view. Was there anything in common? What passions could we tap into? This made us think about a difficult challenge from an unusual perspective giving us a fresh take.

Figure 8.3 Idea-finding tools

Idea-finding tools

Ideas are like rabbits. You get a couple and learn how to handle them, and pretty soon you have a dozen.
John Steinbeck, writer, 1947

Many creativity techniques use the principle of substitution to get a new perspective and stimulate new lines of thought. In this example you swap your current thinking for someone else's with often varied and surprising results.

Idea-finding tool 1: Identity theft

What is it? When you hit a brick wall, a brilliant way to inject a new spark into proceedings is to imagine how someone else would deal with your problem to get a fresh perspective.

How to do it:

- Create the list of people, dead or alive, fantasy or real in the session by writing the letters of the alphabet A-Z on a flip chart and asking people to shout out names of people who they want at their fantasy dinner party.

- There's no end to the list you can use, but some of our favourites are a gaggle of creative brains consisting of Barack Obama, a Hobbit and Lady Gaga. Any of these, we're pretty sure, would have an entirely new take on that marketing idea for your business, that new biscuit campaign or press release that has been leaving you scratching your head.

- Share your well-formed problem statement with the group. For example, how can we improve customer service? Pick one of your 'advisers', eg Lady Gaga. Ask yourself what would she do with your problem?

- Write down everything that comes to mind about it (don't worry whether or not it seems directly relevant at this stage) and try to use your own or the group's thoughts to generate more ideas and considerations.

- Choose the thought or idea that seems to have the most promise then brainstorm ideas about your subject for 5–10 minutes. Keep working through your panel, choosing a different adviser when you run out of steam. This is part of the tool's effectiveness – don't overthink it, just change it around when ideas dry up.

You can break into smaller teams to each take a different person and work through the challenge for 10 minutes, reporting back to the group.

Variation

Use different companies to give you a different perspective. What would Disney or Virgin or Apple do? Or use a customer profile or persona to imagine what they would do with your problem.

Why it works: We talk about 'not being able to see the wood for the trees'. Kyle Emich and Evan Polman ran four studies that all showed that distancing oneself from a problem had a positive effect on ideas. My experience is that it allows you and others to quickly and easily step out of your own way of thinking, and adopt another point of view. It allows distance from 'silly' or wild ideas because Kermit or Donald Trump thought it, not you.

Who it's for: This is a universally popular entry-level tool. It's good for straightforward problems and requires almost no prep in a group setting. It's deceptively simple but can have an amazing effect on idea generation. Work by yourself, in pairs or in smallish teams (around five).

Good for: it's quick, it's fun, you get a large volume of ideas, gives variety, gets you out of a rut.

Not good for: developing strategy or unravelling complex problems that may have many component parts. If you want to be more targeted, eg how to engender trust amongst our online banking customers, then you can use related worlds technique that follows to 'borrow' from a world where trust is important.

Experience required: Creative rookie.

Kapow! Wonder Woman meets banking

Superheroes can be a brilliant way to really take a detour from your own thinking. I worked with a banking client and we wanted to explore some new ways into an issue. We chose to imagine what Wonder Woman would do with our challenge. As unlikely as it sounds that this would bear any realistic ideas for such a corporate and traditional organization, we wrote down all the attributes of Wonder Woman – words like comic, transformation, secret identity, power, costume and immortality came to the fore. Her weapon – the lasso of truth rendered anyone she captured unable to lie.

We used the lasso as stimulus and it led us to consider what would happen if banks had to tell the truth to their customers, what would that mean for how they behaved and communicated? What would it mean if customers were given a forum to ask the hard questions of the bank and the truth had to be told? From these unlikely beginnings we explored the concept of improving transparency and authenticity between the bank and its customers, an idea which we refined and discussed with the bank.

Tip: you don't always have to share where the idea came from, particularly in more conservative settings. This idea was rooted in a genuine business issue for the bank, we just used the stimuli to take a mental detour.

Idea-finding tool 2: Related worlds

What is it? This technique assumes that somewhere in the world your problem (or a version of it) has been faced, and solved. You brainstorm similar but different 'worlds' to get new ideas.

How to do it:

- Ask yourself: exactly what is the problem to be solved? For example: going back to our earlier B2B business problem statement: how do we get our foot back in the door with lapsed customers?

- If we restate that as: how to generate desire for our products and services?

- Ask yourself, where else in the world has a brand or individual solved this challenge (or any variation of)?

- Who is good at creating desire?

- How about Apple, Chanel or Mercedes? Choose one, eg Chanel and then explore that related world to see what you can 'borrow' to bring back to your task.

- So Chanel has beautiful packaging, is expensive, exclusive, luxury, limited availability, has waiting lists, does a catwalk show twice a year, creates access points via 'cheaper' products like perfume.

- Can you take any of these to apply back to your real territory? Leading to ideas like:

  - Could we create a sales offer that has very limited availability?

  - What's our equivalent of a catwalk show? How can we show off what we're selling in a different way?

- Perhaps we can create an invite-only event where there is an opportunity for customers to network and see the advances in our 'collection' – get hands-on with technology or see what we have planned for the future. We could do it somewhere unusual (think Chanel's supermarket show).

- The Chanel catwalk show is twice a year – what seasonal approach could you take to talking to your customers? Chanel creates beautiful visuals and Instagram opportunities.

- Chanel collaborates with different people and organizations like musician Pharrell Williams and H&M. Who could you work with to give you extra appeal to your customers?

Why it works: This tool uses analogy to compare one thing with another and allows you to put distance between you and the problem to find new ways into the challenge.

Possible worlds to explore: Politics, sport, nature, film, food, another country, another culture, history

Who's it for? For anyone who wants to get out of their own category or bust industry conventions.

Good for: mitigating risks by considering what's successfully worked elsewhere. Getting out of a rut when you keep revisiting what you always do in a given situation.

Not so good for: ideas at breakneck speed.

Experience required: Creative middleweight.

CASE STUDY   What's our equivalent to turning the lights off?

It's easy to think that an idea must be completely new to the world to be radical, but an existing idea can be groundbreaking if applied in a different context. NHS Change Day shows how two related words inspired a game-changing idea in another space.

The NHS campaign was informed by Marshall Ganz's organizing principles for empowering social movements (adopted by the Obama for his presidential campaign) and #Earth Hour, the highly successful World Wildlife Fund (WWF) global initiative that encourages people to turn off their lights for just one hour to show they care about the planet.

Figure 8.4 The Related Worlds tool explores where else in the world your problem may have been tackled and what you can borrow to bring back to your challenge

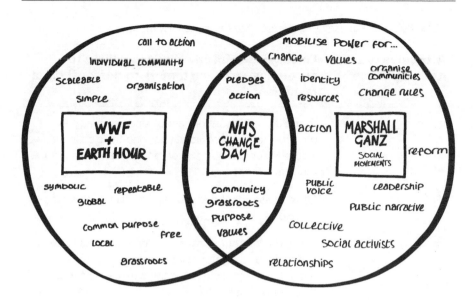

Idea-finding tool 3: Random stimulus

What is it? Anything at all that is used to stimulate ideas or make connections; often objects, images or words.

How to do it:

- Make like a magpie and gather ephemera from your weekend: ticket stubs, a pine cone, a menu, postcard, a picture you took.

- Keep them in a box wherever you work and bring it out when you need a new angle in a brainstorm. Or ask people to bring an object with them to a workshop.

- Either let people take an item randomly or have a selection of items on a tray for people to make their own connections to an item. Frame the question for using the random stimuli, eg this item is like... (the area you are exploring)... because... What does this item/word tell us about our challenge?

- If someone is blocked, move on and come back to them. Remind people that first thoughts are good enough! Keep going with this until you feel you have something new to explore.

You can also get the participants to list the attributes of the item. So if you had a rose, you might list these attributes, which inspire related ideas:

Table 8.2 How to use random stimuli to generate new ideas

Attributes of the item, eg a rose.	Forcing ideas for my challenge: 'how to encourage more customers to our local pizza restaurant?'
kindness	Come up with a random act of kindness day every month where you could pay for one table's dinner as a surprise or just complimentary drinks or dessert to regulars on that day.
gift	Offer a giftcard where you can buy dinner and wine for two.
scent	Focus on different senses – to focus on smell offer a blind-folded tasting or even one course. Create a menu that indulges each of the senses separately in different courses.
only last a week	Create an offer that is short-lived. Create a week-long themed Italian/pizza festival and offer pizza-making classes, food demonstrations, tastings and activities.
love	Who *really* loves your pizza? Create a club for your regulars/biggest fans and give them exclusive offers or one-off supper club invites with bragging rights and freebies.
thorns	Are there thorny issues that you are not tackling? What are you ignoring?

Why it works: If you agree with Steve Jobs that creativity is 'just connecting things' (1996) then you need to find more things to connect! The clue is in the name – by adding in a random aspect to your thinking you cannot predict the outcome and you will make unexpected and unusual connections. We also think in metaphor and our *unconscious mind* Um will make connections for us.

USING RANDOM STIMULI – REAL-WORLD EXAMPLE

One of my favourite examples of how this tool can bring fresh thinking to a challenge comes from pioneering food brand Pret A Manger, a company that revolutionised lunch on the high street 30 years ago (established in 1986) when there wasn't yet an avocado or a crayfish in sight. The operations team at Pret were familiar with the random stimulus technique,

Figure 8.5 Pret's Joy of Pret initiative was inspired using random stimuli

as part of their Academy training, to enable them to look at problems and challenges from a different perspective. One of Pret's values is to develop a 'happy teams and happy customers', through acts of kindness that drives great customer service. While brainstorming a name for their initiative to allow this value to be embraced in the shops, like offering a free coffee for a regular or deserving customer, the team had a seemingly unlikely piece of random stimulus. The book *The Joy of Sex* initially made the group laugh but with further discussion sparked the name for the initiative, 'The Joy of Pret'. It's a great example of how a team's willingness to be playful and experiment can lead to useful business ideas.

Variation: deliberate stimulus'. Bring in stimulus that has a bearing on your business challenge or problem. I was asked to help a local government department with ideas for their annual winter road safety campaign. The team felt that they constantly re-visited what worked but needed some fresh ideas. Since they often worked with senior members of the council they did not feel that they could use random stimulus and for it to be considered credible. So we decided to use a collection of images associated with the season as stimuli – from snowball fights to skids left in the road following an accident on an icy road. This gave the group new stimuli and perspectives on an old challenge. I often use business trend data from sites like www. springwise.com or www.trendwatching.com in this way to being a seemingly unrelated but fresh piece of information to a business issue.

Random word association is a well-known take on this technique.

Good for: getting your brain warmed up, speed, high volume of ideas, variety, getting out of a rut. It's fun. Also helpful for developing existing ideas or products. Working by yourself.

Not so good for: devising strategic solutions, very serious or corporate environments without some explanation. Individuals who like a very logical process.

Experience required: Creative rookie.

Figure 8.6 The avocado word cloud from Chapter 4 shows us how we can throw up unexpected and creative links between disparate thoughts, concepts and memories

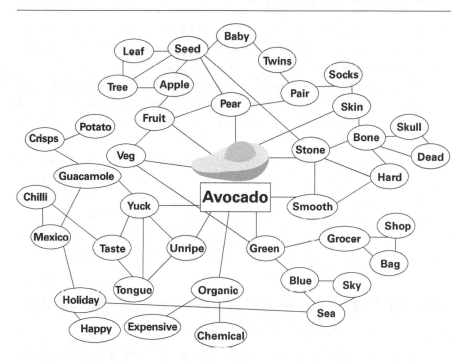

Idea-finding tool 4: break glass in case of creative emergency!

Nine thought-provoking questions to get you out of a creative rut quickly. Ask:

- What ideas do you already have?
- What's the fun thing to do?
- What's the easiest thing to do?
- What's the fastest thing to do?
- What's the bravest thing to do?
- What's the provocative thing to do?' (Bungay Stanier, 2010)
- What's the counter-intuitive thing to do?
- What would your competitors do/never do?
- What would get you fired?

They may forget what you said – but they will never forget how you made them feel.
Carl W Buehner, Mormon preacher, 1971

Using *emotion* [Em] as the lens through which to view your challenge offers a rich seam for creativity and many variations. This is one of my favourite ways to crack a problem.

Think about the last time you responded to a piece of communication, an ad, a direct mailer, an experience or shared a piece of viral content. Or a story that you told someone about a product? Why did you share it? Was it because it stirred an emotion?

Content analysts at Buzzsumo analysed the top 10,000 articles shared online over a given period, and mapped them to a corresponding emotion. The most shared were: awe (25 per cent), laughter (17 per cent), amusement (15 per cent) and joy (14 per cent). The least shared were anger (6 per cent), empathy (6 per cent), surprise (2 per cent) and sadness (1 per cent) (Ordork, 2014). It's an interesting lens through which to generate new ideas.

Idea-finding tool 5: Adapted from new emotion, good fortune (Eat Big Fish, 2010)

What is it? Use different emotions as a way to generate ideas, substituting one for another. It's a simple, but powerful tool based on human behaviour and it opens up many different options.

How to do it:

- Think about something that you're currently working or that you want to generate ideas for. Or take an existing idea you've already developed. Does it currently evoke any emotion? What is it?

- Is it the same emotion as you want your target audience to feel when they think about your product, service or idea?

- You can try taking an emotion and substituting it for another, less obvious one to generate fresh ideas. I first came across this way of thinking on the brilliant Eat Big Fish website and I have adapted and used it many times over the years to generate ideas.

- Eat Big Fish (eatbigfish.com, 2010) suggest that you want to find 'a genuinely new emotion that would surprise, disrupt and provoke... If this emotion was forced into the heart of your identity, if it governed everything that you do, how would your behaviour change?'

- Think about how the following emotions could inspire ideas to make your audience: happy, delighted, joyful, curious, lustful, fearful, angry, surprised?

Ask yourself:

- 'How would introducing this emotion change the way your consumers experience your existing products and services?
- What would it mean to use this emotion as a brief for new product or services development?
- What new usage occasion, distribution opportunities and brand partnerships might this new emotion help to create?' (See eatbigfish.com, 2010.)

Why it works: Often we think about things from the point of view of our product or service or company rather than the end user. There's an emotional convention in a category too that we may be following. This would fall into the 'cliché' section of Heineken's creative ladder that we saw in Chapter 1. Consider the banking sector we referred to earlier – trust is the emotion banks want to instil, but fear, suspicion and mistrust would be more typical of the sector. First Direct set out to bust some of those conventions with its humorous and quirky personality and in the process changed the sector forever.

Who it's for: Anyone wanted to explore the benefits of leveraging a range of emotional triggers for any kind of campaign.

Variation

Find an emotion wheel online, print it off and laminate it. This will provide you with emotional fodder aplenty.

Good for: thinking strategically about what your idea, product or service is trying to achieve.

Not so good for: rookie facilitators or inexperienced groups – it can take a bit of practice to flex this particular muscle – but try and it keep practising!

Experience required: Creative middleweight/Ninja

Another take on using emotion comes from Jonah Berger's brilliant *Contagious: Why things catch on* (2013). Evaluating thousands of *New York Times* articles Berger has documented why some ideas go 'viral' and others don't.

Idea-finding tool 6: Get to your emotional core (Berger, 2013)

What is it? Berger's exercise to help you get to what he calls your company's 'emotional core' to engage with your target audience.

How to do it: Berger writes: 'If finding the emotional core is tricky, you can try asking the *Three Whys*:

- First, why do people use your product or idea?
- Second, why do they want or need that?
- Third, why do they want or need that?'

List three ways you could use either existing or new emotions to drive people to talk about your product or idea.

Why it works: Berger found that emotions are key to shareable content. He says 'when we care, we share. High arousal emotions – like excitement, anger, and awe – fire people up. This activation, in turn, drives them to share'. We saw from the IPA's research in Chapter 4 that emotional engagement and messaging is far more powerful than rational messaging.

Who it's for: individual or group work. In groups give people or pairs different emotions to consider and work on, then bring them back to the session.

Good for: creating shareable content ideas. Thinking about what currently moves your target audience and how you can leverage their feelings to motivate them to take the action you're looking for. It's simple but can yield excellent insights and ideas.

Not so good for: quick idea generation.

Experience required: Creative middleweight.

Storytelling is also key to shareable content, according to Berger. Here are four ways to think about it

> *Stories are like Trojan Horses: Information travels under the guise of idle chatter. People are more likely to share a memorable story than a list of technical facts and features about a product.*
> **Jonah Berger**

Storytelling is one of the oldest forms of sharing information. But how do you go about practically telling stories for your brand, product or service or yourself?

I love storytelling, as it is a great way to generate creative ideas and find angles on your problem that you may never have considered.

Idea-finding tool 7: Think like a Chief Creative Officer

Petra Sammer is a best-selling author and expert on storytelling, as well as Chief Creative Officer for international PR agency Ketchum Europe. She says that, 'stories set your whole brain to work'. Here are her top three ways which she should with me to help bring your story to life.

1 Change the perspective.

How to do it: You read a story to the group of participants in a brainstorm. For example a brand story or the story of the foundation of a company. Now group into smaller teams of two or three. Each team has to rewrite the story from a different perspective, eg from the perspective of the founder's wife or from the perspective of a child. Share these back with the group.

What do you get? New story angles and lots of fun.

2 Change the tone and style.

How to do it: Read a story to the group of participants in a brainstorm. For example, a brand story or the story of the foundation of a company, as above. Each participant (or small groups) has to rewrite this story using different styles, eg as a graphic novel, as a photo story, as a love story or as a western. Pick your favourite genre or try one of the story plots above. Share these back with the group.

What do you get? A new look and feel for your brand's story. More fun.

3 Transform a speech.

How to do it: Many presentations and speeches are written in 'corporate language' – long and complex sentences and so on. The brainstorming group has to listen to a speech or video and will also get the script. Their task is to rewrite the speech with 'normal' words. Transform the presentation into ordinary language (how you would talk to your baker, friend or your mum).

What do you get? Storytelling needs 'normal' language and many managers have forgotten to use this kind of language in business (or they shy away as they think they sound 'stupid' when they talk frankly and simply). So they need to practise doing so amongst their colleagues. It sounds easy. But it isn't.

Idea finding tool 8: Think like Pixar!

What is it? Emma Coats is a former storyboard artist and director at Pixar who worked on the movies *Brave* and *Monsters University*, amongst others. A few years ago she shared some of what she'd learned with her series of Tweets which make up her *Pixar's 22 Rules of Storytelling* It's brilliant advice for any budding writer and can also be applied as creative ways to get over blocks or think about your problem in a new way. For example:

Rule 8 'Finish your story, let go even if it's not perfect. In an ideal world you have both, but move on. Do better next time.' A great piece of advice for any creative.

Rule 22 'What's the essence of your story? Most economical telling of it? If you know that, you can build out from there'. This rule chimes with the one word technique above – cut to the essence of your brief, your problem and your target audience's needs.

We're going to play with Coats' **rule 4.** She writes that all Pixar stories have the six-sentence structure below.

How to do it: Take each of the sentence starters in turn and use them to inspire and shape your story.

- Once upon a time there was ___.
- Every day, ___.
- One day ___.
- Because of that, ___.
- Because of that, ___.
- Until finally ___.

The first time you do this just play with it. Try and write a story about something, anything using the structure. This is a good exercise to warm up with in a group brainstorming session.

Next try using the story structure to help shape and challenge your thinking about your product, service or existing story. Think about writing the story from the point of view of one of your customers (perhaps an existing happy or dissatisfied one) or a potential customer.

Why it works: It uses the story structure as a constraint in which to direct your thinking. It explores the consequences of actions and it can give you a totally fresh perspective. If it's good enough for Pixar....

Good for: warming up your brain. Someone once asked me for tips on how to 'procrastinate creatively' – voila! Getting a totally fresh angle. Using a constraint to help think about your problem in a fresh way. Envisioning what you want (or don't want) in the future.

Not so good for: a facilitator lacking confidence, a closed-minded group, ready-made answers. You'll need to use what you create as a jump-off point for your ideas.

Experience required: creative rookie alone, creative middleweight in a group

Figure 8.7

Solution-finding tools

The key question is never what the idea is, but what the idea has to do.
Dean Poole, Creative Director, 2016

Think about the last time you thought something was creative. What was it?

What criteria did you apply to decide whether it was creative?

The envy factor is often how I judge creative ideas – when I think, 'ooh, I wish I'd thought of that!' If you read Chapter 4 on the creative mind, you'll recognize that our first reaction is *always* emotional (system 2), based on what we feel, rather than on logic (system 1).

As Barry J Gibb writes in *The Rough Guide to the Brain* (2007):

> ... as the mind moves through a number of possible choices, it is the emotions that give the thumbs up or down, by fleetingly providing an insight into how the consequences of a specific choice would make us feel. However much it goes against our conception of ourselves as rational creatures, the role of the emotions in decision-making cannot be overstated.

Knowing that this is all going on unconsciously, these tools offer practical advice to balance emotional and logical thinking.

Being objective matters whether you're a scientist, a judge, a fashion designer or a marketer. Reviewing ideas is 'where personal tastes and preferences can collide with process and consensus. It requires imagination, leadership and trust. Inevitably it leads to conflict' (IPA, 2005).

Solution finding tool 1: Evaluation matrix (Isaksen et al, 2011)

What is it? A systematic tool from the CPS process for judging more fully formed ideas against pre-agreed criteria.

How to do it: Create a matrix. Create a list of the options you want to assess and write them down the left-hand side of the matrix. Identify the criteria you're using to evaluate your options and write these along the top of the matrix. Choose a scoring system that makes sense to you eg 0–10.

'It is important to go down the (vertical) columns, rather than across the (horizontal) rows. If you were to select your favourite option and work across all the criteria, you might score this option higher because of a halo effect' (Isaksen *et al*, 2011).

It helps to frame the options and criteria into a sentence that you can systematically work through. 'If… to what extent will it…?' (Isaksen, 2011).

Why it works: The matrix can be used not just as a simple 'numbers game' to assess your ideas but also to evaluate whether an idea has strengths or weaknesses. This should enable you to potentially improve upon them.

Who's it for? Anyone who wants to evaluate a list of options or ideas in more detail without shutting down any possibilities.

Experience required: Creative rookie

I've also used Edward De Bono's well-known *Six Thinking Hats* – a tried and tested way to get different perspectives. It's widely available online and worth trying if you haven't already.

Solution-finding tool 2: Murder Board (Michalko, 2006)

What is it? Borrow from the CIA and convene a 'murder board': a posse of people who have had nothing to do with the concept whose aim is to 'terminate' bad ideas.

How to do it: Get your board to mercilessly critique your idea, find holes with it and bombard you with difficult questions. The aim is to either kill the idea if it is fatally flawed or to make it more robust if it has potential. If you don't address awkward questions at some point in the process you can bet your life that someone further down the line will!

Who's it for? Anyone wanting to find holes in their ideas.

What it's good for: when your ideas have been developed past the embryonic stage. When you want an unemotional, honest, outside opinion.

Not so good for: the early stages of the creative process when ideas are still fragile.

Experience required: Creative rookie.

REAL-WORLD MURDER BOARD

I like to get to three or four concepts that are pretty well formed before exposing them to a potentially grizzly death. A few years ago, when preparing for a big pitch, I created a war-room and invited everyone in the business to come and act as the murder board for the six ideas we'd worked up. We asked everyone to pop by for just five minutes during their day to add questions and remarks to the ideas pasted around the room. By the end of the day we had six ideas that had been exposed to over 30 different potential assassins and we killed a few and revived others. We won that pitch (worth £1 million, delivered in 10 slides), I'm sure due, in no small part, to opening the ideas up to that level of scrutiny.

Solution-finding tool 3: My master checklist

Informed by the definitions in Chapter 1 and concepts discussed throughout the book, here are some of my favourite questions to ask when you're assessing your own or someone else's ideas.

- Is it novel or new? Give it an out of 10 rating.
- Is the idea surprising? Give it an out of 10 rating.
- Who is the idea valuable to?
- Does it have a story?
- Is there any higher purpose to the idea?
- Is it contagious?
- Will it get people talking?
- Will it impact culture?
- Does it meet the original brief and objectives?
- Is it feasible?
- Is it on budget?
- Will it change anything?
- Does it have longevity?

Have a think about what questions you would add to standardize your idea evaluation.

Technology and the future

This next section explores the impact of technology on creative thinking and considers what the brainstorm of the future might look like. Thirty years ago, the internet barely existed. Now technology is everywhere, in the digital tools that we all use on a daily basis in our laptops and phones, and this gives us access to creative inspiration and tools as never before. Dr Sara Jones, Senior Lecturer, Creative Interactive System Design at the Cass Business School in London shared some of her favourite tech tools with me. 'Technology is ever-changing and so the specifics of exactly what tech tools to use for creativity are also constantly changing. Who knows where developments in AI, robotics, internet of things, big data and block chain technology will take us over the next thirty years? Here, I've made some general suggestions about how to choose your tools, and given examples of where current tools can help.'

How to choose your tool

'So first, when choosing a tech tool, always consider which parts of your creative process a digital tool or technology could help with, and which you should perhaps still leave to the humans (see 'could a robot do my job?). Computers are great at processing, storing and letting you search through huge amounts of information, but not so great, yet anyway, at empathy, emotion, and being creative without human assistance. 'When is it worth using digital pens, Post-its or whiteboards, and when should you stick with the old-school versions?'

'Digital pens, for use on whiteboards, tablets or plain old paper have come a long way in the last few years, but all still require at least some set-up, and few have the familiarity and flexibility of the non-digital equivalent in terms of immediate ease of use. Digital Post-its now also come in many forms with increasingly sophisticated functionality, with some tools, like Post-it Plus, offering perhaps the best of both worlds, in which you can write down your ideas using old-school pen and Post-it style paper, but then capture these digitally. This enables you to share ideas with colleagues who missed the session they were generated in, reorganize them on the fly, and incorporate them into future digital project documentation.

'A final consideration is the extent to which a tool has been specifically developed to support creative processes. Of course, a lot can often be gained from using everyday digital tools, for media sharing, communication, project planning and the like, in a creative way, as part of a creative process, and in the context of a creative climate, as discussed elsewhere in the book. But an increasing number of tools are more or less explicitly aimed at supporting creative professionals. Tools like Canva, a free graphic / content design programme, allows you to quickly and easily pull together slick, brilliantly designed presentations, posters, blog posts and graphics with no design skill required (www.canva.com) can be really useful.

'There are also several online mind-mapping tools, including Coggle (https://coggle.it), Stormboard (www.stormboard.com) and Popplet (http://popplet.com) that allow you to share ideas online, perhaps after a creative session. Search tools, like Yossarian (https://yossarianlives.com) offer a more creative approach to searching for information online than more conventional alternatives.

'Digital tools aimed specifically at supporting creative processes can be categorized based on the work of creativity researcher Todd Lubart (2005) who suggested that computer-based tools could enhance creativity in four different ways: by acting as nannies (who help with things like project planning), pen pals (who make it easier to communicate your ideas), colleagues (who help you generate ideas when you're stuck), or coaches (providing information about potentially useful techniques that you might want to use on your project). In the rest of this section, I've focused on tools that can act as coaches and colleagues.'

Tool: Digital coaches

What is it? 'Several digital tools are available to help you choose what other tools and techniques you want to use for your creative process, and offer guidance on how to do this. The Creative Whack Pack app, based on the work of Roger von Oech or the IDEO Method cards app, based on methods included in IDEO's design thinking approach, both give instructions for different creative thinking techniques and are available on your smartphone. The becreative service available at http://becreative.city.ac.uk makes suggestions for what techniques to use when, as well as guidance on how to use them.'

How to do it: 'Just download the app or visit the website and start playing!'

Who's it for? 'Just about anyone.'

What do you need? 'A smartphone or access to a web browser.'

What do you get? 'Advice on how to use a range of creative tools and techniques, and sometimes also advice on what tools or techniques might work particularly well for you and your creative process.'

Experience required: Creative rookie.

Tool: Digital colleagues

What is it? 'Almost every week new apps and websites appear, all of which are designed to help you use some of the tried and tested creative thinking techniques and tools that you already know. Some of these just provide what you need to use the technique in digital form, for convenience – like the Brightsparks tool, available from http://brightsparks.city.ac.uk that provides everything you need to use the Hall of Fame technique. Others do some of the hard work for you. For example, the Carer tool (Maiden *et al*, 2013), designed to help carers of people with dementia come up with creative solutions to challenging situations in care homes, uses natural language processing and case based reasoning to find creative solutions to problems by searching a large database of examples of best practice in related areas.'

How to do it: 'For some of these tools, such as Brightsparks, you can just download the app or visit the website. To use others, like Carer, you need more specific knowledge of the subject area they have been designed to be used in.'

Who's it for? 'Some are suitable for just about anyone, some work better for professionals working in particular areas.'

What do you need? 'Usually a smartphone, tablet, or access to a web browser.'

What do you get? 'Help with generating creative ideas.'

Experience required: Creative rookie or creative middleweight.

CASE STUDY   Brainstorm of the future?

Duane Holland, Founder at Cross-Discipline Creative Consultancy, DH READY is working with University College, London (UCL) on AGENCY 2030, a project exploring how science, technology and culture will impact the marketing landscape of the future. He told me how emerging technologies could impact idea generation and brand experiences.

'There are many new technologies that can enhance the overall creative output for individuals and groups. One specific area is the correlation between environments and mood enhancement, which can be hugely powerful in identifying, enabling or sharing people's psychological and emotional states. The Centre of Advanced Spatial Analysis (CASA) at UCL developed an experiment that used EEG technology to track brainwaves in an office that was then represented as colours to show people's true mood such as happiness, sadness or anxiety. The colours became an indicator to other people in the office helping them emotionally connect with that person without using words. Taking the same application, imagine if we organized brainstorms when people felt most creative and not at scheduled times. Using brainwave technology we could pull people in during their 'golden hour' (optimal time) rather than being distracted by other psychological detractors that could impact on their creative ability.

Taking future technologies further, a recent study called 'beaming' explored the idea of teleportation and successfully transported a real person, to a real location, in real-time using combined emerging technologies and methods, such as virtual reality, augmented reality, haptics (applying touch to interact with computer systems), neuroscience, robotics and 360-degree cameras. This opens up the opportunity for individuals and groups to take part on 'telepresence tours'; journeying through new spaces and meeting new people to find new ideas and inspiration when geographic distance and access is no longer a barrier. Imagine a brainstorm session for a fashion brand where you could visit and observe street wear tribes in Harajuku, Williamsburg and Berlin all in an hour.

There are early signs that this is already happening with 'mini-beam' case examples in the automobile industry with McLaren's elite VR systems and Mercedes' 'virtual showrooms', to the leisure and entertainment worlds with Marriott Hotels' 'Magic of Miles' teleporter hubs – a 4D virtual travel experience allowing people to leap from one holiday destination to another using 'Oculus Rift'.

This final section brings the toolkit together, and we'll hear how a sales team is using the tools in practice.

For anyone wanting a bit more information on how the tools work together, here's my typical approach:

For a written brief I read it once fully, then re-read it, armed with a high-lighter. I pull out key phrases, try and identify gaps in the brief or my own knowledge. I have a pack of Post-its and Sharpies and I write key issues, insights from the brief or words that I think are important; one per Post-it and start my 'crazy wall'. My mind will start fizzing with possible solutions but I try and keep myself in check a little while I establish what the problem I need to work on really is.

Often I will use the empathy map to help me get inside the target audience's head in relation to the problem. That might throw up more gaps or new information and insights in terms of where they are now and where we want them to be and so what the real problem is.

I'll do some desk-research and fact-finding. Again, I'll create notes and ideas, one per Post-it as I go. All this gets added to the crazy wall. At some point I will establish whether I have enough information to proceed into generating ideas.

I write down my problem statement and play around with this using the tools below to get different versions of it.

Different problem statements can take you off into different creative directions. So I have to decide whether I'll pursue several or whether one seems most appropriate (if you work in a team or with a client you can sanity check with them). This highlights gaps and assumptions and can start to identify (or rule out) creative territories.

Once I've landed on a problem statement I'm happy with I distil the problem down into one word.

I often do a good old-fashioned SWOT (Strengths, Weaknesses, Opportunities and Threats analysis) to get the key information in one place. Then there's the 'so what' factor with all the information. What does the data tell me?

With my problem statement, one word and research I leave it alone a while. This is where Webb Young's 'tentacles of the mind' (1965) come into play or the element of the 'wandering mind'. My colleague Elizabeth uses the metaphor of a child's snowglobe for this phase – throwing everything up and seeing where and how it settles. If you don't like where it lands you can shake it again.

This detailed preparation should you give a strategy and a clear direction from which to take your creative ideas. The next stage is where idea generation tools help. If I'm finding ideas difficult it is often because the question is poorly formed or the brief is missing something. Revisiting that often helps.

My favourite tool is using emotion to generate ideas because it's rooted in basic human needs and motivations. If I have to be creative in a very short time frame I go for a Creative Safari (with a well-formed question primed in my head) or use related worlds.

My weakness is the nitty-gritty of evaluating the ideas. But it must be done so I almost always use Michalko's (2006) 'murder board' (asking what would my worst enemy and brand competitors say about the ideas). I also force myself to use the CPS evaluation matrix to add logic to my emotional responses.

To end this chapter, here's how one business is using the tools day today.

CASE STUDY   Creativity on demand at Sky Media

Sky Media is the advertising sales arm for broadcaster Sky, representing over 130 channels across entertainment, news and movies. Working in a highly competitive sales environment, the Creative Solutions team of 8 is responsible for answering around 40 proactive and reactive responses briefs from media agencies and brands every month. This is in addition to live deals where the team is evolving campaigns that are running or in production or development.

With a vast number of possible channel, platform and buying options, from straight spot sales to sponsorship, product placement and branded content, the team need to be nimble and creative thinkers – and they need to do it at speed. Jason Hughes heads up the Creative Solutions team who have been trained in a variety of problem solving tools (including some of those included here) to tackle the briefs. Jason told me what difference using tools has made to the creative output of the team.

'It's provided more of a focus having a toolkit to use. It's not so much had an impact on the quantity but certainly the quality and focus of thinking has improved. It's also made idea generation more structured. It's a common trap to fall into going straight to a disorganized brainstorm and the tools help prevent that from happening. There's no doubt individuals who regularly practice the techniques become more at ease and more confident with their ability to generate ideas.'

Which tools are particularly useful?

'Identity theft is the most popular and you do observe the occasional brainstorm where people are picking people like Donald Trump or brands like Apple to think laterally.'

Have there been any challenges in terms of implementing process and tools?

'In all honesty what it needs is for it to become a habit. Like all big businesses focus and priorities move and change which has meant keeping the momentum and enthusiasm up beyond the core evangelists becomes a challenge. There does need to be a level of pragmatism with how this is adopted in larger organizations.

Time is still a significant barrier. If there are unreasonable time pressures placed on you by an agency or client then more often than not it will hamper the best ideas coming through. That said, the tools provide a good platform from which to quickly generate good ideas without immediately narrowing the creative funnel of possibilities.'

What advice do you have for anyone leading the creative charge in their business?

Take time to always take a step back from everything and see the bigger picture – how far have you turned the dial, has there been improvement? Have trust and confidence in your team and let them grow and learn from their projects without interference, coaching is better than instruction – don't micro manage but at the same time don't over-delegate.

Table 8.3 Review the creative tools

Tool	Key questions	Rate the tool out of 10 in terms applicability to your work. Diarize a time to try some of the tools that are new to you.
Brainstorm.	How can you manage and plan your brainstorms to incorporate tools, navigate different personalities and tailor them to best meet your challenge?	
Problem statement.	Have you explored the problem sufficiently and crafted a compelling problem statement?	
Empathy map.	Ask questions relating to the target audience relating to their personal needs.	
One word.	Boil the problem down to its essence.	
Identity theft.	Who can help you find a new angle on the challenge?	
Related worlds.	Where else in the world has another person or company solved your problem?	
Random stimuli.	What stimuli can you use to add a new and unknown element into your thinking?	

Table 8.3 *continued*

Tool	Key questions	Rate the tool out of 10 in terms applicability to your work. Diarize a time to try some of the tools that are new to you.
Break glass in creative emergency.	Use these provocations to get you out of a creative jam.	
New emotion, good fortune.	How can you generate ideas using different emotions?	
Get to your emotional core.	Why should anyone care about your idea or product?	
Change perspective, change tone and style, transform a speech.	Can you create an interesting, shareable story for your product or service using the storytelling methods?	
Think like Pixar.	How can you use a simple story structure to inspire your thinking?	
Murder board.	What would your worst critics say about your idea?	
Evaluation matrix.	Systematically evaluate your options	
Checklist.	Use these or develop your own to decide how you'll evaluate ideas.	
Technology.	Are you up to speed with the latest technologies to help you be creative?	

REVIEW THE CHAPTER

Reflect on the tools in this chapter:

- Do you have new tools in your arsenal and a better understanding of how and when to use them?
- Which creativity tool appeals most?
- When can you try and incorporate a new tool into your kit to generate ideas?
- How confident do you feel about trying something new?
- Is there one new tool you could try *today* that would have a positive impact on your team and business?
- Are there any barriers to using tools with your team or company? What can you do to overcome them?

IN A NUTSHELL

This whole book is about the art and the science of creativity and in my opinion facilitating and using tools, particularly for groups, is definitely where these two things collide. As we've seen, there are many different ways to think about what creativity tool might fit your challenge, not least establishing the kind of ideas that you need and cutting your cloth accordingly.

Keep pushing yourself to try new things, even if they don't work first time. Using a new tool for the first time is just like learning guitar chords, or trying out a new recipe; you just have to go for it and keep practising until you are cooking with gas!

DIG DEEPER

Berger, J (2013) *Contagious: Why things catch on*, Simon & Schuster, New York

Isaksen, S G, Dorval, K B and Treffinger D J (2011) *Creative Approaches To Problem Solving*, 3rd edn, Sage, London

Michalko, M (2006) *Thinkertoys: A handbook of creative-thinking techniques*, 2nd edn, Ten Speed Press; California

Putting it all together

Change will not come if we wait for some other person or if we wait for some other time. We are the ones we've been waiting for.
Barack Obama, 2008

Hey, well done – you made it this far!

Or maybe you just cut straight to the chase by coming to this chapter first. Either way I want to make it easy for you to make sense of it all – so here's the bottom line on putting it all together.

> With self-awareness you have a **50:50** chance of demonstrating self-management; you only have a 4 per cent chance without it. (Burckle and Boyatzis, 1999)

This chapter is jam-packed with coaching questions and tips to help unlock your own creative potential or that of your team or organization. So let's crack on!

So where do you want to focus?

1 your individual creativity;
2 helping teams to be more creative;
3 creating a climate for organizational creativity.

There are several ways to use this chapter.

Just show me the money!

Skip straight to our advice as to what to do next. Based on the research and elements discussed throughout the book I've suggested a potential creativity formula for individuals, teams, organizations and leaders.

If you want to review your strengths and weaknesses, based on your reflections following the exercises in the book, and consider your own personal formula, then you can do that too.

Review your strengths and weaknesses

You may have systematically worked through the coaching questions and experiments, or dipped into the areas of most interest to you. As you've worked through the book you'll have considered:

- What are you great at already? Let's figure out how you can play even more to your strengths.

- Where are your blind spots? More focus could give you a big return on your creative investment. After all, getting out of your comfort zone is the essence of creativity!

- Come on in, the water's lovely.

If you've worked your way through the various chapters and recorded your thoughts then write your scores from the tables into the grid below.

You'll record the two elements that you scored as your greatest strength and biggest area for development following the exercises in the four relevant chapters on people, values, culture and purpose.

It will look something like this:

Table 9.1 Review your scores from the values, people, culture and purpose chapters

Chapter	Greatest strength and your score	Biggest area for development and your score
Values	Freedom 9	Grit 7
People	Failure 7	Rebellion 3
Culture	Leadership 8	Idea support 2
Purpose	Social good 6	Money 5

Note your personal scores here:

Table 9.2 Review your scores from the values, people, culture and purpose chapters

Chapter	Greatest strength and your score	Biggest area for development and your score
Values		
People		
Culture		
Purpose		

You might want to work through individually, and then again on behalf of your team or organization. For example – you may put risk-taking as high personal priority for you, but this may not be so appropriate for your company.

Review your scores:

- What do you notice at first glance?
- Review all your strengths – what are you like at your creative best?
- What are your areas for development? What are you going to do to improve your scores? List your actions and diarize them.
- What would you do if you knew you could not fail?
- List three things you're going to do differently having reviewed the list.
- Now envisage the next three to six months.
- Imagine you're writing a postcard to yourself from the future you in a year's time – what will it say that you've achieved? Done differently? What will your creative life be like?
- If you had to choose one area that represents your biggest interest for further exploration from the whole Periodic Table of Creative Elements what would it be?
- You should now have a clear focus for your creative energy and efforts and can think about the elements that make up your personal creative formula.

What's your personal creativity formula?

Using a combination of system 1 and system 2 thinking, heart and head, consider which three (or more) elements would make up your formula – it may be your strengths, weaknesses or areas of interest, in any combination.

So for example, my creativity formula is made up of *curiosity* $\boxed{\text{Cs}}$, *motivation* $\boxed{\text{Mo}}$ and *social good* $\boxed{\text{Sg}}$ based on where I am right now – my strengths and area of greatest interest.

Social activist Jackie Lynton's personal creative formula is made up of the elements of *courage* $\boxed{\text{Cg}}$, *money* $\boxed{\text{M}}$ and *social good* $\boxed{\text{Sg}}$ – representing her biggest strength, her biggest area of development and her biggest area of interest.

For Elizabeth Lovius, her formula would be based on all three of her greatest areas of interest as of today – *curiosity* $\boxed{\text{Cs}}$, *incubation* $\boxed{\text{Ib}}$ and *love* $\boxed{\text{L}}$.

What would your personal creativity formula be?

THE THREE ELEMENTS YOU CAN'T IGNORE TO DEVELOP YOUR INDIVIDUAL CREATIVITY

A successful formula for individual creativity = *Openness* $\boxed{\text{O}}$ + *Self-belief* $\boxed{\text{Sb}}$ + *Motivation* $\boxed{\text{M}}$

- Cultivate an open mind.
- Believe in yourself, your ideas and your ability to sell them.
- Follow your curiosity, passion and purpose.

Key questions for individuals:

- Start a journal or scrapbook and make notes about when you are creatively 'in the zone' and when you're not so hot. What's going on?
- Are any of the elements at play?
- Consider whether having a creative mentor or buddy would be useful.
- Could you work through some of the exercises in the book together?
- Think about your strengths – what are you like at your creative best?
- What are your areas for development? What are you going to do to improve your scores? List your actions and diarize them.
- What can you do in the short term? List three things to do within the next month.
- What do you want to achieve in the long term?

CREATIVE EXPERIMENT **WE COULD BE HEROES**

Take a moment to think about who your creative heroes are. These are people who you admire, who rock your world, who inspire you creatively. It might be someone you work with, a musician, a scientist, an artist or a friend. If there is an element that you really want to develop (perhaps your biggest weakness) can you find someone who embodies that element for you and include them in your list?

List at least three of your heroes. Who's on the list? What qualities do they have that you admire? Take few moments to list them.

See if you can find any commonalities amongst them – are any of the values in this chapter showing up? My list would definitely include Björk for her fearlessness and freedom, Alexander McQueen for his vision and daring, Emmeline Pankhurst for challenging the status quo, journalist Christiane Amanpour for her relentless curiosity about people and my nana for embracing life at full creative blast. All characteristics I could do with a bit more of in my own creative life.

Think about who you admire and how you might steal some of their creative prowess for your own work. Can you find a creative mentor who has the qualities you admire?

Gather your creative council

If you're so inclined, grab a picture of each of your heroes and pin them somewhere you can see them. When you need inspiration ask your 'creative council' how they would approach your problem then apply those principles back to your challenge from your new perspective.

The three elements you can't ignore to develop team creativity

A successful formula for team creativity = *Vision* $\boxed{vi}$ + *Collaboration* $\boxed{c}$ + *Freedom* $\boxed{F}$

- Have a shared creative definition and vision for the team.
- Embrace diversity of thought. Structure teams and assignments for collaboration.

- Autonomy can take many forms – to make mistakes, to take decisions, to fail, to explore, to work flexibly, to disagree, to break the rules, to have free time and to decide where to work.

Key questions for teams:

- How would you describe your team's current approach to creativity?
- Do you have any processes in place?
- How much of a priority is developing creativity for your team?
- Who will lead the overall drive for creativity?
- What can you do in the short term? List three to do within the next month.
- What do you want to achieve in the long term?
- Ensure you have cross-functional teams and you continually seek to harness diversity.
- Set up a group either inside or outside your company to discuss creativity.

KICKSTART THE TEAM CONVERSATION

Organize an offsite to discuss some of the themes and experiments raised in the book and plan your next steps as a team.

Set up your own version of Adobe's red innovator Kickbox starter kit that we saw in Chapter 5. What's included:

- Money. Agree a budget to kick-start small projects without breaking the bank.
- Instructions – a process checklist – think about what processes you currently use (or could adopt from Chapter 8) and make your own.
- Tools – you can pick tools from Chapter 8 and add your own.
- Find out more: https://kickbox.adobe.com/what-is-kickbox

The six elements you can't ignore in order to develop organizational creativity – for leaders, management and HR teams

Starting with the three elements leaders can't ignore.

A successful formula for leading creativity = *Leadership* [Lp] + *Vision* [Vi] + *Trust* [T]

- Leaders need followers.
- A shared vision will inspire others to follow you.
- Trust is fundamental to enabling all the other behaviours associated with innovative working – such as risk-taking and debate.

Key questions for leaders:

- If you are a creative leader, why would anyone follow you?
- What vision are you creating and sharing with your people?
- What goals and rewards are in place for creativity and innovation?
- What meaning or purpose are you creating for people to believe in?
- Are company values aligned with creativity and are they well-understood?

CREATIVE EXPERIMENT
THE BIG WHY (SHOULD I FOLLOW YOU)?

As a creative leader, you will need to answer a big question that captures people's hearts and minds. *Why?* Why should we do it differently? Why should we follow? Here are three ways for you to answer that:

1 *What do you stand for?*
- Review the creativity values in Chapter 1 – which one has your name on it?
- What story (ideally from your own life experience) exemplifies that value for you?
- How could you tell that story in a fresh and original way?

2 *What purpose are you creating for people to believe in?* Core purpose is the reason for being. It is like a guiding star, forever pursued but never reached. It:

- inspires change;
- stimulates progress;
- captures the soul of a person or enterprise;
- guides decision making;
- answers the question

3 *Why are we here?*

It is not – a number, result, outcome and definitely not about money. Begin with a simple mission statement that answers the questions:

- What do we do?
- Who do we do it for?
- What value do we add?

Having answered these questions, ask *why is that important*? Ask it FIVE times.

You'll know you've hit on something when it is super simple (usually three to five words) and you have goosebumps because it inspires *you*. And if it inspires you, you will inspire others.

What will it be like? What vision are you creating?

First, establish a bold creative goal – this will contain an element of challenge and you will need others to achieve it. This is like describing what mountain you want to climb. It is best if this is a measurable but not a financial goal.

What would it be like to achieve that goal? What is your vision?

Consider what it would be like to achieve the goal. Imagine the possibilities. Describe what it will be like. Describe the process of achieving it. Be as descriptive and use as many sensory words as you can.

What will you and others see? Hear? Feel? Notice?

This is like describing the journey to and the view from the top of the mountain.

A good way to do this is to grab a pack of Post-its, write each response on a separate Post-it, without editing, then once you have the ideas, group them into themes, then structure the themes into a story. If you are more visual, you could also do a vision as a series of images that express the feeling of your vision.

Developing organizational creativity

The three elements you can't ignore (once leadership is established)

A successful formula for developing organizational creativity = *Freedom* Fr + *Risk-taking* Rt + *Motivation* M

- Autonomy can take many forms – to make mistakes, to take decisions, to fail, to explore, to work flexibly, to disagree, to break the rules, to have free time and to decide where to work.

- Risk-taking allows room to try something new versus playing it safe.

- Employee motivation is significantly affected by leaders and managers and is a key influence on creative output and innovation.

Key questions for organizations

- Does the organization have a shared understanding of creativity? See how organizations like Heineken and Google use one to focus their efforts in Chapter 1. You can also use Kouzes and Posner's 'credo' memo (page 29)

- Is this shared and well-understood by everyone in the company?

- How much of a priority is developing creativity within the business?

- Who will lead the overall drive for creativity in the organization?

- What's the budget? Think in terms of both time and money.

- Which elements from Chapter 5 (Culture) do you think have impacted the company's successes (or challenges) to driving creativity to date?

- Are there set goals for creativity or innovation? If not, set some.

- Is debate and dissent encouraged and managed within the organization?

- Are employees encouraged to take risks and how is this managed?

- How is trust fostered in the organization?

- What working practices and structures are in place (or could be) to allow employee freedom?

For HR teams

One of the findings from my work with teams required to deliver creativity is that the HR function is often disconnected in terms of appraisals, rewards and incentives.

Think about the following aspects if you want to directly link your working practices with creative output:

- *Recruitment* – how do you assess for creativity at interview stage?

- *Training* – is there a formal training creativity skills programme in place?

- *Appraisals* – how is creativity appraised?

- *Incentives* – how is creativity acknowledged, rewarded and incentivized? Are intrinsic and extrinsic motivations considered?

- *Pay and bonuses* – is there any financial incentive to be creative or innovate?

- *Reputation* – what is the company's reputation in relation to creativity and innovation?

- *Aptitude* – do you use any psychometric tools to assess an individual's attitude to creativity?

Whether it's for yourself, your team or your business set SMART (Specific, Measurable, Attainable, Realistic and Time-bound) creative goals for the short, medium and long term.

You may be at the end of the book, but you're just at the start of the next stage of your own creative journey. Use the questions in this chapter and the topics raised throughout the book to start a conversation with a like-minded friend, team mate or boss about how you can bring your creative ambitions to life.

> There is a vitality, a life force, an energy, a quickening that is translated through you into action – and because there is only one of you in all time, this expression is unique. And if you block it, it will never exist through any other medium and it will be lost. The world will not have it.
> Martha Graham (1943)

Author's note

Before you can play to your strengths, you've got to work out what they are. Before you can marshal your mental resources, you've got to know their limits. When you're running low on gas or turning into an imaginative cul-de-sac it pays to notice quickly and re-route. In pursuit of creative goals, keep the ancient Greek maxim 'know thyself' in mind.

Taking time out to reflect what makes us tick is what helps us grow and move forward. This book is the result of my own search to make sense of this wonderful thing called creativity, and to share insights from my studies and experiences at the sharp end of corporate life. I've had to take my own advice at times whilst writing the book – to dig deep and find grit when the going got difficult, to accept that making mistakes is part of the creative process and the joy of a thing obsessed over, critiqued and finished.

Research and thinking into creativity is ever-evolving, with advances in technology, neuroscience and psychology constantly improving our knowledge. What makes me most happy in my day-to-day work with professionals upping the ante in their own creative lives is hearing how their confidence has improved, how tools have made their creative work easier and how tackling the blank page has become a less scary thing.

I wish you the best of luck in your creative endeavours and would love to hear your feedback too. To join the conversation please share your experiences with me at www.nowgocreate.co.uk or follow me on Twitter @nowgocreate. Let me know how you're using the Periodic Table of Creative Elements and what elements you think should be added!

Picture credits

1 Definitions
Figure 1.1 Visual created by Man v Beast © Claire Bridges 2016
Figure 1.2 Visual created by Man v Beast © Claire Bridges 2016
Figure 1.3 Visual created by Man v Beast © Claire Bridges 2016

2 The values of creative people
Figure 2.1 Visual created by Man v Beast © Claire Bridges 2016
Figure 2.2 Photo by Brinkhoff/Mögenburg
Figure 2.3 Reproduced with permission Memac Ogilvy and Mather, Dubai
Figure 2.4 © Escape The City 2016
Figure 2.5 and 2.6 © ANZ Bank Gay TM 2015. Images reproduced with permission of Australia New Zealand Banking Group Ltd

3 The characteristics of creative people
Figure 3.1 Rupert and Claire Callender. Reproduced with permission
Figure 3.2 Graphic by Nigel Holmes
Figure 3.3 © Bombay Spirits Company Ltd
Figure 3.4 Michael Acton Smith: reproduced with permission of Mind Candy

4 The creative mind
Figure 4.1 © Bridges and Martynoga 2016
Figure 4.2 © Bridges and Martynoga 2016
Figure 4.3 © Bridges and Martynoga 2016
Figure 4.4 © Bridges and Martynoga 2016
Figure 4.5 © Bridges and Martynoga 2016
Figure 4.6 © Bridges and Martynoga 2016

5 Culture
Figure 5.1 Gerry Hopkinson and Nik Done. Photographer Sara Lincoln
Figure 5.2 Ribena Play, photographer Ben Barker © Unity
Figure 5.3 Paddy Power Nigel Farage. Photographer Andy Fallon
Figure 5.4 Racepoint Global. Photographer Sonia Carneiro
Figure 5.5 Mother London office. Reproduced with permission of Mother London

6 Purpose

Figure 6.1 Jackie Lynton © Chloe Lynton 2014

Figure 6.2 B Corps logo reproduced with permission

Figure 6.3 Patagonia ad campaign. Reproduced with permission

Figure 6.4 Vinnie Jones/BHF hardman advert reproduced with permission of Grey London and British Heart Foundation

Figure 6.5 Volvo Lifepaint reproduced with permission of Grey London and Volvo

7 The creative process

Figure 7.1 Visual created by Man v Beast © Claire Bridges 2016

Figure 7.2 © Claire Bridges 2016

Figure 7.3 © Claire Bridges 2016

Figure 7.4 © Damien Newman. Reproduced with permission

Figure 7.5 © Bridges and Martynoga 2016

Figure 7.6 Visual created by Man v Beast © Claire Bridges 2016

8 The creative toolkit

Figures 8.1–8.4 and 8.6 All visuals created by Man v Beast. All images © Claire Bridges 2016

Figure 8.5 © Pret A Manger 2016

Passim

Periodic table of creative elements © Claire Bridges 2016

REFERENCES

Introduction

Online

Csikszentmihalyi, M (1996) [accessed 14 April 2016]

The Creative Personality, *Psychology Today* (Reviewed 2011) [Online] https://www.psychologytoday.com/articles/199607/the-creative-personality

Forrester Consulting (2014) [accessed 11 May 2016] Adobe Creative Dividends Report (2014) [Online] http://landing.adobe.com/en/na/products/creative-cloud/55563-creative-dividends.html

Gov.UK (2014) [accessed 11 December 2015] 'Creative industries worth £8 million an hour to UK economy' *Press Release* [Online] https://www.gov.uk/government/news/creative-industries-worth-8million-an-hour-to-uk-economy

IBM (2010) [Accessed 16 December 2015] 'IBM 2010 Global CEO Study: Creativity Selected as Most Crucial Factor for Future Success' *News Releases.* [Online] https://www.03.ibm.com/press/us/en/pressrelease/31670.wss

World Economic Forum (2015) [accessed 11 May 2016] Unlocking the Potential of Technology, *World Economic Forum New Vision for Education*, Prepared in collaboration with http://widgets.weforum.org/nve-2015/

Chapter 1: Definitions

Books

Adrià, A and Soler, J (2012) *A Day at elBulli*, 1st edition, Phaidon Press, London, p 72

Boden, M (2004) *The Creative Mind: Myths and mechanisms*, Routledge, London

Catmull, Ed (2014) *Creativity Inc: Overcoming the unseen forces that stand in the way of true inspiration*, Bantam Press, London, p 158

Gilbert, E (2015) *Big Magic: Creative living beyond fear*, Bloomsbury Publishing, London, p 67

Govindarajan, V and Trimble C (2010) *The Other Side of Innovation: Solving the execution challenge*, Harvard Business Review Press, Boston

Torrance, P and Sternberg, ER (1988) *The Nature of Creativity*, Cambridge University Press, p 43

Wallas, G (1926) *The Art of Thought*, Solis Press, London (2014)

Articles

Hernandez, R (2012) Big ideas: Research can make a big difference, *Millward Brown Points of View*, June

Isaksen, S, Dorval, B and Treffinger, D (1994) Nollers theories analysed, and expounded, creative problem solving: The history, development and implications for gifted education and talent development – Paper for CPSD, *Gifted Child Quarterly*, Fall 2004, **49** (4), p 6

Rhodes, M (1961) An analysis of creativity, *Phi Delta Kappan*, **42** pp 305–10

Online

Andrew, J (2014) [accessed 4 May 2106] SIMPLES! Aleksandr the Meerkat makes £220 million fortune for insurance tycoon on the back of popular advertising campaign for comparison website, *Daily Mail* [Online] www.dailymail.co.uk/: news/article-2231270/Meerkat-man-doubles-fortune

Campaign, (2009) [accessed 26 May 2016] APG Creative Strategy Awards comparethemarket.com 'Meerkat Campaign' by VCCP, *Campaign* [Online] www.campaignlive.co.uk/article/apg-creative-strategy-awards-comparethemarketcom-meerkat-campaign-vccp/930643

Carlin, J (2011) [accessed 5 May 2016] If The World's Greatest Chef Cooked For A Living, He'd Starve, *Observer Online Foodie* [Online] www.theguardian.com/observer/foodmonthly/futureoffood/story/0,,1969713,00.html

Catmull, E (2008) [accessed 14 May 2016] How Pixar fosters collective creativity, *Harvard Business Review*, September [Online] http://hbr.org/2008/09/how-pixar-fosters-collective-creativity/ar/1

Hodges, J (2011) [accessed 2 May 2016] Keys assessment checks Langley innovation climate, *Researcher News* [Online] www.nasa.gov/centers/langley/news/researchernews/rn_keyssurvey.html

Jack, L (2015) [accessed 7 April 2016] How Cannes' Marketeer Of The Year Codifies Creativity, *Fast Co Create*, [Online] www.fastcocreate.com/3047609/behind-the-brand/how-cannes-marketer-of-the-year-codifies-creativity

Lader, Phil (2014) [accessed 4 April 2016] WPP AGM Trading Update [Online] www.wpp.com/wpp/investor/financialnews/2014/jun/25/wpp-agm-trading-update/

Levy, S (2013) [accessed 4 May 2016] Google's Larry Page on why moon shots matter, *Wired Business* [Online] www.wired.com/

Levitt, T (2002) [accessed 2 May 2016] Creativity is not enough, *Harvard Business Review*, August [Online] https://hbr.org/2002/08/creativity-is-not-enough

Macleod, I (2014) [accessed 4 May 2016] WPP Chairman complains some businesses see creativity as 'lipstick to make a product look more appealing' *The Drum* [Online] www.thedrum.com/news/2014/06/25/wpp-chairman-complains-some-businesses-see-creativity-lipstick-make-product-look

Magee, K (2015) [accessed 20 May 2016] Why Heineken embraces creativity, *Campaign* [Online] www.campaignlive.co.uk/article/why-heineken-embraces-creativity/1352351

Maher, M L, Fisher, D (2012) [accessed 4 May 2016] Using AI to evaluate creative designs, lecture at the 2nd International Conference On Design Creativity, Glasgow, 18–20 September [Online] www.vuse.vanderbilt.edu/~dfisher/ICDC-2012-final.pdf

NESTA (2010) [accessed 27 May 2016] Demand and innovation, how customer preferences shape the innovation process, *NESTA the Work Foundation Working Paper 2010*, no named authors [Online] https://www.nesta.org.uk/sites/default/files/demand_and_innovation.pdf

Noller, R, (2001) [accessed 2 May 2016] Online interview for Buffalo State University, New York, Buffalo State University [Online] http://creativity.buffalostate.edu/multimedia/videos/interview-dr-ruth-noller-2001

Oxford English Dictionary (2016) [Online] www.oxforddictionaries.com

Robinson, K (2013) [accessed 4 May 2016] To encourage creativity, Mr Gove, you must first understand what it is, *The Guardian* [Online] www.theguardian.com/commentisfree/2013/may/17/to-encourage-creativity-mr-gove-understand

Robinson, K (2006) [accessed 4 May 2016] *TED Talks* 'Do schools kill creativity?' www.ted.com

Wilkinson, C (2014) [accessed 4 May 2016] Interview on designing spaces for new ways of working – Spaces, *Designboom* [Online] www.designboom.com/design/clive-wilkinson-on-designing-spaces-for-new-ways-of-working-03-17-2014/

Interviews

Acton Smith, M, interviewed by Peake, M (15 September 2015)
Daisley, B, interviewed by Bridges, C (6 October 2015)
Dromey, H, interviewed by Bridges, C (30 October 2015)
Haq, A, interviewed by Bridges, C (September 2016)
Lynton, J, interviewed by Bridges, C (22 April 2016)
Maguire, V, interviewed by Magee, K (10 February 2016)
Trinetti, M, interviewed by Peake, M (8 September 2015)

Chapter 2: Values

Books

Beam, L S (2008) *The Creative Entrepreneur: A DIY visual guidebook for making business ideas real*, Quarry Books, Beverly, MA

Cameron, J (1995) *The Artist's Way: A course in discovering and recovering your creative self*, Pan, London

Covey, S (2013) *The 7 Habits of Highly Effective People: Powerful lessons in personal change*, 25th anniversary edition, Simon & Schuster, London

Gilbert, E (2015) *Big Magic: Creative living beyond fear*, Bloomsbury Publishing, London, pp 23–26

Isaksen, S G, Dorval, K B and Treffinger D J (2011) *Creative Approaches to Problem Solving*, 3rd edition, Sage, London

Kelley, T in Pink, D (2011) *Drive: The surprising truth about what motivates us*, Canongate Books, Edinburgh, p 90

Kouzes, J and Posner, B, (2008) *The Leadership Challenge: How to make extraordinary things happen in organizations* 3rd edition, Jossey-Bass, San Francisco, p 69

Nin, A (1971) *Diary of Anaïs Nin*, Volume 3 1939–1944, Mariner Books, New York

Articles

Biederman, I, Vessel E A (2006) Perceptual pleasure and the brain, *The American Scientific Journal of Research Journal, Sigma* 2006 Xi, p 247–258

Dollinger, Stephen J, Burke Philip A and Gump Nathaniel W (2007) Creativity and Values, *Creativity Research Journal*, **19** (2–3) pp 91–103

Ekvall, G (1996) Organizational climate for creativity and innovation, *European Journal of Work and Organizational Psychology*, 5 (1), 105–123 p 108

Ingham, A G, Levinger, G, Graves, J, Peckham, V (1974) The Ringelmann Effect: studies of group size and group performance, *Journal of Experimental Social Psychology*, 10(4), pp 371–384

King, L A, McKee W L and Broyles, S J (1996) Creativity and the Five-Factor Model, *Journal of Research in Personality* 30, pp 189–203

McCord, P (2014) How Netflix reinvented HR, *Harvard Business Review*, January/February Issue, pp 1–14

Parnes, S J (1961) Effects of extended effort in creative problem solving, *Journal of Educational Psychology*, **Vol 52** (3), June, pp 117–122

Patterson, F, Kerrin, M, Gatto-Roissard, G (2009) Characteristics and behaviours of innovative people, *Organisations for Literature Review*, a paper prepared for NESTA Policy and Research Unit (NPRU) City University, London, p 36

Zanna, Mark P (1992) Advances in experimental social psychology, *ScienceDirect* **vol 25**,? Elsevier ?P iii-ix?

Online

Best, J (2013) [accessed 4 May 2016] Watson: The Inside story of how the jeopardy winning supercomputer was born and what it wants to do next, *Technorepublic*, [Online] www.techrepublic.com/article/ibm-watson-the-inside-story-of-how-the-jeopardy-winning-supercomputer-was-born-and-what-it-wants-to-do-next/

Brown, T (2008) [accessed 21 March 2016] Tales of creativity and play, *TED Talks Education*, filmed on 8 November 2008, [Online] ted.com

Chamorro-Premuzic, T (2014) [accessed 4 May 2016] Curiosity is as important as intelligence, *Harvard Business Review* [Online] https://hbr.org/2014/08/curiosity-is-as-important-as-intelligence/2014

Csikszentmihalyi, M (1996) [accessed 14 April 2016] The creative personality, *Psychology Today* Reviewed 2011 [Online] https://www.psychologytoday.com/articles/199607/the-creative-personality

Duckworth, A L (2013) [accessed 21 March 2016] Grit: The power of passion and perseverance, *TED Talks Education*, Filmed April 2013 Available at ted.com

Escape the City (2015) www.escapethecity.org [accessed 14 May 2016]

Gray, P (2008) [accessed 4 May 2016] The Value of Play 1: The definition of play gives insights, *Psychology Today* [Online] www.psychologytoday.com/blog/freedom-learn/200811/the-value-play-i-the-definition-play-gives-insights---changed

Hastings, R (2009) [accessed 14 May 2016] Responsible people thrive on freedom, and are worthy of freedom, *Netflix Slide Share*, [Online] www.slideshare.net/reed2001/culture-1798664/41

Helm, B (2012) [accessed 4 May 2016] Dyson: How I did it: James Dyson, *Inc Com Magazine* [Online] www.inc.com/magazine/201203/burt-helm/how-i-did-it-james-dyson.html

Kapadia Pocha, S (2012) [accessed 4 May 2016] Rejection letters sent to famous people, *Stylist* [Online] www.stylist.co.uk/stylist-network/rejection-letters-sent-to-famous-people

Madison, A (2010) [accessed 10 May 2016] *Persist!* [Online] http://theanimatorlettersproject.com

Nightingale, E *Creative Thinking* audiobook and test on i-Tunes [Online] https://itunes.apple.com/us/album/creative-thinking/id445242877

Perry, G (2013) [accessed 16 May 2016] BBC Reith Lectures, Playing to the Gallery, Lecture 4, 'I found myself in the art world', recorded at St Martin's School of Art, BBC Broadcast Radio 4 [Online] http://downloads.bbc.co.uk/radio4/transcripts/reith-lecture4-csm.pdf

Schwartz, S H (2012) [last accessed 14 May 2016] An overview of the Schwartz theory of basic values, *Online Readings in Psychology and Culture*, 2 (1) [Online] http://dx.doi.org/10.9707/2307

St George, A (2013) [accessed 4 May 2016] Leadership lessons from the Royal Navy, *Mckinsey Insights Quarterly 2013* [Online] www.mckinsey.com/insights/organization/leadership_lessons_from_the_royal_navy

Interviews

Acton Smith, M interviewed by Peake, M (15 September 2015)

Dromey, H interviewed by Bridges, C (30 October 2015)

Hopkinson, G interviewed by Bridges, C (14 August 2015)

Lynton, J interviewed by Bridges, C (22 April 2016)

Moutran, R interviewed by Bridges, C (16 May 2016)

Reinhard, K (2015) Berlin School at Cannes Lions Festival of Creativity 2015, personal remarks reproduced with permission

Trinetti, M Interviewed by Peake, M (2015)

Chapter 3: Characteristics

Books

Amabile, T (1987) *The Motivation to be Creative*, in Isaksen, S (ed), *Frontiers of Creativity Research: Beyond the basics*, Bearly Limited, Buffalo, NY, pp 223–254

Boden, M (2004) *The Creative Mind: Myths and mechanisms*, Psychology Press, London, p 15

Carroll, L (1865) *Alice's Adventures in Wonderland*

Csikszentmihalyi, M (2008) *Flow: The psychology of optimal experience*, Harper Perennial Modern Classics London, p 4

Csikszentmihalyi, M (1996) *Creativity: The psychology of discovery and invention*, reprint edition August 2013, Harper Perennial, London, pp 58 and 73

Gilbert, E (2015) *Big Magic: Creative living beyond fear*, Bloomsbury Publishing, London

Gladwell, M (2009) *Outliers: The story of success*, Penguin, London

Jay-Z (2011) *Decoded*, Spiegel & Grau, New York, p 141

Kelley, D, Kelley T (2013) *Creative Confidence: Unleashing the creative potential within us all*, William Collins, London

Pink, D (2011) *Drive: The surprising truth about what motivates us*, Canongate Books London, pp 205, 207 and 208

Articles

Rothenberg A (1971) The process of Janusian thinking in creativity, *Arch Gen Psychiatry*, **24** (3) pp195–205, doi:10.1001/archpsyc.1971.01750090001001

Online

Alda, Alan (1980) [accessed 14 May 2016] 62nd Commencement speech at Connecticut College [Online] http://web.archive.org/web/20110429024820/ [Online] www.conncoll.edu:80/events/speeches/alda.html

Braddock, K (2007) [accessed 2 May 2016] Fame Academy: The Brit School. *The Independent on Sunday*, January 2007 [Online] www.independent.co.uk/news/uk/this-britain/fame-academy-the-brit-school-433652.html

Burkeman, O (2012) [accessed 28 May 2016] Happiness is a glass half empty, *Guardian* [Online] www.theguardian.com/lifeandstyle/2012/jun/15/happiness-is-being-a-loser-burkeman

Cameron, J (2015) [accessed 28 May 2016] Video: 'Visionaries', meet James Cameron (interview with Sergio Rodriguez) *The Amazing Start Up* [Online] http://theamazingstartup.com/video-visionaries-meet-james-cameron/

Carpenter, J (2013) [accessed 28 May 2016] Nigel Kennedy on his accent, Aston Villa and playing violin with the greats, *The Daily Express* [Online] www.express.co.uk/entertainment/music/384354/Nigel-Kennedy-on-his-accent-Aston-Villa-and-playing-violin-with-the-greats

Cellon Jones, R (2015) [accessed 1 May 2016] Could a robot do your job? An investigation into new technology. *BBC News* [Online] www.bbc.co.uk/news/technology-34231931

Cleese J (1991) [accessed 26 January 2016] Creativity in management, *videoarts.com* Available from: [Online] www.videoarts.com/Vintage-Video-Arts/creativity-in-management/

Contagious.com (2016) [accessed 7 June 2016] Thinx wins most contagious 2015 startup award www.contagious.com/blogs/news-and-views/70695045-thinx-wins-most-contagious-2015-startup-award

Dilts, R (1996) [accessed 21 May 2016] Strategies of Genius, Article of the Month for *Nlpu*, [Online] www.nlpu.com/Articles/article7.htm

Dweck, C (2016) [accessed May 2016] Interview with Carol Dweck on Mindsetonline, mindsetonline.com

Dyer, J H, Gregerson C, Christensen M (2009) [accessed 1 May 2016] The Innovator's DNA, *Harvard Business Review* December Issue [Online] https://hbr.org/2009/12/the-innovators-dna

Gaskin, T (2012) [accessed 28 May 2016] www.Twitter.com 9.08am 29 August

Heatherwick.com (2016) [accessed 4 May 2016] Company website

Henry, T (2016) [accessed 4 May 2016)] Get Over Yourself: How your ego sabotages creativity, *99u* [Online] http://99u.com/articles/19327/get-over-yourself-how-your-ego-sabotages-your-creativity

Jones, G (2015) [accessed 28 May 2016] Grace Jones Slays Rihanna, Miley, Gaga and Kanye In This Exclusive Extract From Her Autobiography, *Time Out* [Online] www.timeout.com/london/music/grace-jones-autobiography-extract-rihanna-miley-gaga-kanye

Jung, R (2013) [accessed 1 May 2016] Speaking of Psychology: The neuroscience of creativity Series of papers for *The American Psychological Association* [Online] www.apa.org/research/action/speaking-of-psychology/neuroscience-creativity.aspx

Kaufman, S B (2015) [accessed 1 May 2016] The Imagination Institute Awards, Nearly $3M to Advance the Science of Imagination, Report for *The Scientific American* [Online] http://blogs.scientificamerican.com/beautiful-minds/the-imagination-institute-awards-nearly-3m-to-advance-the-science-of-imagination/

Melford S, (2015) [accessed 1 May 2016] Thomas Heatherwick's Adaptive Designs, Interview for *The Wall St Journal*, [Online] www.wsj.com/articles/thomas-heatherwicks-adaptive-designs-1446689067

Patterson, F, Kerrin, M, Gatto-Roissard, G, Coan P (2009) [accessed 15 May 2016] *NESTA* Everyday innovation: How to enhance innovative working in employees and organisations, *www.nesta.org.uk* p 18

Perry, G (2013) [accessed 16 May 2016] BBC Reith Lectures, Playing to the Gallery, Lecture 47. I found myself in the art world, recorded at St Martins School of Art, BBC Broadcast Radio 4 [Online] http://downloads.bbc.co.uk/radio4/transcripts/reith-lecture4-csm.pdf

Plimpton, G (1958) [accessed 3 April 2016] Interview with Ernest Hemingway on the Art of Fiction, *The Paris Review* [Online] www.theparisreview.org/interviews/4825/the-art-of-fiction-no-21-ernest-hemingway

Schwartz, S H (2011) [accessed 4 May 2016] An Overview of the Schwartz Theory of Basic Values, Online Readings in Psychology and Culture, Article 8, *The International Association for Cross Cultural Psychology* [Online] http://scholarworks.gvsu.edu/cgi/viewcontent.cgi?article=1116&context=orpc

Smith, W (2015) [accessed 6 May 2016] Will Smith in conversation with Zane Lowe, Beats 1 Radio Posted on YouTube on 1 May [Online] https://www.youtube.com/watch?v=CT4zlcKgOm8

Van Dyck, H (2016) [accessed 1 May 2016] What happens when you disrupt the White House: Haley Van Dyck speaks at *TED2016*. United States Digital Service TED talk [Online] http://blog.ted.com/what-happens-when-you-disrupt-the-white-house-haley-van-dyck-speaks-at-ted2016/

Ward, O (2012) [accessed 1 May 2016] Interview with Thomas Heatherwick, *Time Out Magazine*, [Online] www.timeout.com/london/art/interview-thomas-heatherwick

Wroe P (2012) [accessed 1 May 2016] Thomas Heatherwick: The new Leonardo of Design, article for *The Guardian online* [Online] www.theguardian.com/artanddesign/2012/may/18/thomas-heatherwick-da-vinci-design

Interviews

Acton Smith, M interviewed by Peake, M (15 September 2015)

Callender, C interviewed by Bridges, C (25 January 2016)

Callender, R interviewed by Bridges, C (25 January 2016)

Daisley, B interviewed by Bridges, C (6 October 2015)

Dromey, H interviewed by Bridges, C (30 October 2015)

Wardley, J interviewed by Peake, M (17 August 2015)

Reinhard, K, 2015 Berlin School at Cannes Lions Festival of Creativity 2015, personal speech remarks reproduced with permission

Song lyrics

Fields, D, Kern J (1936) Pick Yourself Up, Lyrics from the film, *Swing Time*

Chapter 4: The creative mind

Books

Binet, L and Fields, P (2013) *The Long and the Short of It*, Institute of Practitioners in Advertising, London, (Free slide download via IPA website)

Crick, F (1990) *What Mad Pursuit*, Basic Books, New York, p 141

Eagleman, D (2011) *Incognito*, Canongate Books, London

Gladwell, M (2006) *Blink: The power of thinking without thinking*, Penguin, London, p 115

Kahneman, D (2011) *Thinking, Fast and Slow*, Penguin Books, London

Lynch, D (2006) *Catching the Big Fish: Meditation, consciousness, and creativity*, Tarcher Perigee, New York p 1

Pratchett, T (2016) *Seriously Funny: The endlessly quotable Terry Pratchett*, Penguin, London, p 28

Seuss Geisel, T (1975) *Oh, the Thinks You Can Think*, Random House, New York

Articles

Baas, M, Nevicka B, Ten Velden FS (2014) Specific Mindfulness Skills Differentially Predict Creative Performance, *Pers Soc Psychol Bull*, **40**, 9, pp 1092-1106

Baird, B, Smallwood J, Mrazek M D, Kam J W, Franklin M S, Schooler J W (2012) Inspired By Distraction: mind wandering facilitates creative incubation. *Psychol Sci*, **23**, 10, pp 1117–22 (October)

Beaty, R E, Benedek M, Silvia P J, Schacter D L (2016) Creative cognition and brain network dynamics, *Trends Cogn Sci*, **20** (2), pp 87–95 (February)

Beaty, R E and Silvia P J (2012) Why do ideas get more creative across time? An executive interpretation of the serial order effect in divergent thinking tasks *Psychology of Aesthetics, Creativity, and the Arts*, **6**, 4, p 309

Brunyé, T T, Gagnon S A, Paczynski M, Shenhav A, Mahoney C R, Taylor H A (2013) Happiness by association: breadth of free association influences affective states, *Cognition*, **127**, 1, pp 93–8 (April)

Cai, D J, Meditionick S A, Harrison E M, Kanady J C, Meditionick S C (2009) REM, not incubation, improves creativity by priming associative networks, *Proc Natl Acad Sci USA*, 106, **25**, pp 10130–34 (December)

Colzato, L S, Ozturk A, Hommel B (2012) Meditate to create: the impact of focused-attention and open-monitoring training on convergent and divergent thinking, *Front Psychol*, **18** (3), p 116 (April)

Cowan, N (2001) The magical number 4 in short-term memory: A reconsideration of mental storage capacity, *Behavioral and Brain Sciences*, **24**, pp 87–185 (February)

Creswell, J D, Bursley J K and Satpute A B (2013) Neural reactivation links unconscious thought to decision-making performance, *Soc Cogn Affect Neurosci*, **8** (8), pp 863–69 (December)

De Dreu, C K, Nijstad B A, Baas M, Wolsink I, Roskes M (2012) Working memory benefits creative insight, musical improvisation, and original ideation through maintained task-focused attention, *Pers Soc Psychol Bull*, 38 (5), pp 656–69 (May)

Dijksterhuis, A, Meurs T (2006) Where creativity resides: the generative power of unconscious thought, *Conscious Cognit*, 15 (1), pp 135–46 (March)

Fink, A, Benedek M (2014) EEG alpha power and creative ideation, *Neuroscience and Biobehavioral Reviews*, Volume 44, pp 111–123 (July)

Forgas, J P (2013) Don't worry, be sad! On the cognitive, motivational, and interpersonal benefits of negative mood, *Current Directions in Psychological Science*, 22, pp 225–232 (June)

Isen, A M, Daubman K A, Nowicki G P (1987) Positive affect facilitates creative problem solving, *J Pers Soc Psychol*, 52 (6), pp 1122–31 (June)

Jia, L, Hirt E R, Karpen S C (2009) Lessons from a Faraway land: the effect of spatial distance on creative cognition, *Journal of Experimental Social Psychology*, Volume 45 (5), pp 1127–131 (September)

Jung, R E, Wertz C J, Meadows C A, Ryman S G, Vakhtin A A, Flores R A (2015) Quantity yields quality when it comes to creativity: a brain and behavioral test of the equal-odds rule, *Front Psychol*, 25 (6), p 864 (June)

Jung-Beeman, M, Bowden E M, Haberman J, Frymiare J L, Arambel-Liu S, Greenblatt R, Reber P J, Kounios J (2004) Neural activity when people solve verbal problems with insight, *PLoS Biol*, 2 (4), p 97 (April)

Kenett, Y N, Anaki D, Faust M (2014) Investigating the structure of semantic networks in low and high creative persons, *Front Hum Neurosci.* 10 (8), p 407

Killingsworth, M A, Gilbert DT (2010) A wandering mind is an unhappy mind, *Science*, 330, 6006, p 932 (November)

Liu, S, Chow H M, Xu Y, Erkkinen M G, Swett K E, Eagle M W, Rizik-Baer D A and Braun AR (2012) Neural correlates of lyrical improvisation: an FMRI study of freestyle rap, *Sci Rep.* 2, 834 (November)

Liu, S, Erkkinen M G, Healey M L,Xu Y, Swett KE, Chow H M and Braun A R (2015) Brain activity and connectivity during poetry composition: toward a multidimensional model of the creative process, *Hum Brain Mapp*, 36 (9), pp 3351–72 (September)

Lustenberger, C, Boyle M R, Foulser A A, Mellin J M and Fröhlich F (2015) Functional role of frontal alpha oscillations in creativity, *Cortex*, Volume 67, pp 74–82 (June)

Maddux, W W, Galinsky AD (2009) Cultural borders and mental barriers: the relationship between living abroad and creativity, *J Pers Soc Psychol.*, 96 (5), pp 1047–61 (May)

Martindale, C, Hines D (1975) Creativity and cortical activation during creative, intellectual and E E G feedback tasks, *Biol Psychol*, 3 (2), pp 91–100 (September)

Meditionick, S A (1962) The associative basis of the creative process, *Psychological Review*, 69, pp 220–232

Nemeth, C, Personnaz, M, Personnaz, B, Goncalo, J (2004) The liberating role of conflict in group creativity: A cross-cultural study, *European Journal of Social Psychology*, **34**, pp 365–374

Ostafin, B D and Kassman K T (2012) Stepping out of history: mindfulness improves insight problem solving, *Conscious Cogn*, **21** (2), pp 1031–36 (June)

Pinho, A L, Ullén F, Castelo-Branco M, Fransson P, de Manzano Ö (2015) Addressing a paradox: dual strategies for creative performance in introspective and extrospective networks, *Cereb Cortex*, pp 1–12 (June)

Salvi, C, Bricolo E, Franconeri S L, Kounios J, Beeman M (2015) Sudden insight is associated with shutting out visual inputs, *Psychon Bull Rev*, **22** (6), pp 1814–19 (December)

Simonton, D K (1997) Creative productivity: A predictive and explanatory model of career trajectories and landmarks, *Psychological Review*, **104** (1), pp 66–89 (March)

Subramaniam, K, Kounios J, Parrish T B, Jung-Beeman M (2009) A brain mechanism for facilitation of insight by positive affect, *J Cogn Neurosci*, **21** (3), pp 415–32 (March)

Tang, Y Y, Hölzel, B K, Posner MI (2015) The neuroscience of mindfulness meditation, *Nat Rev Neurosci*, **16** (4), pp 213–25 (April)

Whitehead, A N (1925) Religion and Science, *The Atlantic*, (August)

Zedelius, C M, Schooler J W (2015) Mind wandering 'Ahas' versus mindful reasoning: alternative routes to creative solutions, *Front Psychol*, **17** (6), p 834 (June)

Online

Cameron, J (2016) [accessed 18 May 2016] *Morning Pages* [Online] http://juliacameronlive.com/basic-tools/morning-pages/

Cleese, J (1991) [accessed 26 January 2016] Creativity In Management, videoarts. com Available from: [Online] www.videoarts.com/Vintage-Video-Arts/creativity-in-management/

Gaiman, N (1997) [accessed 26 January 2016] Where Do You Get Your Ideas? *neilgaiman.com* [Online] www.neilgaiman.com/Cool_Stuff/Essays/Essays_By_Neil/Where_do_you_get_your_ideas%3F

Jarrett, C (2012) [accessed 26 January 2016] Why The Left-Brain Right-Brain Myth Will Probably Never Die [Blog] *Psychology Today* [Online] www.psychologytoday.com/blog/brain-myths/201206/why-the-left-brain-right-brain-myth-will-probably-never-die

Kaufman, S B (2014) [accessed 26 January 2016] The Messy Minds of Creative People [Blog] *Scientific American* [Online] blogs.scientificamerican.com/beautiful-minds/the-messy-minds-of-creative-people/

Kreider, Tim (2012) [accessed 26 January 2016] The 'Busy' Trap [Blog] Opinionator blog, *New York Times* [Online] opinionator.blogs.nytimes.com/2012/06/30/the-busy-trap/

LeDoux, J E (2007) [accessed 26 January 2016] Emotional memory, *Scholarpedia*, **2** (7), p 1806 [Online] www.scholarpedia.org/article/Emotional_memory

Martynoga, B (2014) [accessed 26 January 2016] Beware The Neuroplasticity Hype [Blog] Medium.com [Online] medium.com/@mountainogre/beware-the-neuroplasticity-hype-e448d4efd119#.vpc8xsqmt

Michalko, M (2014) [accessed 26 January 2016] Writing A Letter To Your Unconscious Self [blog] *creativethinking.net* [Online] creativethinking.net/writing-a-letter-to-your-unconsciousness/#sthash.NNo5UUCP.lihAsL7l.dpbs

Whiteside, S, (2015) [accessed 12 May 2016] Procter & Gamble Research Validates Emotional Marketing [Online] warc.com

Interviews

Trinetti, M interviewed by Peake, M (8 September 2015)

Whiston, J interviewed by Bridges, C (8 March 2016)

Yeardsley, S, interviewed by Bridges, C (September 2016)

Chapter 5: Culture

Books

Currey, M (2013) *Daily Rituals*, Picador Books, London, p 64

Hemingway, E (1953) *Ernest Hemingway Selected Letters 1917–1961*, edited by Carlos Baker, Scribner Classics, p 805

Isaksen, S G, Dorval, K B and Treffinger D J (2011) *Creative Approaches to Problem Solving*, 3rd edition, Sage, London, p 88

Govindarajan, V and Trimble, C (2010) *The Other Side of Innovation, Solving the Execution Challenge*, Harvard Business School Press, Boston, pp 3, 8, 10, 15, 16

Kline, N (2002) *Time to Think: Listening to ignite the human mind*, Ward Lock, London

Kouzes, J and Posner, B (2008) *The Leadership Challenge: How to make extraordinary things happen in organizations* 3rd edition, Jossey-Bass, San Francisco, p 111

Nin, A (1971) *Diary Of Anaïs Nin Volume 3 1939–1944*, Houghton Mifflin Harcourt

Ries, E (2011) *The Lean Startup: How today's entrepreneurs use continuous innovation to create radically successful businesses*, Crown Business, London

Webb Young, (2003) *A Technique for Producing Ideas*, McGraw-Hill, New York, p 29

Articles

Ekvall, G (1996) Organizational climate for creativity and innovation, *European Journal of Work and Organizational Psychology*, 5 (1), pp 105–23

Straus, L S (1997) Putting Your Company's Whole Brain to Work *Harvard Business Review*, July /August p 2

Online

Alter, A (no date) [accessed 4 May 2016] How to Build a Collaborative Office Space Like Pixar and Google, [Online] http://99u.com/articles/16408/how-to-build-a-collaborative-office-space-like-pixar-and-google

Best, Jo (2016) [accessed 25 May 2016] IBM Watson: The inside story of how the *Jeopardy*-winning supercomputer was born, and what it wants to do next [Online] www.techrepublic.com/article/ibm-watson-the-inside-story-of-how-the-jeopardy-winning-supercomputer-was-born-and-what-it-wants-to-do-next/

Catmull, E (2014) [accessed 10 July 2016] Inside the Pixar Braintrust *Fast Company* [Online] www.fastcompany.com/3027135/lessons-learned/inside-the-pixar-braintrust

Catmull, E (2008) [accessed 25 May 2016] How Pixar Fosters Collective Creativity [Online] https://hbr.org/2008/09/how-pixar-fosters-collective-creativity

D'Onfro, J (2015) [accessed 14 May 2016] The Truth About Google's Famous '20%' Time Policy, *The Business Insider, UK* [Online] http://uk.businessinsider.com/google-20-percent-time-policy-2015-4?r=US&IR=T

Hackman, J (2009) [accessed 13 May 2016] Why Teams Don't Work, by Diane Coutu, *Harvard Business Review* [Online] https://hbr.org/2009/05/why-teams-dont-work

Halliday, J (2011) [accessed 3 May 2016] Mind Candy – the monster that lurks on Silicon Roundabout. *The Guardian* [Online] www.theguardian.com/media/2011/jul/17/mind-candy-monster-silicon-roundabout

Milton, F, Brown, M (no date) Price WaterhouseCoopers Innovation Survey, Originally available to buy from www.pricewaterhousecoopers.com p.28, no longer available

Nisen, M (2013) [accessed 26 May 2016] Zappos is Building an Intentionally Inconvenient Office In Downtown Las Vegas [Online] www.businessinsider.com/zappos-new-downtown-las-vegas-office-2013-3?IR=T

Perry, G (2013) [accessed 16 May 2016] BBC Reith Lectures, Playing to the Gallery, Lecture 4: I found myself in the art world, recorded at St Martins School of Art, BBC Broadcast Radio 4 [Online] http://downloads.bbc.co.uk/radio4/transcripts/reith-lecture4-csm.pdf

Wilkinson, C (2014) [accessed 2 May 2016] Clive Wilkinson Interview On Designing Spaces For New Ways Of Working, *Interview for Designboom at Design, indada 2014* [Online] www.designboom.com/design/clive-wilkinson-on-designing-spaces-for-new-ways-of-working-03-17-2014/

Interviews

Barratt, F interviewed by Bridges, C (12 April 2016)

Clark, Wendy comments from Cannes Lions Festival of Creativity Masterclass (June 2016) reproduced with permission and interviewed by Bridges, C (9 July 2016)

Daisley, B interviewed by Bridges, C (6 October 2015)

Dromey, H interviewed by Bridges, C (30 October 2015)

Gallery, C interviewed by Bridges, C (9 May 2016)

Hopkinson, G interviewed by Bridges, C (14 August 2015)

Lynton, J interviewed by Bridges, C (22 April 2016)

Middleton, S interviewed by Bridges, C (18 May 2016)

Statt, D interviewed by Bridges, C (20 May 2016)

Reinhard, K, 2015 Berlin School at Cannes Lions Festival of Creativity 2015, personal speech remarks reproduced with permission

Chapter 6: Purpose

Books

Csikszentmihalyi, M (1998) *The Nature of Creativity*, edited by Sternberg, R Cambridge University Press Cambridge p 314 and p 326

Gardner, H (1998) *The Nature of Creativity*, edited by Sternberg, R Cambridge University Press, Cambridge p 314

Loye, D (2007) *Darwin on Love*, Benjamin Franklin Press Philadelphia

Torrance, E Paul (1998) *The Nature of Creativity*, edited by Sternberg, R Cambridge University Press Cambridge p 67

Milligan, A, Smith S (2015) *On Purpose: Delivering a branded customer experience people love, Kogan Page, London*

Pink, D (2011) *Drive: The surprising truth about what motivates us*, Canongate Books, Edinburgh, p 208

Online

Amabile and Kramer (2012) [accessed 22 February 2016]

What Doesn't Motivate Creativity Can Kill It, *Harvard Business Review*, 25 April [Online] https://hbr.org/2012/04/balancing-the-four-factors-tha-1/

B. Corp Community (2016) [accessed 4 May 2016] *Corporations are leading a global movement to redefine success in business*, Video Certified B [Online] www.bcorporation.net

Bokova, Irina (2012) [accessed 4 May 2016] Protecting Culture in the Time of War, *Address to The Academie Diplomatique International. Paris*, [Online] http://unesdoc.unesco.org/images/0021/002186/218626E.pdf

Confino, J (2015) [accessed 4 May 2016] Will Unilever Become the World's Largest Internationally Traded B Corp? Report from Davos, *The Guardian*, [Online] www.theguardian.com/sustainable-business/2015/jan/23/benefit-corporations-bcorps-business-social-responsibility

Cookfood (2016) [accessed 4 May 2016] Company Statement and Values [Online] cookfood.net

Edelman, D (2016) [accessed 7 May 2016] The 2016 Eldeman Trust Barometer: Global results, *Slideshare –presentation* [Online] www.edelman.com/insights/intellectual-property/2016-edelman-trust-barometer/executive-summary/

Escape the City (2015) [accessed 4 May 2016] 'Diagnosing Job Satisfaction' *Escape the city* report 2015 [Online] www.escapethecity.org

Hurman, J (2011) [accessed 28 April 2016] The Case for Creativity, Spikes, *Slide-Share for in:slide share*, [Online] www.slideshare.net/jameshurman/the-case-for-creativity-spikes-2011

Jackman, D (2015) [accessed 1 May 2016] 'Dear Corporates' Open Letter [Online] www.escapethecity.org

Jobs, S (2005) [accessed 30 March 2016] 'You've got to find what you love', a prepared text of the Commencement address delivered by Steve Jobs, CEO of Apple Computer and of Pixar Animation Studios, *Stamford University* [Online] https://news.stanford.edu/2005/06/14/jobs-061505/

Lader, P (2014) [accessed 30 March 2016] AGM highlights vital role of 'applied creativity', *E Wire, WPP News Bulletin*, No 185, July [Online] www.wpp.com/wpp/press/enewsletter/2014/e-wire-185-july-2014/

Marcario, R (2016) [accessed 14 May 2016] Repair is a Radical Act, *Personal Statement for Patagonia*, [Online] patagonia.com

Percival, A (2015) [accessed 30 April 2016] Adele at the BBC, *Huff Post Entertainment* [Online] www.huffingtonpost.co.uk/2015/11/06/adele-hello-performs-live-first-time-bbc-special_n_8486840.html

Sinek, S (2009) [Accessed 9 May 2016] Start with Why; How Great Leaders Inspire Action, *Video Lecture for TED*, September [Online] https://www.ted.com/talks/simon_sinek_how_great_leaders_inspire_action?language=en

Stengel, J (2011) [Accessed 9 May 2016] Millward Brown in partnership with Jim Stengel Reveals the 50 Fastest-Growing Brands in the World and Uncovers the Source of Their Success, *Report for Business Wire Spring*, [Online] www.businesswire.com/news/home/20120117005066/en/Millward-Brown-Partnership-Jim-Stengel-Reveals-50

TED (2013) [accessed 14 March 2016] Ads Worth Spreading, *Report for TED Initiatives* [Online] http://storage.ted.com/aws/TED-Ads-Worth-Spreading-Report.pdf

Wyman, O, Blake, J and Milligan, K, Social Innovation (2016) [accessed 8 May 2016] A guide to Achieving Corporate and Societal Value, *Insight Report for SCHWAB Foundation,World Economic Forum* [Online] www3.weforum.org/docs/WEF_Social_Innovation_Guide.pdf

Interviews

Daisley, B interviewed by Bridges, C (6 October 2015)
Finnegan, K interviewed by Bridges, C (11 March 2016)
Gallop, C interviewed by Magee, K (22 January 2016)
Lynton, J interviewed by Bridges, C (22 April 2016)
Maguire, V interviewed by Magee, K (10 February 2016)
Wardley, J interviewed by Peake, M (17 August 2015)

Chapter 7: Process

Books

Boden, M (2004) *The Creative Mind: Myths and Mechanisms*, Psychology Press, London, p 15
Bullmore, J (2006) *Apples, Insights and Mad Inventors: An Entertaining Analysis of Modern Marketing*, John Wiley & Son, London p 151
Freedman, L (2013) *Strategy, a History*, Oxford University Press, p x
Gogatz, A and Mondejar R (2005) *Business Creativity: Breaking the invisible barriers*,
Palgrave Macmillan, London, p 139
Guilford, J P (1967) *The Nature of Human Intelligence*, McGraw-Hill, New York
Isaksen, S G, Dorval, K B and Treffinger D J (2011) *Creative Approaches to Problem Solving*, 3rd edition, Sage, London, p 28
Kaufman, J and Sternberg R J (2010) *The Cambridge Handbook of Creativity*, Cambridge University Press, p xiii
Rothenburg A and Hausman, K, Editors (1976) *The Creativity Question*, Duke University Press, p 64
Wallas, G (1926) *The Art of Thought*, new edition Solis Press, London, 2014 pp 38, 39
Webb Young, J (2003) *A Technique for Producing Ideas* McGraw-Hill, New York, p 29

Online

Brown, T (2008) [accessed 5 May 2016] Design Thinking; How To Deliver A Great Plan *Harvard Business Review* p 84 [Online] https://www.ideo.com/images/uploads/thoughts/IDEO_HBR_Design_Thinking.pdf
Drell, B (1993) [accessed 3 May 2016] Intelligence Research Some Suggested Approaches, *Paper for The Central Intelligence Agency*, Approved for release 22 September [Online] https://www.cia.gov/library/center-for-the-study-of-intelligence/kent-csi/vol1no4/html/v01i4a08p_0001.htm

Elsbach, K D (2003) [accessed 4 May 2016] How to Pitch a Brilliant Idea, *Harvard Business Review*, [Online] https://hbr.org/2003/09/how-to-pitch-a-brilliant-idea

Hindo, B (2007) [accessed 9 May 2016] At 3M, A Struggle Between Efficiency And Creativity, *Cover Story Podcast Bloomberg News 11 June* [Online] www.bloomberg.com/news/articles/2007-06-10/at-3m-a-struggle-between-efficiency-and-creativity

Jacobs, M (2011) [accessed 3 May 2016] The Creative Process, *Video Interview with Julien Ebhar* [Online] https://vimeo.com/27007803

Meng, Tham Khai (2014) [accessed 9 May 2016] When Big Data Meets Big Creativity, You Get Pure Sex, *Campaign US*, 20 September [Online] www.campaignlive.com/article/when-big-data-meets-big-creativity-pure-sex/1314992#OsBx6UQ1z6ssWouy.99

Newman, D (2010) [accessed 5 May 2016] The Squiggle of Design, *Article for Central Office of Design 2011* [Online] http://cargocollective.com/central/The-Design-Squiggle

Pasteur, L (1854) [accessed 4 May 2016] Inaugural Lecture As Professor And Dean Of The Faculty Of Science, University Of Lille, Douai, France, 7 December — *A Treasury of the World's Great Speeches*, ed Houston Peterson, p 473 (1954) [Online] www.bartleby.com/73/174.html

Resources For Practitioners [accessed 3 May 2016] *Creative Problem Solving* www.creativeproblemsolving.com

Shlain, T (2013) [accessed 4 May 2016] *The Future Starts Here. Clips of her best selling American Television Series* Pro [Online] http://on.aol.com/shows/the-future-starts-here-shw517951318

Tylee, J (2005) [accessed 26 May 2016] The 10 Best Advertising Anecdotes... Ever! *Campaign, July* [Online] www.campaignlive.co.uk/article/10-best-advertising-anecdotes-ever/488746#

Tyson, M (2012) Bernadino.M. [accessed 9 May 2016] Mike Tyson explains one of his most famous quotes, *Sun Sentinel*, 9 November 2012[Online] http://articles.sun-sentinel.com/2012-11-09/sports/sfl-mike-tyson-explains-one-of-his-most-famous-quotes-20121109_1_mike-tyson-undisputed-truth-

Wood, S (2016) [accessed 2 May 2016] Series Of Nine Interviews Covering Her Company Unruly And How She Has Developed The Business *Creative Business Leaders* [Online] www.creativebusinessleaders.com/interviews/sarah-wood/

Interviews

Clark, Wendy comments from Cannes Lions Festival of Creativity Masterclass (June 2016) reproduced with permission and interviewed by Bridges, C (9 July 2016)

Newman, D, interviewed by Bridges, C (19 May 2016)

Whiston, J interviewed by Bridges, C (8 March 2016)

Chapter 8: Toolkit

Books

Berger, J (2013) *Contagious: Why things catch on*, Simon & Schuster, New York

Buechner, C W (1971) *Richard Evans' Quote Book*, Publishers Press, Shepherdsville. Kentucky

Bungay, Stanier, M (2010) *Do More Great Work*, Workman Publishing, New York, p 111

Cummings, E E (1938) *Introduction to the Collected Poems*, original out of print; reprinted in 1997 by The Book of The Month Club, 1st Thus edition, Montreal

Gibb, B T (2007) *The Rough Guide to the Brain*, Rough Guides Limited, London, p 96

Gladwell, M (2006) *Blink: The power of thinking without thinking*, Penguin, London

Isaksen, S G, Dorval, KB and Treffinger D J, 2011, *Creative Approaches to Problem Solving*, 3rd edition, Sage, London pp 72, 74 and 123

Kahneman D (2011) *Thinking, Fast and Slow*, Penguin Books, London

Michalko, M (2006) *Thinkertoys: a handbook of creative-thinking techniques*, 2nd edition, Ten Speed Press, California

Steinbeck, John (1947) Interview with Robert van Gelder, as quoted in *John Steinbeck: A Biography* (1996) by Parini, J Henry Holt & Co (P), 1st Owl Book Ed edition (March 1996) p 35

Webb Young, J (2003) *A Technique for Producing Ideas* McGraw-Hill, New York, p 29

Articles

Emich, K, J Polman E (2011) Decisions for others are more creative than decisions for the self, *Personality and Social Psychology Bulletin* 37 (4), pp 492–501

Maiden, N, D'Souza, S, Jones, S, Müller, L Pannese, L, Pitts, K, Prilla, M, Pudney, K, Rose, M, Turner, I and Zachos, K, (2013) Computing technologies for reflective, creative care of people with dementia, *Communications of the ACM*, 56 (11), pp 60–67

Online

Adobe State of Create Global Study, (2012) [accessed 26 May 2016] www.adobe.com/aboutadobe/pressroom/pdfs/Adobe_State_of_Create_GlobalBenchmark_Study.pdf, p 32

Berger, J (2013) [accessed 27 May 2016] Crafting Contagious Workbook, [Online] http://jonahberger.com/resources/

Bullmore, J (2004) [accessed 1 May 2016] Why is a Good Insight Like a Refrigerator? *WPP Annual Report*, 2004 [Online] www.wpp.com/wpp/marketing/marketresearch/why-is-a-good-insight-like-a-refrigerator/

Coats, E (2011/2012) [accessed 26 May 2016] *Pixar's 22 rules of storytelling* @lawnrocket, www.twitter.com

Collister, P (2007) [accessed 26 May 2016] 'Judging Creative Ideas' best practice guide [Online] www.ipa.co.uk/Page/Best-Practice-Guides#.V0GpgKtOJFI

Ganz, M Website (no date) [accessed 4 May 2016] with interviews, lectures and comprehensive information, available from [Online] http://marshallganz.com

Jobs, S (1996) [accessed 26 May 2016] Steve Jobs: The Next Insanely Great Thing, interviewed by David Wolf, for *WIRED* [Online] www.wired.com/1996/02/jobs-2/

New Emotion, Good Fortune, The Challenger Project for *Eat Big Fish*, (no date) [accessed 26 May 2016] [Online] www.eatbigfish.com/wp-content/uploads/2010/11/new-emotion-good-fortune.pdf

Orkdork, (2014) [accessed 1 May 2016] Why Content Goes Viral: What Analyzing 100 Million Articles Taught Us [Online] http://okdork.com/2014/04/21/why-content-goes-viral-what-analyzing-100-millions-articles-taught-us/

Poole, D (2016) [accessed 26 May 2016] How I Got The Idea: Interview with Mark Sinclair for *The Creative Review*, 29 February [Online] https://www.creativereview.co.uk/cr-blog/2016/february/how-i-got-the-idea/

Saatchi, M (2010) [accessed 26 May 2016] Maurice Saatchi On His 'Brutal Simplicity Of Thought' Interview With Steve Armstrong, *Guardian Online* [Online] www.theguardian.com/media/2010/sep/06/maurice-saatchi-brutal-simplicity

Interviews

Holland, D interviewed by Bridges, C (10 May 2015)

Hughes, J interviewed by Bridges, C (5 May 2016)

Jones, S. interviewed by Bridges, C (20 May 2016)

Milligan, A interviewed by Bridges, C (20 May 2016)

Sammer, P interviewed by Bridges, C (22 January 2016)

Chapter 9: Putting it all together

Books

Burckle, M and Boyatzis R E (1999) quoted by Feldman, J and Mulle K *Put Emotional Intelligence to Work: Equip yourself for success*, ATD Press 2008 edition, Alexandria, p 53

Graham, M (1943) quoted by Horosko, M in Martha Graham *The Evolution of Her Dance Theory and Training*, University Press of Florida, 2nd revised edition 2002, p 92

Online

Obama, B (2008) [accessed 1 May 2016] The Transcript Of Senator Barack Obama's Speech To Supporters After The Feb 5 2008 Nominating Contests, As Provided By Federal News Service, *New York Times* [Online] www.nytimes.com/2008/02/05/us/politics/05text-obama.html?_r=1

INDEX

Italics indicate a figure or table in the text.